STORMING THE STATE HOUSE

STORMING THE STATE HOUSE

*The Campaign that Liberated Alabama
from 136 Years of Democrat Rule*

MIKE HUBBARD
WITH DAVID AZBELL

AND WITH A FOREWORD
BY U.S. REPRESENTATIVE MIKE ROGERS

NEWSOUTH BOOKS
Montgomery

NewSouth Books
105 S. Court Street
Montgomery, AL 36104

Library of Congress Cataloging-in-Publication Data

Hubbard, Mike.
Storming the State House : the campaign that liberated Alabama from 136 years of
Democrat rule / Mike Hubbard with David Azbell ; and with a foreword by
Mike Rogers.

p. cm.

Includes index.

ISBN-13: 978-1-58838-283-2 (hardcover)
ISBN-10: 1-58838-283-4 (hardcover)
ISBN-13: 978-1-60306-117-9 (ebook)
ISBN-10: 1-60306-117-7 (ebook)

1. Alabama. Legislature—Elections, 2010. 2. Elections—Alabama—History.
3. Political campaigns—Alabama—History. I. Azbell, David. II. Title.
JK45932010 .H83 2012
324.9761'064—dc23

2012003262

Printed in the United States of America

༚

For more information about this book, visit
www.newsouthbooks.com/statehouse
or www.StormingtheStateHouse.com

The authors will donate their portion of profits from this book
to John Croyle's Big Oak Ranch. For more information about
this Christian home for children needing a chance, visit www.
bigoak.org.

TO SUSAN, CLAYTE, AND RILEY,
WHO HAVE STOOD WITH ME ALWAYS

TO GOVERNOR BOB RILEY,
MENTOR, ROLE MODEL, AND FRIEND

AND TO THE REPUBLICAN CANDIDATES, PARTY STAFFERS,
VOLUNTEERS AND VOTERS WHO MADE CAMPAIGN 2010 A SUCCESS

CONTENTS

(16 pages of photos follow page 132)

ACKNOWLEDGMENTS

Over the past several months, I have discovered that writing and publishing a book is not terribly different from planning and carrying out political campaigns. In order to be successful, both require a team of dedicated individuals with different talents and duties all focused on a common goal. Thankfully, I have been blessed to have worked with truly remarkable people and incredible teams in my political life as well as in the writing of this book.

I am forever indebted to the following individuals, not only for their support of this book project, but also for the important roles they have played and continue to play in my life and career.

My beautiful and amazing wife, Susan, whose love, advice, and patience has sustained me for each of the twenty-five years of our marriage; and my sons, Clayte and Riley, who always make me proud.

The other women in my life, Tracy Ledbetter at the Auburn Network and Alley Jackson in the Speaker's Office, who along with Susan, always keep me headed in the right direction, on task and on schedule.

My partner in this book project, David Azbell, who has spent countless hours to help put this story down on paper. David is a talented writer and I thank him for being such a valued advisor and a loyal friend.

The entire staff of the Speaker's Office, which I consider to be the hardest-working and most dedicated team in the State Capitol complex. The long hours and tireless efforts of Josh Blades, Jason Isbell, Boone Kinard, Todd Stacy, Stephen Tidwell and Sommer Vaughn are appreciated by me as well as countless others. Thank you for always making me look good.

My current and past colleagues on both sides of the aisle in the Alabama Legislature, both mentioned and not mentioned in the book. Thank you for accepting an untested rookie legislator from Auburn into your ranks.

Our wonderful friends who have walked door-to-door in campaigns and attended dozens of political banquets and events to support me and only because I asked.

Jon Cole, Chris Hines, and the entire staff at the Auburn Network who hold down the ship at my "real" job while I am carrying out my public service duties in Montgomery.

Our entire 2010 freshman Republican legislative class who fulfilled their promises and demonstrate daily that the future of our Caucus is in good hands; former Alabama Democrat Party Chairman Joe Turnham, my good friend and a worthy, yet honorable, opponent during several election cycles.

Each and every contributor to the Governor's Circle and Campaign 2010 whose financial commitment and generosity fueled our effort to storm the State House; everyone who agreed to be interviewed for this book whose recollections, confirmations of dates, facts, and events, as well as individual perspectives, added greatly to the content.

And to my "kitchen cabinet" of advisors who always offer sound guidance and candid thoughts.

Finally, our book editor, Randall Williams, who showed great patience and never allowed his differing political views to affect the words we wrote, and NewSouth's publisher, Suzanne La Rosa, who believed the story of our 2010 campaign was historical enough to publish.

FOREWORD

U.S. REPRESENTATIVE MIKE ROGERS

Taking control of the legislature after Democrats held it in their grasp for 136 years could well be the most monumental political achievement of our time in Alabama. Accomplishing it took not only blind faith and self-confidence but other characteristics that most politicians, frankly, just do not possess. It also required vision, leadership, and a healthy dose of self-sacrifice.

As the architect of the Republican takeover effort, Mike Hubbard demonstrated each of these qualities along with an incredible work ethic, determination, and the self-discipline to pull it off. The story you are about to read will make that abundantly clear. Hubbard, along with a team of young political party staffers, seasoned political consultants, and a combination of veteran and rookie candidates accomplished one of the most significant political victories in Alabama history.

Prior to the 2010 election cycle, serving as a conservative, pro-family, pro-business Republican state legislator was frustrating. Not only were the Democrats in each chamber much more liberal than the electorate they represented, but the legislative process was not the fair, impartial, and even-handed one we learned about in high school civics class. The Alabama Education Association, a large and aggressive liberal labor union, had absolute control over the leadership in the House along with the Democrats that made up its majority. As a result, attempts to make much-needed reforms to improve the state's public education system were futile. Similarly, in the even more liberal Senate, the AEA shared control with the Alabama Trial Lawyers Association, which successfully worked to block any tort reform efforts. Together, they bought and paid for control of the legislature and played it like a violin.

Many legislators became numbed and accustomed to the fact that this was the way it had always been—and would probably always be. Fortunately for Alabama, Mike Hubbard is not like most members.

I first met Mike in 1998 when he joined our minority caucus in the Alabama House of Representatives as a freshman legislator. I had played a role in an effort to take the majority during that election cycle which, unfortunately, proved to be grossly inadequate once the results came in. My colleagues had been telling me about an impressive candidate in Auburn who was a real winner, but I had no contact with him during the campaign since I had been assigned to other races. From the first time I met him, though, I knew he was going to be a leader, a committed conservative and a tenacious opponent to those who stood in his way.

Storming the State House outlines the long and tortured process that brought about historic changes in our state. Since Mike and I are close friends who talk regularly, I was aware of his plans from their genesis and was in contact with him throughout the effort. Reading this book, however, gave me a whole new perspective on just how difficult and complicated the campaign to capture the House and Senate really was.

One of the critical elements in the success of this process was the involvement of State Senator Del Marsh. Just like Mike, Del came from humble beginnings and became a successful businessman. I had the privilege of serving in the same legislative delegation with Del during his first term in the Senate and found him to be exactly the kind of citizen-legislator Alabama needs. Mike and Del are both involved in public service for all the right reasons and I deeply appreciate their commitment and sacrifice for our state.

In the book, Mike gives me the credit for convincing my Republican colleagues in the Alabama congressional delegation to join the Governor's Circle fundraising program by agreeing to commit $40,000 in contributions toward the Campaign 2010 effort. The fact is it really wasn't that difficult a deal to close. Once Mike sat down with us and outlined the plan, including the time, money, and resources he was prepared to devote to Republicans taking control of the Alabama legislature, every member of the delegation was immediately sold.

As it turned out, none of the Governor's Circle investors—myself included—would be disappointed. The 2010 election brought a tidal wave of anti-Obama and anti-Pelosi voters to the polls. While this created a favorable environment for the takeover, it wouldn't happen in a vacuum. It required a well-thought-out, properly funded, and perfectly executed plan. Hubbard, Marsh, and the dedicated staff they assembled pulled it off. *Storming the State House* tells the complete story with candor and fascinating behind-the-scenes insight.

Several years ago, I predicted that the GOP would take control of the legislature and that Hubbard would one day become the first Republican Speaker since Reconstruction. Mike, of course, always shrugged it off as improbable—as did most everyone else—since Republicans were deep in the minority.

I am proud to say that my prediction came true.

STORMING THE STATE HOUSE

1

ELECTION DAY 2010

November 2, 2010, started with the same routine as any other Tuesday during the school year. I wake up about 6 A.M. and rouse my two boys, Clayte and Riley. While Susan prepares breakfast for them, I shave, shower, and put on a suit and tie. Then I drive Riley to Dean Road Elementary School.

After that I normally go directly to my office at the Auburn Network on East University Drive in Auburn. But this was, in fact, no normal day. It was Election Day 2010. On this day, I drove right past the building. My friend and employee Andy Burcham was inside hosting his popular morning show on WANI NewsTalk 98.7 FM and 1400 AM. Just as I turned into the Lexington Inn, only 150 yards from my office, I heard Andy remind his listeners that the polling places were now open and would remain open until 7 P.M.

I had gone straight to the polling place where Susan and I vote. The lines were full, but not overwhelmingly long. As I waited in the "F–H" line, friends were wishing me luck or giving me a "thumbs up" sign.

I was on the ballot for reelection to a fourth term as the state representative for District 79, but the butterflies in my stomach were not from anxiety about my race, because I had no opposition. The prize today was much larger and infinitely more historic.

I had been working and planning for this day, along with a team of incredibly talented and hardworking people, for four years. I sat down to cast my ballot with one very quick mark with the black Sharpie pen—a straight Republican ticket.

After voting, I visited with folks outside the polling place and then headed to the office. The butterflies increased, as they would for the remainder of the day.

I called John Ross, the executive director of the Alabama Republican Party, who was already at the GOP headquarters in Birmingham following a late night of last-minute campaigning and logistics preparation. It would be the first of more than a dozen phone calls to John, whom I had selected as my right-hand man during my four-year tenure as state party chairman. John, a trusted and highly capable young man, wise beyond his 32 years, gave me a status report of our final Get Out The Vote efforts—GOTV, in political circles—and what House and Senate district races we were monitoring throughout the day.

John told me to relax because he had a good feeling about things. I did, too, but after four years of work, it was still hard not to worry and wonder. Had we missed anything in our overall plan to flip control of the Alabama Legislature from Democratic to Republican for the first time since Reconstruction? Had we done a thorough job following the vote totals needed and other data that Michael Joffrion, the party's political director, had laid out for us? Was there a race out there where we could have pulled our candidate over the finish line with just one more mail piece or radio or TV spot?

At this point, worry did no good. Although the campaign was still making phone calls to Republicans across the state to make sure they remembered to vote, most of our work was complete.

Over the next several hours, in between people calling to ask if I had heard any voter turnout reports and friends calling asking who to vote for (I always said, "Just mark straight Republican and you'll be fine"), I called many of the candidates I had helped recruit to run for the legislature to reassure them that, together, we had run a top-quality race and to make sure they were following the Election Day instructions our team had given them.

B<small>Y</small> 3 p.m., I was too anxious to wait around the office in Auburn, so I drove to Birmingham. When the results came in, I wanted to be with the team I had put together. Either a historic night awaited us, or the dreaded hour of disappointment. Regardless, we had all worked hard on this campaign effort, so it was only fitting that we be together to celebrate or to console each other.

At the ALGOP headquarters on Highway 31 in Homewood, everything was set up perfectly, and the electricity in the air enveloped me as soon as I entered the office. There was a section set aside for lawyers who were ready to dispatch legal teams to any courthouse in the event of reports of election tampering. (Thankfully, it would be a quiet night for the lawyers.)

Kate McCormick and Sidney Rue, the party's first full-time fundraisers when I hired them in 2007, had morphed fully into veteran producers of political messaging over the past several months of campaigning. They were the best fundraising and event planners I had ever seen. Kate had also become a TV commercial production coordinator and Sidney our photographer. Both had traveled around the state to help our candidates. Today, though, they were in the headquarters and set to field calls from candidates as soon as results started to roll in.

Michael Joffrion crunched numbers at his computer, as usual, and remained in constant contact with deputy political directors Ryan Cantrell and Ryan Adams, a duo everyone in the office simply referred to as "the Ryans." Joffrion also coordinated the activities of seven field representatives who had been working for months in strategic areas of the state where House and Senate races were in play. Michael and his team had run the largest, most aggressive and most expensive GOTV and Victory programs in the history of the Alabama Republican Party. We would soon find out if the work and investment would pay off.

Meg Eldridge returned for the big day. She had headed our "new media" efforts and had worked with the team at party headquarters for a year and a half before her husband entered seminary in Louisville. Even though I had joked with Meg (the niece of U.S. Senator Dan Coats of Indiana) that it was more important for her to work on Campaign 2010 at our Birmingham headquarters than to be with her husband, she moved to Louisville anyway. But we worked out a great plan so Meg could continue as a productive member of our team by telecommuting to handle our web and e-mail campaigning.

Meg worked as deputy communications director under Philip Bryan.

I jokingly called Philip our "Minister of Propaganda" because he had an uncanny way of getting information out to the public and getting under Democrats' skins at the same time. Even though he had never worked in politics before I hired him, Philip had developed a great relationship with media outlets across the state and had coordinated the best campaign communications program the party had ever produced.

Minda Riley Campbell, the daughter of Governor Bob Riley, was also on hand anxiously awaiting the results. Minda was a 15-year veteran of successful political campaigns and brought some battle scars and experience to our young, talented, and aggressive team. She had been heavily involved in fundraising, coordinating our high-level "Governor's Circle" program, and also produced radio and television commercials for many of our legislative candidates. Now, her work would be judged by the voters as well.

John Ross and Philip were in charge of the "war room," along with Blakely Logan, who had only been on our team for about a year but had been engaged in the campaigns and in Campaign 2010 to the point that the outcome was personal for her, too. Actually, the war room was simply our conference room, but on this night it would be where computers would compile vote counts and telephones would be anxiously answered throughout the night.

BY 7 P.M., WHEN the polls had closed across the state, my good friend, fellow legislator, and the person I tapped as finance chairman for the party when I became chairman, Senator Del Marsh (R-Anniston) was there. During Campaign 2010, Del had concentrated on the Senate races while I oversaw the House races. We made a great team in fundraising and in developing and implementing the overall plan. We both hoped to flip control of our respective houses, but we would consider it to have been a successful effort if only one changed.

The first report we received was not good news. A precinct in House District 81, where Republican Mark Tuggle was facing veteran Betty Carol Graham, came in with Tuggle trailing badly. Graham was a top GOP target because she was a favorite of our nemesis, the teachers' labor union known as the Alabama Education Association. My stomach sank when I heard the report and I wondered if our hard work and optimism for historic change in Montgomery was going to end in failure. As it turned out, that early report was from the worst box in that race; in the end, Tuggle trounced Graham.

The rest of the night blurred. The reports coming in were almost too good to be true. Virtually every one of our targeted races came in better than anticipated, and we had expected to win most of them. I called House candidates once races were called to congratulate them and Del did the same with Senate candidates.

A couple of my House colleagues, Jim McClendon of Springville and Greg Canfield of Vestavia, had camped out with us in the war room during the evening. Around 9:50 P.M., Jim showed me a paper he had been scribbling on throughout the night. He assured me we had taken the majority in the Alabama House of Representatives. I strongly suspected that from my own calculations, but when Jim showed me his results, I let myself finally believe it. Jim later framed his tally sheet from that night and gave it to me and it is now proudly displayed in my State House office.

On the Senate side, the positive news continued. Virtually all of our candidates who were challenging incumbent Democrats were winning as well. Even longtime powerful Democratic senators like Lowell Barron of Fyffe and Zeb Little of Cullman were going down in defeat. The Senate would also fall into Republican control and history was made.

One race that kept me from being completely happy at that point was in House District 38, where my good friend and colleague DuWayne Bridges of Valley had called my cell phone to tell me he thought he had lost his race. DuWayne is one of the finest Christian men I know. His district is right next to mine and we both represent parts of Lee County. I had personally engaged myself in his campaign, where his opponent had falsely attacked him repeatedly. I helped produce radio, television, and print pieces for DuWayne and I really thought we had done what was needed to win. The thought of his losing nauseated me.

I asked DuWayne if all the Lee County boxes were in. He said he didn't think so. "Do NOT concede, DuWayne," I yelled. "Lee County is going to put you over the top. Whatever you do, DO NOT call that guy and concede." DuWayne promised he wouldn't, but he sure sounded down and depressed. I asked John Ross to find out what was going on.

BY 10 P.M. THE major media outlets had called the election. Republicans had won every statewide election, had picked up a congressional seat we had lost in 2008, and had held a seat in a tough congressional race in north Alabama. Most incredibly, the goal we had established back in 2007—to ridicule by the pundits and political insiders—had come true: Republicans would control the House and Senate in the Alabama Legislature for the first time in 136 years.

Philip grabbed me to say that WBRC-TV Fox 6 in Birmingham wanted me live on the set right away. Dax Swatek, one of our top Campaign 2010 consultants, volunteered to drive me to the station. On the way, I talked to Dax about what had taken place and how my head was spinning. I also remember saying over and over that I could not believe that DuWayne had lost and that I felt responsible for not doing more in his campaign.

On Fox 6's Election Night set, I visited on-air with news anchor Rick Journey and political analyst Natalie Davis, a professor at Birmingham-Southern College, about the historic nature of the election, why I thought it happened, and how we were going to govern as the majority party. We took a break for WBRC to go live to Tuscaloosa and I watched on the monitor as Robert Bentley, who had served with me in the House for eight years, delivered his victory speech as the winner of the governor's race over Democrat Ron Sparks. During Governor-elect Bentley's speech, Dax appeared from behind a curtain in the studio, waved to get my attention, and pointed to my cell phone which I had asked him to hold while I was on the air. He mouthed the words, "DuWayne won!"

At that point, the historic margin of our victory and the results of our years of hard work became real. It was a day that would fundamentally change the direction of Alabama, and of my own life, forever.

2

Small Town, Big Opportunities

Hartwell is a small town of around 4,000 people located in northeast Georgia, only eight miles from the South Carolina line. It serves as the county seat of Hart County, the only one of Georgia's 159 counties named for a woman, Revolutionary War heroine Nancy Hart. The town's slogan, "The Best Town by a Dam Site," is proudly displayed on its police cars and references the town's best-known feature, the Hartwell Dam on the Savannah River, which created Lake Hartwell with its more than 960 miles of shoreline.

Hartwell is where I was born in February 1962 and where my brother, Bill, and I were provided the happy, small-town childhood that served as the basis for so many iconic black-and-white family television shows in the 1950s and 1960s. We didn't have a lot of money, but I didn't realize it at the time because we had everything we needed and a lot of what we wanted. My parents would save up so we could go on family vacations once every two or three years, and they always found a way to provide whatever I needed to be involved in extracurricular activities at school. To be honest, my childish perspective convinced me we were rather well off financially.

In the summers, we would ride our bikes to town with no fear for our safety, and we would play outside in the humid, Southern heat from morning until our mothers yelled for us to come home at night. Many of the friendships that were forged from first grade at Hartwell Elementary through my years at Hart County High School still stand strong today.

My parents, both Hart County natives, were high school sweethearts who each went to one year of college—my dad at North Georgia College in Dahlonega and my mom at Georgia State College for Women in Milledgeville, now known as Georgia College. Their one year of separation proved too much, and both decided they wanted to come back to Hartwell and get married.

Both of my parents were government workers, so I have to chuckle when my political opponents sometimes accuse me of being an enemy of public employees. I saw how hard my parents worked and know the hours they put in being of service to others, often without being thanked by those they helped. As a result, government employees hold my respect, not my ire.

My dad, William Hubbard, spent his childhood years growing up in Hartwell's mill village. He told me that he moved from house to house so many times that sometimes he would wake up and not remember where he was. I believe that made him determined to provide a stable home for his family, which he did. I lived in the same house from the day I was born until I left for college. And my dad still lives there. Dad worked for the U.S. Postal Service, starting out his career before I was born as an on-foot mail carrier and eventually retiring as the assistant postmaster in Hartwell's post office.

Dad was the local Boy Scout scoutmaster for years, the chairman of the Board of Deacons at Hartwell First Baptist Church, and chairman of the local Salvation Army, and he was involved in everything my brother and I did. For years, he worked the front window at the post office so he knew just about everyone in town. While I was growing up, people would tell me what a fine dad I had, which made me feel proud and special. I still consider him to be the finest, most honest and ethical man I know.

My mom, Rheba Cordell Hubbard, grew up on a farm in the Sardis community of Hart County. She worked as the administrator of the Hart County Health Department from the time I can remember until she retired after I had graduated from the University of Georgia and had started my career at Auburn. My dad was always supportive, but my mom was really the glue that held our family together. She had what some would call a strong personality, not in a bad way, but she was no-nonsense and always said what she thought.

Mom always pushed me to be the best at everything I did, whether it was in school, 4-H projects, speaking contests, piano competitions, or whatever I was involved in. She made it clear that I was expected to make all A's in school. Second-best was simply not acceptable in her eyes. I believe my drive to win, politically and otherwise, was instilled in me by Mom. She died of lung cancer in November 2000, just four months after the birth of our second son, Riley. I'm thankful she got to see him twice before she died.

ONE MIGHT THINK THAT growing up in a small town would not provide the opportunities that a larger town or city might. But I found it to be quite the opposite. I doubt many large towns would have a 13-year-old working as a radio station disc jockey or writing sports articles for the local newspaper. But in a small town, you can do those things. And I did.

In the winter of 1971, my mom took our Scout troop on a field trip to WKLY, a 1000-watt AM station and the only one in town. I remember being mesmerized from the time I walked in and saw the disc jockey, a high school senior named Don Purvis, playing records and talking on the air. I remember that he played the number one song that week, "Joy to the World" by Three Dog Night, for us and it was the coolest thing I had ever seen. I knew right then that's what I wanted to do.

That night I begged my mom to call the station and ask if I could start coming up there and work, even if it was just emptying the trash. The word came back that a nine-year-old was probably a little too young but to check back when I was older. I didn't forget. I constantly listened to the radio and that Christmas even got a reel-to-reel tape recorder, a big deal back then, which I used to practice being a disc jockey.

By the summer of 1975, I had pestered the manager to the point that he let me come to the station just to hang out and learn. I would get there early in the morning and stay all day just watching and listening and absorbing all that I could. By then, Don Purvis had worked in radio in Athens while in school at the University of Georgia and was back at WKLY. I learned everything he would teach me about radio. One day, he turned the sound control board over to me, told me to give the time and temperature and introduce the next record and left the control room. I did it and played my first song, "Philadelphia Freedom" by Elton John. It was my first time on the air, and I loved it. Being on the air made me feel like an entertainer of sorts, and I enjoyed that people were listening to me to provide them with information and entertainment. It was invigorating. At the age of 13, I was a disc jockey and would work at WKLY through high school. My mentor, Don, incidentally, has been a huge success in the broadcasting industry. He has been on the air in Atlanta, one of the top markets in the country, for more than 32 years, most of it on the legendary station, WSB.

I've never completely gotten over the radio bug. On Saturday mornings, I'm the disc jockey on a Classic Hits radio station I own in Auburn, and every once in a while, I play "Philadelphia Freedom" for old times' sake.

WHILE I WAS STARTING my broadcasting career at the ripe young age of 13, I also enjoyed athletics and wanted to participate. The only problem was I was not an athlete. Not even close. My coach in junior high suggested that I could contribute to the team by using my writing skills and covering the school's sports in the town newspaper, the *Hartwell Sun*.

Again, only in a small town could this happen, but I became a sportswriter for the paper while I was still in the seventh grade. In high school, our head football coach, Don Elam, gave me the title of "Sports Information Director" and treated me as a member of the team. I handled the radio coverage, produced and hosted a weekly coaches' radio show, did voice reports for area radio stations, wrote for the newspaper, called area papers and sent out releases about Hart County in an effort to get coverage. And I kept up with the statistics. Not only did this allow me to be a part of the athletic program, but it honed my marketing skills and eventually led to a college scholarship and an incredible career in big-time college athletics.

A couple of the assistant coaches at my high school were graduates of the University of Georgia and had been involved with the athletic program, one as a baseball player and the other as a football manager. They called the sports information director at Georgia, a great guy named Claude Felton, and told him about this kid in Hartwell who could broadcast on radio, write stories, and promote players on the high school team. Felton agreed to meet with me and I went to Athens to visit him during my senior year.

I also had friends with connections at Clemson and I visited their athletic department and their sports information office. But I really wanted to go to Georgia since I had run the sound control board during the school's college football broadcasts at WKLY every Saturday. It should come as no surprise that when Felton called to offer me a scholarship to work with the Georgia Bulldogs, I readily accepted.

Sometimes it's better to be lucky than good and I was extremely lucky when it came to being at the right place at the right time when I went to Athens for my freshman year in 1980. The most sought-after running back in the country that year was a kid from Johnson County High school named Herschel Walker. He had offers from all over the country but had signed with Georgia.

I actually got to know Herschel before we both got to Athens. I had won the state Veterans of Foreign Wars oratorical competition and, of course, Herschel was a high school All-American football player. We had both been invited to attend an event called the "Academy of Achievement" in Los Angeles. We ended up flying out and back together on the same plane, and since we were both from Georgia, spent a lot of time together.

At the University of Georgia, I lived in the athletic dormitory, Mc-Whorter Hall, and one of my jobs was to meet with Herschel in the evenings to make sure he made all of his media calls. As a freshman, he was a phenomenon and there was no shortage of media attention and demands. We won the 1980 National Championship, and I was fortunate to be a part of one of the top programs in the country.

While I majored in Radio and Television at Georgia on paper, the truth is that I mainly majored in Georgia Athletics. Claude Felton and Vince Dooley—then serving as head football coach and athletic director—gave me a tremendous amount of responsibility during my four years in Athens. Not only did I attend football practice and file daily reports to the media outlets, I was involved in arranging player interviews, working the press box, drafting press releases, filing live radio reports to stations around the country—remember, this was before ESPN and satellite radio—and writing feature articles for the game program. Oh, and I was also a college student. Claude also gave me a great deal of responsibility in working on

Herschel Walker's Heisman Trophy campaign, which he won in 1982.

My college roommate at Georgia was a Texan named Terry Hoage. For some reason, he had not been highly recruited coming out of high school. In fact, only Georgia and Columbia University had shown any interest in him and only Georgia offered him a scholarship. But Terry was incredibly smart, an Academic All-SEC and All-American majoring in Genetics. He also turned out to be an awesome football player, in large part because of his intellect and his uncanny ability to be at the right place at the right time. Since I roomed with him and he was my best friend in college, Claude made me the guy to oversee Terry's publicity and media efforts.

In 1982, Terry had led the nation in interceptions and was one of the top defensive players in the country, making several game-winning plays. Herschel had left Georgia for the upstart USFL after the 1982 season, so, in 1983, Terry Hoage—my college roommate and a player no one had really wanted—was Georgia's star. He was having an incredible year, so I went to Claude midway through the season and asked if I could start a Hoage for Heisman campaign. No defensive back had ever come close to winning the Heisman, but I thought it would be some great publicity. Surprisingly, Claude gave me the go-ahead.

One Sunday afternoon following a Saturday game, Terry and I drove to Dobbins Air Force Base in Marietta and had a photo made of him dressed in his football uniform and holding his helmet, standing next to a fighter jet. I had a poster made with the headline "America's Top Two Defenders" along with some statistics and facts that made the case for Heisman voters to vote for him. He ended up finishing fifth in the 1983 Heisman balloting, the highest finish ever for a defensive back and the highest finish for a defensive player in the SEC. We considered it a victory and the campaign helped my reputation in athletic communications circles. It probably also helped me prepare for some political campaigns to follow because it taught me the need to think creatively to make an impact on the voter.

Terry was a consensus All-American, an Academic All-American, played 13 years in the NFL and is now a member of the College Football Hall of Fame. He and his wife, Jennifer, now own and operate a vineyard and winery, Terry Hoage Vineyards, in Paso Robles, California. We served as best man in each other's weddings and remain close friends.

I will always be grateful to Coach Dooley and to Claude Felton for the opportunities they gave me. Looking back, I can't believe they allowed a young student assistant like me to have so much responsibility. I've told Claude many times that I'm not sure I would have done that if I had been in his shoes. Either he saw some talent in me or he felt sorry for me, but there is no way I would have had the success I've had if he had not shown confidence in me and given me the responsibility that he did.

DAVID HOUSEL WAS THE sports information director at Auburn University and was regarded along with Claude as among the best in the country. I had met David a few times during Georgia's trips to Auburn and the Sugar Bowl, where he assisted in media relations for the bowl game. David and Claude were close friends and I suppose they had a conversation about me at some point.

Auburn had a young running back named Bo Jackson who was a lot like Herschel Walker—big, strong, fast, and getting lots of attention from media across the country. David called me during my senior year at Georgia and offered me a position at Auburn. He even said he would hold the job for me until I graduated in December 1983. The opportunity to work with and learn from someone of David Housel's stature and to work on a Heisman campaign for Bo Jackson was an opportunity I couldn't pass up. So two weeks after I graduated, I was living in Alabama and working for the Auburn Athletic Department, my first full-time job.

Just as Claude Felton had done at Georgia, David Housel gave me unprecedented responsibility and respect at Auburn. I was only 21, but here I was working with a bona fide Heisman Trophy candidate and having my ideas and suggestions taken seriously. Just as I had with Herschel and Terry, I worked closely with Bo on his media obligations. David, of course, oversaw and approved everything to do with the campaign effort, but he allowed me to handle much of the day-to-day work. After practice, Bo would come to my office, and I would have a list of phone calls for him to make. Again, this was before the Internet and football games on dozens of television channels every week, so we had to really work to let Heisman voters know about Bo. We even sent out video tapes with highlights of Bo's incredible feats so voters could see for themselves what an amazing player he was. I spent a lot of time with Bo, and I believe he trusted me.

In 1985, Bo had an outstanding season, but in the Iron Bowl game against cross-state rival Alabama, he was playing with two broken ribs and was in extreme pain. Auburn lost and *Sports Illustrated* staff writer Rick Reilly wrote a cover story arguing that Bo didn't deserve the Heisman because he took himself out of the Alabama game for brief periods—no one knew until later about the broken ribs. That national story, along with other naysayers who wrongly questioned Bo's toughness, made the Heisman race much tighter than anyone had thought it would be.

David went to New York a couple of days before the Heisman announcement, and I stayed behind to handle media requests and travel with Bo when it was time for him to arrive. David called me that night to tell me there was a chance we would not win and that he expected me to not let my disappointment show. He knew how much this meant to me, and he didn't want my emotions to embarrass Auburn. David, who would later become Auburn's athletic director, was always good about thinking ahead to cover all bases, which is just one of many important lessons I've learned from him over the years.

Bo and I drove from Auburn to the Atlanta airport and flew to New York. We stayed at the Downtown Athletic Club where the announcement would be made the next day. The afternoon of the announcement, I went to Bo's room and we went over the logistics, some things to say to the media, and other odds and ends. Right before we left to go downstairs to the Heisman Room where the live broadcast of the ceremony would be made, he asked, "Mike, what do I do if they call my name?" I replied with a grin, "Just stand up, turn around and shake my hand, and then go get your trophy."

The top three Heisman candidates that year were Bo, Chuck Long of Iowa, and Lorenzo White of Michigan State. The room was hot because of the television lights and, since the long program was being broadcast live, we also had to wait through the commercial breaks. After what seemed like an eternity, the time came for the announcement. I kept remembering the conversation David had with me about not showing disappointment on my face if we didn't win, but in the end, although it was the closest vote in the history of the Heisman Trophy to that point, the 1985 winner was, indeed, Bo Jackson of Auburn University.

If you look at the video of the announcement, after his name is called, Bo turns around and shakes my hand.

OF THE MANY PEOPLE who have played important roles in my life and career, former Auburn head football coach Pat Dye is at the top. Like me, Coach Dye is a Georgia graduate who became an Auburn man. He was an imposing figure and I respected him; to be honest, I was also scared of him.

After I had been at Auburn only a few months, I went to Coach Dye, who in those days owned his own TV show, and told him that if he would allow me to produce his TV show, I could make it better and more profitable. To this day, I can't believe I had the audacity to do that. I was a young guy right out of college and I went to the head football coach to convince him to turn his TV show over to me. I may have conveniently forgotten to tell him that I had never produced a TV show before.

Coach Dye agreed. I took over the advertising sales responsibilities of the show and changed the way it was sold and aired. Rather than sharing part of the commercial inventory with the TV stations, I kept 100 percent of the inventory and simply bought a 30-minute block of time from each station. I was betting that I could sell the advertising for more than the cost of the time. By the end of the first season that I produced the show, Coach Dye had gone from making $35,000 to $150,000, and for that reason I believe he has liked me ever since.

Emboldened by my success, I went to Coach Dye and the other athletic administrators following the 1989 season and pitched the concept of putting all of the media offerings under one umbrella. At the time, I was selling and producing the TV show; Colonial Broadcasting was handling the radio network; and the Auburn athletic department was handling the official game day program booklets. There were three entities in the marketplace all legitimately selling Auburn products and, in some ways, competing among themselves. My idea was to create a one-stop shop to eliminate the competition and consolidate everything. I also believed an entity that focused on nothing but Auburn TV shows, radio broadcasts, and publications, as well as other media and publishing rights, would produce better products.

In 1990, the Auburn Network was born as a division of Host Communications. I left Auburn University to become general manager for Host. In 1994, I created my own company, Auburn Network, Inc., to handle the multimedia rights. I'm proud of the fact that we built the radio network into one of the largest in the country and even built a dedicated facility to originate the broadcasts and produce the television shows and highlights videos. When I started the network, Auburn's rights fee was $250,000 per year. When I sold the multimedia rights in 2003 to International Sports Properties, Auburn University was receiving $3.5 million per year.

Coach Dye's coaching career ended following the 1992 season. I remember going up the elevator with him at WSFA-TV in Montgomery, where we produced the TV show prior to doing it in-house at the Auburn Network facility, following the taping of the final show of his career. I thanked him for the opportunities he had given me and for taking a chance on a young 21-year-old to handle his show. In typical Pat Dye fashion, he responded with an expressionless, "Well, if you'd messed it up, I would've fired your ass!" And he would have.

I am no longer scared of Coach Dye, but my immense respect for him has only grown over the years. He was a tremendously successful football coach and is now a legend, with the football field at Auburn named in his honor. What most people don't know about him is that he deeply cares about people and that behind his gruff demeanor is a generous and loving person. He is a great man and I'm fortunate to have worked with him and learned from him.

SOON AFTER I CAME to Auburn from Georgia, I noticed a very attractive college student named Susan Sorrells who was president of the Tigerettes, the group that assisted in recruiting football players to come to Auburn. The recruiting office was just down the hall from my office in the Coliseum and I found all kinds of excuses to walk down there.

When we played in the Cotton Bowl following the 1985 season, there was a nice dinner and ball, and I was allowed to invite someone. When she arrived in Dallas, I asked Susan if she would go with me and, even though she was dating someone else at the time, she agreed. Actually, I think her dad made her go. In fact, she hadn't brought any clothes to wear to a formal ball, so he insisted she and her mother go shopping to buy a dress and some shoes.

I joke around now and say that Susan saw my $16,000 a year salary with the athletic department and started pursuing me because she saw my potential, but quite the opposite was true. I put on a full-court press to convince her that I was the man for her. I would even go by her apartment some mornings and leave breakfast at the door for her and her roommate. I figured if I got her roommate on my side, it would help.

Fortunately for me, Susan relented and we were married on August 1, 1987, in Opp, Alabama. I readily admit that I married way above my pay grade, as everyone who knows us will attest. Susan is now a full professor at Auburn University and is the associate dean of the College of Human Sciences. She has won just about every award you can win at Auburn, including the Pam Sheffield Award given to the outstanding female on the Auburn campus.

Susan is a remarkable wife and mother to our two sons, Clayte and Riley. She has consistently supported me through my career and now, through the trials, tribulations, twists and turns of Alabama politics.

∽ *In Their Own Words* ∽

BO JACKSON
1985 HEISMAN TROPHY WINNER

Mike Hubbard and David Housel ran the campaign for the Heisman Trophy. This was back in the day before the internet when you actually had to campaign for it. I just had to worry about playing football and they handled the media part. Mike came from Georgia and I never thought I would be working with a guy who had been Terry Hoage's roommate. Even after 25 years, he continues to play a major role in my life as one of my closest friends.

3

THE LIFE OF RILEY

In 1996, my life was as calm, complacent, and enjoyable as it had probably ever been. My business was proving to be a great success, and Susan was quickly moving her way up the academic ladder as an Auburn University professor. Our first child, Clayte, had been born a year before, and other than church activities and a few civic involvements, there were few outside demands for my time and attention.

That all changed when a friend asked me to attend a lunch. Patrick Nix had just graduated as Auburn's quarterback, with a school record in passing efficiency. As a sophomore, he had helped lead the Tigers to a perfect 11-0 record. Nix, whose wife, Krista, worked for me at the Auburn Network, called one day to say he knew a man who was running for Congress and asked if I would meet with him. Because of my background in public relations and my experience in promoting Heisman Trophy candidates, which is like running a political campaign, Nix thought I might be able to offer his friend some valuable advice.

My first reaction was that a meeting would be a waste of time because I really wasn't interested in politics and doubted I could be of any help. Plus, I didn't know anything about the friend's campaign and, to be honest, was only vaguely aware that a congressional race was happening. But, as a favor to Nix, I agreed to a meeting. I didn't think any more about it until a few days later when I told Susan before I left for work that I was supposed to meet with some guy who was running for Congress and really wasn't sure why.

I met Bob Riley for the first time at my office in Auburn. Accompanied by his daughter and campaign worker, Jenice, he immediately put me at ease, and it took only a few moments for me to realize that we would get along famously. It was the first time I had seen anyone wear cowboy boots with a suit and actually pull off the look (which, to me, epitomizes who Bob Riley is—you can put him in blue jeans and boots at the corner gas station drinking a Grape Nehi with the boys or in a suit in a Fortune 500 board room with corporate chieftains, and he is equally comfortable and confident in either environment).

We rode a few blocks to the Barbecue House on College Street, and Riley began to tell me a little bit about himself and his reasons for running for Congress. Born in 1944 in the small Clay County town of Ashland, Bob Riley grew up with the Mayberry-like childhood that so many older folks in the South romanticize. It was a time when families did not worry about locking their doors at night, parents taught that teachers were always right and receiving a paddling at school meant another was waiting for you at home.

His father operated a grocery store on the town square, and the father of Patsy Adams, his childhood sweetheart, operated the pharmacy just down the block. He and his older brother, David, sold peanuts and mowed lawns to put some spending money in their pockets. Upon graduating from Clay County High School, he enrolled in the University of Alabama where he tried out for the freshman basketball squad but quickly found out that his 150-pound frame was too small, and his talent too lacking, to make the team.

Riley and his brother lived in a rented room in a Tuscaloosa lady's home, and he sometimes hitchhiked home to spend time with Patsy. He readily admits that academics were never his strong suit in college, but he did enough to get by and graduate.

In 1963, he had a bird's-eye view of one of the most historic events to take place in Alabama at the time—George Wallace's Stand in the Schoolhouse Door. Elected to his first term as governor the year before, Wallace had campaigned for office on a platform of supporting continued segregation in the public schools and had pledged to physically bar anyone who tried to integrate Alabama's education system. Faced with a federal court order to allow African American students James Hood and Vivian Malone to enroll in the University of Alabama, Wallace had a nationally televised confrontation with Deputy U.S. Attorney General

Nicholas Katzenbach. Watching it all from a back window of Farrah Hall, the old law school building that overlooked the site of the stand-off, was the young undergraduate Bob Riley.

Continuing the entrepreneurial spirit that his father had instilled, Riley, along with his brother, began selling eggs in the college town to help defray school expenses. He knew to look for customers that would buy in high volumes, so he approached the fraternity houses on campus and began selling to them all. The brashness of youth led him to ask for a private appointment with legendary Alabama Head Football Coach Paul "Bear" Bryant, and, surprisingly, it was granted. Riley remembered sitting on a low couch with cushions that sank into the base and looking up to see Bryant towering above him like Moses with the tablets. He proposed to the coach that the athletic dorm buy its eggs from him because few groups on campus ate more eggs than the football team, and Riley could deliver. Bryant appreciated his sales pitch, and his moxie, and made a deal. To this day, Riley facetiously credits Alabama's 1965 National Championship to the eggs he sold the team.

Upon graduation with a degree in Business, Riley returned to Ashland, married Patsy, and began a family. They named their first child Robert Renfroe Riley Jr. Three girls, Jenice, Minda, and Krisalyn followed.

He began going door-to-door selling eggs by the dozen under his new label, Uncle Bob's Eggs, and with hard work and determination eventually grew his business into the largest integrated poultry product company in the southeast. In addition to his multi-million dollar poultry enterprise, Riley diversified into a number of other businesses including a trucking company, a Ford dealership, a cattle farm, and substantial real estate holdings.

Riley explained that he was running for Congress due to a convergence of circumstances. He told me he was watching a television news report shortly after the birth of his first grandchild, and it mentioned the portion of the outrageous national debt that children like her would be responsible for repaying. It angered him that future generations would be saddled with the debt created by his generation and he wanted to address the issue.

At roughly the same time, his brother, David, undeniably Riley's best friend, died unexpectedly. The loss hit him hard. Riley, who had just turned fifty, put a few pairs of jeans and some t-shirts into the cargo seat of his motorcycle, and set out on a long, solo trip from Ashland to Key West. He camped by the road at night and spent the days motorcycling through the Keys, befriending strangers and making new friends. He also did a great deal of thinking. When he returned home, he gathered his family together and told them he had decided to run for Congress.

Sometimes you meet someone and, for some reason, you just like them. Well, I liked Bob Riley. I liked him a lot, actually. I was impressed with his personal story, the fact that he openly shared his Christian faith with me, and I believed that he genuinely was seeking public office for all the right reasons. We concluded lunch by talking about some of the conservative views he and I shared on a number of issues, and I told him he had sold me. I was willing to help his campaign anyway I could, and we sealed the deal with a handshake—one of the most important handshakes of my life.

At the time, Alabama's Third Congressional District was by no means a Republican stronghold. In fact, it was a coin-toss district that could be won by either party, with Democrats carrying a slight advantage. The southern part of the district included Macon County, populated predominantly by African Americans and considered among the state's most heavily Democratic areas. The northern part of the district was friendlier to GOP candidates but included large swaths of traditional white Democrats. Most of the area had also been hit hard by job losses in the textile industry when many businesses that provided this essential economic base moved their operations out of the country as a result of the North American Free Trade Agreement.

The district had been represented for several terms by Glen Browder, a relatively moderate Democrat who had decided to run for the U.S. Senate seat being vacated by Howell Heflin rather than seeking reelection. Browder would run a strong Senate race, but he finished second in the 1996 Democratic primary to State Senator Roger Bedford (D-Russellville), one of the most liberal members of the Alabama Legislature. Bedford was defeated in the general election by U.S. Senator Jeff Sessions, who continues to serve with distinction today.

Several candidates in both parties lined up to run for Browder's congressional seat, but I had placed my money on Riley to win. Just a couple of weeks after our first meeting, Riley called one night to ask if I would produce some radio ads for his campaign. I told him that I would write the spots, record his audio, voice the disclaimer personally, and cut them for time. That began a tradition that continued until the end of his last term as governor—every radio ad for every Riley campaign included my voice in its content.

Running in a multi-candidate Republican field, Riley landed in a run-off with Braxton Bragg Comer, the great-grandson of a well-known Alabama governor with the same name. Riley defeated Comer by a wide 64 to 36 percent margin and turned his attention toward the fall's general election contest.

Democrats, meanwhile, had nominated State Senator Ted Little (D-Auburn), who represented my district in the State House's upper chamber. By a 61 to 39 percent margin in the primary, Little had defeated State Senator Gerald Dial (who still serves his legislative district today as a Republican).

The general election was a competitive and spirited contest with Riley putting more than $200,000 of his own money into his race, and Little contributing more than $100,000 of his money into his. As a Democrat, Little tried to divide the district among racial and economic lines by saying Riley would not be responsive to minorities or the poor. He even aired a television commercial that referred to Riley as a "used car salesman" with a photo of him riding off in an animated little red car. But Riley showed the charisma and compassion that served him so well throughout his career and refused to concede votes even in traditionally Democratic pockets.

Having never been deeply involved in politics, I found myself energized by the hand-to-hand combat style of the campaign and the excitement that surrounded such an important race. I was on call to the Riley camp around the clock and was ready to help on a moment's notice with a radio ad that needed production or a print ad that needed to be laid out on a looming deadline.

I began to know the Riley family very well during this race because he viewed his campaigns as an opportunity for his entire family to bond. No task was too big or too small for anyone and every member did it all. The family would put up yard signs in the heat all day and then change clothes in gas station restrooms to go to fundraising events that evening. His daughter, Jenice, served as the chief fundraiser while Minda developed the media campaign and Rob ran the day-to-day operations and also devised campaign strategy with his father. Krisalyn, the least political of the Riley children, helped wherever and whenever necessary, and her always-cheerful demeanor earned her father a lot of votes. Patsy, his devoted wife, served as a surrogate speaker and helped shore up the important female vote.

The hard work paid off when the results came in on election night, and Riley had earned a close 50 to 47 percent victory. Given the makeup of the district and its history, Riley's win surprised a number of pundits who took it for granted that Democrats would hold the edge.

Susan and I were both invited to the Rileys' beautiful home in Ashland for a celebration a few days after the election. I remember a cake that Patsy had made with the words "Mr. Riley Goes to Washington" written in icing, a reference to the old Jimmy Stewart movie about a man with unwavering values and the determination to make a difference who is elected to Congress. I was touched and honored when Riley called to invite me to join him in Washington for his swearing-in ceremony. I told Susan that I'd probably never have an opportunity like that again, so I accepted. Watching my new and valued friend taking his oath touched me deeply, and it unlocked a door in the back of my mind.

As I walked among the U.S. Capitol, the Supreme Court, the Library of Congress, and other symbols of our nation's power on the way back to my hotel that evening, I began to ask myself if public service might be in my future. It was certainly nothing I had considered before, but Riley's ascension had inspired me, and I had certainly enjoyed my time in the political bubble. The more I walked, the more determined I became.

I didn't know whether it would mean running for the city council, seeking an appointment to the local school board, or some other role, but public service, I decided, would definitely be in my future. I just did not realize it would happen so soon.

⌒ In Their Own Words ⌒

BOB RILEY
U.S. CONGRESS 1996–2002; GOVERNOR 2003–2011

There are some people you meet in life that you instantly like. For me, that perfectly describes my introduction to Mike Hubbard. We just hit it off. He was bright, energetic and gifted. Even now, Mike is one of my closest friends and among the most talented people I know.

I remember he asked during that meeting with me why I was running for Congress. I had never been in politics before so it was a fair question. I told him I believed in a conservative philosophy, and our nation was going down the wrong path. I also told him that a citizen-statesman was essential to my belief. I did not want to go to Washington and make Congress a new career. I pledged to serve three terms and then return to my life running businesses. But, I also told him that someone needed to go and make the changes that our country so desperately needed at that time. Someone who didn't care about being re-elected but about doing the right thing, no matter the cost.

Back then, as today, balancing the budget was paramount to our message. The crushing debt, I believed, was immoral and placed an unthinkable burden on our children and grandchildren. It would take people, businesspeople especially, to make the tough decisions and rein in the spending and cut the deficit. Mike agreed with that unequivocally. And once Mike Hubbard believes in something, he is totally committed. From that moment on, he began to help lay out everything our campaign was doing. His talent plus his dedication to a cause is a powerful combination.

Within the first two months of meeting him, Mike became, in effect, the Lee County Chairman of my first campaign. I had other strong supporters in Lee County. But none more committed, dependable or loyal as Mike. He became the person I called whenever we needed anything. And he never failed to come through.

He had a little radio station in Auburn, and he started cutting my radio ads there. Then, he started consulting on our mailers and campaign materials. His eye and ear for marketing a product, in this case our message, was essential to our success. Before I knew it, he was one of the key players in our campaign. By the end of the race, he was indispensable.

As with everything else in his life, excellence was the standard for Mike Hubbard. The only standard. Failure was never and is never an option. Mike has always done whatever it takes to accomplish the goal. I wish there were more people like him.

4

THE FIRST CAMPAIGN

The closest I had come to serving in elected office was being voted senior class president at Hart County High School. The position required me to deliver the welcome at the graduation ceremony and I also led an effort to build a new exterior sign for the school, so it wasn't exactly a high-pressure position. I figured it would be my first and only time as a candidate for anything.

That's not to say I didn't enjoy learning about civics and, as an avid history student, seek opportunities to be exposed to it. As a junior in high school, I was selected to attend Georgia Boys State held that summer at North Georgia College in Dahlonega. We spent a week learning about our political system and holding mock elections. On the final night at Boys State, it was announced that I was one of two selected to go to Boys Nation in Washington for a week at American University. I considered it an interesting free trip to the nation's capital more than an introduction into politics.

The main thing I remember about Boys Nation, other than touring the national monuments, is that former Georgia Governor Jimmy Carter was president and the folks from the American Legion, who sponsored the program, were unable to secure a meeting at the White House for our group. Supposedly, past presidents had met with participants of Boys Nation as a group, as evidenced by the famous photo of a boyish Bill Clinton shaking hands with JFK in the White House Rose Garden. Since I was from Georgia, the boys from other states kidded me about it. I knew my parents didn't vote for Jimmy Carter as governor, so this meant I didn't care for him, either. And that was before I had any idea about his political ideology.

While in Washington, each boy had an opportunity to have lunch with one of their U.S. senators. My lunch was with Senator Herman Talmadge, a former governor, the son of a former governor, and nothing short of a legendary Georgia political figure. We ate at the Senate dining room in the U.S. Capitol, and at his insistence I ordered the famous Senate Bean Soup. We had a pleasant conversation discussing my hometown, my college plans, and general small talk. He also told me about his father, Gene Talmadge, being governor and the impact growing up in politics had had on his life and political career. At the end of the lunch, he took his U.S. Senate Dining Room menu, pulled a pen from his coat pocket and wrote on the cover "To Mike Hubbard, my good friend," signed his name and handed it to me as we shook hands and left the dining room. I was, of course, impressed with him and called my parents that night to tell them what a fine senator we had representing us.

In October of that year while working a shift at the radio station, I read on the air a wire story that Talmadge had been "denounced" by an 81–15 vote of the Senate for improper financial conduct. "So much for honest politicians," I thought to myself. "I'll just stick with radio."

Years later, I found the signed menu Talmadge gave me, had it framed, and it is displayed in my office. Understandably, visitors often ask why I have an autograph from a Democrat hanging on my wall.

As a student at the University of Georgia, I concentrated on two things: journalism school and working in the Georgia Athletic Department. I was not involved with and had no interest in the Student Government Association or anything to do with politics, campus or otherwise. I remember that a fellow student named Ralph Reed was big into it, though. As I walked to and from class, he would often be handing out political materials on the bridge behind the stadium. Dr. Ralph Reed would later become a powerful political figure in national Republican politics and the conservative movement as head of the Christian Coalition.

Interestingly, in high school I had defeated Ralph in a VFW "Voice of Democracy" oratorical competition. He is originally from Stephens County, not far from Hart County, and we competed for the district title in Athens, Georgia. I went on to win the state championship that year.

Years later, I had a meeting with Ralph in his Atlanta office and casually mentioned the contest and the fact that I had won. His body language let me know he didn't appreciate being reminded of a defeat, even if it was in a high school oratorical contest. I quickly dropped the subject, but I still have the newspaper article as proof.

FOLLOWING MY TRIP TO Washington for Congressman Riley's swearing-in and my decision to look for a role to play in public service, I stayed in contact with him and, when he was in town, talked to him about my running for an office. One morning in early 1998, Riley called to say he had just been told that Pete Turnham, the state representative for my district, was retiring. If true, he said, it was the perfect opportunity for me.

After some phone calls, I determined that the news about Turnham retiring was not just idle rumor. Turnham was a highly respected political figure and citizen in Lee County and the state. I was only 36; he had been in the legislature for 40 years. Now, after 10 terms, the respected dean of the Alabama House of Representatives was hanging it up.

I didn't know very much about the Alabama Legislature. In fact, I had to do some quick research to educate myself about the district lines, qualifications to run, when the sessions were held, and other basic facts. I also made some calls and talked to local people I trusted.

To say that I was discouraged with the feedback I received would be an understatement. Everyone I talked to told me the same thing—I could not win.

The simple fact was that Jan Dempsey, a popular and effective mayor of Auburn for almost two decades, was already the "chosen one" to replace Turnham. She had decided not to seek another term as mayor in the upcoming August municipal election just so she could run for the District 79 seat in the Alabama House. Apparently, all of this had already been decided, and I was out of the loop and late to the game. Plus, I would be running against an established candidate with high name identification, a seasoned political team, and established financial support . . . in a district where a Republican had never been elected.

Despite the discouragement from friends and local leaders, as well as from Susan at home, I just couldn't get the idea out of my head. I met with Lee County GOP leaders, who were anxious to have a Republican on the ballot in that race, and word quickly made it to Montgomery and the House Republican Caucus.

Representative Chris Pringle (R-Mobile), the chairman of the heavily outnumbered House Republican Caucus, called and invited me to come to Montgomery to meet with him, along with some other Republican House members. I made my first ever visit to the Alabama State House, watched a little bit of a session from the gallery, and then visited with Pringle and Representatives Mike Hill (R-Columbiana) and Mark Gaines (R-Homewood) in the fifth floor lobby for about 10 minutes amid chaotic and distracting activity all around us. They were encouraging me to run and said a group wanted to come to Auburn soon to help convince me to get into the race.

I really did need some convincing at that point. Even one of my closest friends, local banker Gene Dulaney, was not encouraging. I asked him if he would consider serving as the treasurer of my campaign should I decide to run. I thought having his name on my campaign taglines would help me because of Gene's popularity and respect in Auburn and Opelika. I was surprised when he responded that he couldn't because of Dempsey's connections at the bank and in the community. That really discouraged me because I had always trusted Gene's advice and opinions.

It seemed like everyone in town, including Bill Ham, a city councilman who would become the next mayor of Auburn, tried to talk me out of running. Bill, who was and is a good friend, even called me several times—at Dempsey's urging, I would later discover—to ask whether I had decided to enter the race. Dempsey herself came to my office one day to try and talk me out of running and laid out the many reasons I could not beat her.

Instead of being dissuaded, I began to think that some folks were actually concerned about my potential candidacy.

My best friend, biggest supporter, and most trusted advisor was, and still is, my wife. Susan and I had been married for 10 years and at that time our son, Clayte, was only two and a half years old. Susan is one of the smartest people I know and possesses uncanny intuition. Her points against getting involved in politics were, as usual, right on target: I was building a business and the time required to serve in office would be a liability; it would be almost impossible to defeat Dempsey; we had a young son who didn't need to be subjected to all that comes with a campaign; our life was pretty good and this would do nothing but complicate it; I was well-liked and respected in the community and a campaign against a popular local figure like Mayor Dempsey could only create enemies.

Susan was right, I decided. Running for the Alabama Legislature was a dumb idea. After all, the only people encouraging me to run were Bob Riley and some members of the House Republican Caucus. I decided I would call Riley and Pringle the next day and let them know that I had decided to look for another way to be involved in public service.

Before I spoke with them, though, Gene Dulaney called to tell me that he had thought it over and wanted me to know that if I decided to run, he would be honored to serve as my treasurer and to support me 100 percent in the campaign. I appreciated his willingness to help a friend despite overwhelming odds and at the risk of complicating his career. I told Gene what a great friend he was but that I had pretty much decided not to run. (Incidentally, Gene still serves as treasurer of my campaigns and I even later helped convince him to run for Auburn City Council, a position he still holds.)

When I called Pringle, he asked if Representatives Gaines, Hill, and Johnny Curry (R-Bessemer) could come over to Auburn the next night to have dinner and talk things over before I made a firm decision. I agreed.

I remember telling Susan that I was going to have dinner with them "just to be nice." She gave me a look that told me she knew exactly what I was thinking and that I still had running in the back of my mind.

During the dinner at The Hotel at Auburn University, the trio of legislators delivered a great sales pitch. They brought a map of the district and were armed with some statistics to show that a Republican could win. They told me all of the great, fun things that come with serving in the Alabama Legislature and how my family would enjoy it. The time required would not be that much, they told me, and they thought Republicans had an excellent shot at taking the majority and that I would be a key in the takeover.

I now joke with them about all the lies they told me that night, but driving home from the dinner I knew I really wanted to run, even though Susan was not on board and my close friends and people I trusted were telling me I could not win.

I called Congressman Riley the next day and asked him again for his opinion. Looking back, I suppose I was looking for him to give me an out and tell me that this might not be the race to launch my political career. He said just the opposite.

"Mike, you can win," he said. "The timing is right and I'll help you campaign and raise money. We need people like you in public office, but you just have to decide for yourself and move on one way or the other. If it were me, I'd do it."

The man who had inspired me to get involved in public service in the first place definitely wasn't making it easy for me.

Over the next week, I vacillated on whether I should qualify. While I was wrestling with a decision, someone else qualified to run as a Republican, so there would be a primary race. Dempsey, however, would have a free ride to the general election. It was lining up to be exactly what I had been told early on, a perfect race for Dempsey to win and for the Democrats to retain the seat.

On the morning of the final day of qualifying, I told Susan before we each left the house for work that I had decided not to run. She was relieved and assured me that I had made the right decision. I walked in my office intending to call the few people still encouraging me to run and let them know my decision.

Before I could muster the resolve to pick up the phone, Susan called. "Have you made your calls yet?" she asked.

"Not yet, but I'm going to do it right now," I replied.

"Well, don't. Something just happened and I think you ought to do it."

She told me that a colleague, Betty Higginbotham, whose husband, Dutch, had once served in the legislature and was currently on the state school board, had dropped by her office in Spidle Hall on the Auburn campus. Susan relayed the conversation to me.

"Someone told me Mike's thinking about running for the legislature," Betty asked.

"Yeah, he's been looking at it, but he's decided not to run," Susan replied. "We just don't think the timing is right."

Betty shared with Susan the reasons why I should run and laid out a pretty good argument. The conversation lasted only a couple of minutes, but Susan really believed Betty Higginbotham's unplanned conversation was actually an answer to prayers asking for guidance about this decision. Susan knew deep down that I wanted to run and now she was convinced it was something I was supposed to do. She told me to go to Birmingham and qualify.

After getting the green light from my wife, I drove to Birmingham and signed the qualifying papers with the Alabama Republican Party about 30 minutes before qualifying closed. I even took two of my Auburn Network employees, Ceil Morris and Evie Simpkins, with me to make sure I didn't back out. That night, I called Bob Riley to tell him that I was going to give it a shot. He again assured me that I could win and that he would make calls on my behalf to help me start raising money for my brand new campaign.

I was officially in the game, but I remember having a sick feeling in my stomach that I might have made a bad mistake. Even if I won the GOP primary, I would likely get embarrassed in the general election.

A victory would be a historic win for the GOP and for the minority caucus in the legislature.

It would also be a miracle.

As IT TURNED OUT, having a primary race was a blessing. It forced me to put a campaign organization together, including recruiting volunteers, sending out fundraising letters, organizing events, and developing campaign materials and lists. But the most important thing for me was learning how to campaign. This wasn't like the Heisman Trophy campaigns I'd been involved with in the past. In those, we knew exactly who the voters were and the candidate was a football player with solid credentials. Now, I had to figure out who the voters were, and the candidate was me.

I actually learned much of how to develop a campaign from a book. Barry Mask, who was Auburn University's very first Aubie, the school's beloved costumed mascot, and I had become friends through Auburn circles. When he heard I was running for the legislature, he gave me a book on how to run a campaign. I called it my "Campaigning 101" manual, but since I was engaged in on-the-job training, it served as a valuable roadmap and guide. Years later Barry would win a special election for the House and become a key member of my leadership team.

A major part of any political campaign is fundraising. It's also the worst part of a campaign. No candidate enjoys asking friends for their hard-earned money. Campaign donations are not tax deductible and you can't guarantee success. But if you can't raise the necessary resources, it's almost impossible to win. I had to force myself to make fundraising calls, both in person and by telephone. I figured it would cost around $25,000 to run both the primary and general election campaigns, which seemed like an impossible sum to raise.

I won the Republican primary in June 1998 by a fairly wide margin, so as I turned my sights toward the general election and Jan Dempsey, I was feeling much better about my chances. My team was solid, my campaign message seemed to have been well-received, and I had a better understanding of the issues and how a campaign should operate. I really thought I was in great shape.

I was wrong.

AFTER I BECAME THE Republican nominee, a friend named Stan Mc-Donald suggested I call a transplanted New Yorker named Billy Canary. Stan, whose father had held statewide office as Alabama's Commissioner of Agriculture and Industries, was married to Coach Pat Dye's daughter, Missy, and was big into GOP politics. He had worked in Governor Guy Hunt's administration and his brother-in-law, Robert Aderholt, won an improbable 1996 race for the U.S. Congress. Stan told me that Canary was the architect behind Robert's victory and was one heck of a smart guy.

I met Billy in his Montgomery office on Union Street a few days later and I immediately knew I was in way over my head. On the walls of his office were incredible photos of dozens of national political leaders and elected officials. The impressive part was that he was in the photos with them. There was one of him briefing President George H. W. Bush aboard Air Force One and another of him with the president in the Oval Office.

It quickly became evident that I was meeting with a national-level political consultant. I wondered why someone who had worked on presidential campaigns, the Republican National Committee, and in the White House was wasting his time with a guy running for state representative.

Nevertheless, this meeting would be a pivotal point for me in my political and governmental career and the beginning of a great friendship with one of the smartest and most remarkable people I know.

Billy Canary was born in Queens in New York City, was raised on Long Island, and worked his way through college and law school. He had run for and won elected office in Suffolk County, New York, and then moved on to national politics. He worked actively on President George H. W. Bush's 1988 campaign, was appointed to serve in the White House as a special assistant to the President, and was then appointed chief of staff at the Republican National Committee. Canary would later serve as president of the American Trucking Associations in Washington and go on to become the president and CEO of the Business Council of Alabama.

On a trip to the then-Soviet Union, he met Leura Garrett, a beautiful and intelligent attorney from Alabama and was fortunate enough to later marry her. Leura would eventually be appointed by President George W. Bush as the United States Attorney for the Middle District of Alabama. The Canarys wanted to live in and raise their family in Alabama, not Washington.

Lucky for me, Billy now lived in Montgomery and was willing to meet with a 36-year-old guy running for the Alabama Legislature from House District 79.

I told him what I had done in my primary race and that I had about $15,000 left in my campaign account, and I laid out my campaign materials and general election plan. Since I had won the primary by a wide margin, I figured I would just keep doing the same thing and I'd be fine.

"First, let's get a survey done and see where we are," Canary said after listening to my story. "Then, we'll decide what to do."

"That sounds good," I replied, not having a clue what he was talking about.

I had a sick feeling in my stomach when he told me it would take roughly $7,000, almost half of what I had left, to conduct a comprehensive survey of general election voters. But I figured he knew what he was doing, so I agreed.

The survey, as it turned out, was a public opinion poll. Canary developed a series of questions to determine how the race stood at that particular point in time. We hired Fabrizio, McLaughlin & Associates, a respected national Republican research firm out of Alexandria, Virginia, to conduct the research.

When the results came back, Canary called. "Mike, come to my office and we'll go over the survey results together," he said. "And bring your wife."

The news was not good and Billy laid it all out to Susan and me.

"If the election was held today, you would lose by 19 points," he said without any emotion.

Losing by 19 points isn't just getting beat, it's a slaughter. Even after a primary race, my name identification was extremely low and Dempsey's was incredibly high. People viewed her as the conservative candidate and it turned out that even self-identified Republicans were supporting her over me.

I was dumbfounded.

After delivering the bad news, he told us that after studying the numbers, he had also found some good news in the survey.

In fact, he had one question circled on page 73 of the cross tabulations, which breaks down each question response by gender, party affiliation, ideology, and just about every other demographic you can imagine. He explained that he was prepared to map out a winning strategy in my race but warned that it would be hard work and an expensive campaign to wage.

Canary wanted the two of us to think hard about it and decide if we were up to it. Susan and I looked at each other and immediately decided that we were in it to win.

I put Canary's campaign plan into action, followed his instructions to the letter, and learned from him along the way.

The question Canary had circled on page 73 of the survey told us that if people knew both of us equally, they were more likely to vote for me. To achieve that level of name identification and message development, it would mean lots of radio, cable television, and mail to increase my visibility district-wide to all households. It also meant having to raise our original $25,000 budget to run both the primary and general election campaigns to $150,000.

Susan and I, along with our friends and the two employees who had accompanied me to Birmingham to qualify, Ceil and Evie, also put in many long hours of campaigning door-to-door, making phone calls, stuffing envelopes, and putting out yard signs. My parents came over from Georgia on weekends to walk door-to-door as did Susan's parents and sisters from Opp. But we weren't operating in a vacuum. The Dempsey campaign was in high gear as well, with most of her mail pieces—and there were a lot of them—coming out of the Alabama Education Association in Montgomery.

By city ordinance, sixty days from the election is the first day campaign signs could be placed in yards in Auburn and Opelika. We had collected what we thought was an impressive and long list of people who had requested signs and were anxious to put them out. Some politicos jokingly refer to campaign signs as the "flowers of democracy" because they seem to bloom overnight just before an election is held.

When the day arrived, Susan and I along with our volunters set out to deliver them. But so was the Dempsey team and they had a longer list. It seemed like there were 15 Chevy Surburbans with Jan Dempsey magnets on them buzzing around every neighborhood putting out signs. By day's end, there were five Jan Dempsey signs for every one Mike Hubbard sign. It was demoralizing and probably the low point of the campaign for me. If signs were an indicator of things to come, I was going to get killed on Election Day.

But over the next several weeks, we stuck to our plan, worked hard, and raised the money to run the campaign. I could feel the momentum shiffting as the Dempsey signs starting coming down and more and more Hubbard signs went up. I also learned that signs don't vote. One week out from Election Day, a new survey indicated that not only had I erased the 19 point deficit from the early weeks of the general election campaign, but I had actually pulled ahead.

When the votes were counted on Election Day, I won the election by 16 points. In my first attempt at elected office, I had become the first Republican state representative in the history of District 79. A miracle had indeed taken place.

I was on the road to Montgomery . . . a journey that would forever change my life.

AROUND THE STATE, HOWEVER, the 1998 election wasn't so good for Republicans. The incumbent Republican governor, Fob James, had been trounced, the Senate had lost Republican seats, and the House had no gains with only 36 of 105 seats. As it turned out, my race was one of the few legislative victories for the GOP; the much hoped-for Republican takeover of the legislature had been a bust.

Prior to the election, the House Republican Caucus had arranged for veterans and newly elected representatives to meet in Birmingham the week following the election. I had looked forward to the meeting and the opportunity to meet my fellow legislators. The meeting, however, was somber. Instead of a strategy session for the upcoming organizational session, it was a wound-licking occasion.

I listened as Mike Hill relayed a conversation he had with the new Speaker-designate, Representative Seth Hammett (D-Andalusia). In an emotionally charged meeting of the House Democratic caucus the day before, the Democrats decided that Republicans would no longer be allowed to serve as committeee chairmen, as they had been able to under the previous Speaker, Jimmy Clark (D-Eufaula). The membership of all committees would also be divided proportionally, meaning the GOP caucus would have even less influence than before. The veteran members looked as though they had just lost their best friend.

At that very first House Republican caucus meeting, I quickly realized that being a member of the minority party in the Alabama Legislature was not going to be a lot of fun.

One positive from that trip to Birmingham for me was meeting Representative Mike Rogers (R-Anniston) for the first time. Mike had just been reelected to the House for a second term and we immediately hit it off. He was elected Minority Leader and became a great friend as well as my mentor in the House.

I would need one.

~ *In Their Own Words* ~

BOB RILEY
U.S. CONGRESS 1996–2002; GOVERNOR 2003–2011

When I called Mike and encouraged him to run for the state legislature, he told me he very unsure about what he should do. You could tell he was torn. I, more than most, understood that. But, I told him again that it is people like him who need to get involved in politics.

We didn't need more professional politicians who saw public service as a paycheck. They had run the country and the state for long enough. We needed people from every walk of life, who wanted to serve for the right reasons, not for glory or personal gain. We needed people who understood that decisions made in legislative chambers had a real and practical impact on businesses and the lives of our citizens. And we needed people who understood there is a consequence for every law that is passed.

In my life, I have sold many things. But, I probably sold Mike Hubbard on the idea of public service as hard as I ever have. Still, he was not convinced. After all, he had a great life, a successful career, a beautiful family and time to enjoy it all.

Ultimately, however, to my relief and gratitude, he decided to run. And I'm not sure Susan has forgiven me to this day.

5

A Rookie Legislator

The Alabama governor's private office is both an impressive and, oftentimes, intimidating environment for meetings, especially for a wet-behind-the-ears, freshman House member making his first official visit.

The walls of the office are finely detailed dark mahogany with heavy doors that disappear into the woodwork when closed, much like in the Oval Office in the White House. A marble fireplace accents the room, which is dominated by a 15-foot-long antique conference table surrounded by red leather chairs, all set at a height lower than the governor's chair at the head. Behind the desk stand the U.S. and Alabama flags along with the governor's military flag signifying him as state commander of the national guard. Illuminating the entire space is an impressive crystal chandelier that once hung in the Hearst Castle in California.

A corner of the office conceals a small, phone booth-sized private elevator that leads to the governor's parking space just outside the capitol. The elevator was installed, in the days before handicapped-accessible buildings became the norm, to accommodate four-term former Governor George C. Wallace, who was paralyzed and confined to a wheelchair as the result of gunshot wounds from an assassination attempt during his 1972 presidential campaign.

This is where I was summoned shortly after the start of my first legislative session when word came that Governor Don Siegelman would like to meet with me in his office.

If ever there was a "political animal" in Alabama politics, Siegelman personified the label. A Democrat, he is the only person in state history to have held the constitutional offices of Secretary of State, Attorney General, Lieutenant Governor, and Governor. It seemed that wherever he went, controversy chased him, and on several occasions throughout his career, ethical red flags were thrown.

As secretary of state in the early 1980s, Siegelman decided to get his private pilot's license but did not want to pay the high costs for lessons and flying time. Instead, he offered to let a private aviation firm use his name and likeness—and, by association, his office—as an endorsement in its advertising. The company turned down his offer and the newspapers barbecued him for his audacity.

While serving as attorney general, he held a meeting with representatives of the Mothers Against Drunk Driving organization that was so intense, he screamed curses at the women and stormed out of the room. His ugly display hit the headlines soon after.

According to published reports, Siegelman, during his time as lieutenant governor, would scan the newspaper for stories on high-profile accidents, consumer disputes, and similar disagreements. Using personal stationary that looked remarkably like his official office letterhead, he would write the involved parties and seek to represent them as a plaintiff's trial lawyer. He never tried the cases himself but would refer the clients to other trial attorneys and collect a hefty finders' fee in the process.

These are only a few of the publicly reported examples of questionable conduct; dozens more from his career could be cited. Yet, his charisma and the Clintonian way he faced such ethical questions with no hint of shame earned him the nickname "Teflon Don"—long-term political damage never seemed to stick to him.

He was elected governor in 1998 by defeating incumbent Fob James, one of the last of the colorful, old-style Southern politicians whose personality, rhetoric, and rumpled appearance did not transfer well to the modern television age. James, an All-American running back at Auburn University in the 1950s who had briefly played in the Canadian Football League, had made national headlines by his promise to call out the Alabama National Guard if a federal judge ordered the removal of a Ten Commandments display in a small-town Alabama courtroom. He also demonstrated his opposition to teaching evolution in public school classrooms by personally pantomiming the stages of journey from ape to man at a State School Board meeting.

Siegelman ran a relentless campaign accusing the incumbent James of leadership failures in economic development, law enforcement, and other areas. But he focused most of his attention on promoting one issue—the creation of an "education lottery" in Alabama. His proposal was based upon the HOPE scholarship lottery implemented in Georgia by Governor Zell Miller. Siegelman intended to provide high school students earning at least B-averages with tuition-free rides to attend the four-year public college or university of their choice in Alabama. Students earning C-averages could attend community colleges or trade schools. His plan would also devote a portion of lottery proceeds toward pre-kindergarten programs and school technology initiatives.

During the campaign, capital press corps journalists in the state used to joke that Siegelman remained on message to the point that if you talked to him about the weather, he would note the sun was shining brightly—but added it would shine even brighter once his lottery and scholarship program were passed. Another joke said if you asked Siegelman for the time, he would tell you it was time to pass a lottery in Alabama.

His tenacious campaign, coupled with the fact that James was seriously damaged by a bruising Republican primary and run-off challenge in his reelection bid, resulted in a landslide 58-42 percent win for the Democratic candidate. Governor-elect Siegelman wasted no time in making it clear that turning his lottery dream into a reality was his first, top, and only priority. He even had Governor Miller travel from Georgia to swear him in at his inauguration, though it was determined that Miller did not have the authority to do so and a second, legal oath of office was later administered in Siegelman's private office.

When I arrived at the capitol for our meeting, I was quickly ushered into the governor's office, where Siegelman and his chief of staff, Paul Hamrick, awaited me. The governor, smiling and back-slapping, put on a full charm offensive as he explained the reason for my invitation was to gauge my support for his lottery legislation. Because Alabama's 1901 Constitution expressly forbids "games of chance" such as a state lottery, Siegelman would have to pass a constitutional amendment that required a three-fifths supermajority vote of both houses before it could appear on the ballot. Thus, he was seeking support anywhere he could find it, including on the Republican side of the aisle.

I paused for a moment while gathering my thoughts and explained as candidly as possible that I had campaigned as an opponent of the lottery and felt obligated to fulfill my pledge to my constituents once elected. Furthermore, my opposition to the lottery was rooted in three simple facts that I believed deeply then and still think hold true today.

To begin, I explained, I do not believe in state-sponsored gambling or that the government should spend millions of dollars on advertising trying to convince its citizens to participate in a lottery that the overwhelming odds showed few, if any, would ever win. For the government to try and convince Alabamians to invest in little more than a pipe dream was wrong and deceptive, in my book.

In addition, gambling is an unreliable and unstable source of revenue upon which to base education funding, especially since participation rises and falls on the whims of a cyclical economy. If you look at the struggles that gambling-centric states like Nevada are suffering in today's Obama recession, I believe my reasoning continues to be validated. And, with surrounding states like Georgia and Florida—and, later, Tennessee—offering lotteries with exponentially larger jackpots than Alabama's population could ever afford, there was no guarantee we could compete.

Finally, I told Siegelman, the lottery-funded HOPE scholarship in Georgia resulted in the poorest citizens of the state, who bought the most tickets, subsidizing the educations of the wealthiest students in the state, who routinely produced the grades necessary to qualify for free tuition. Add in the fact that there was no guarantee lottery revenues would remain at the level necessary for the state to keep its commitments to all who qualified, and my reservations grew even larger.

Suddenly, the genial governor who welcomed me into his office with open arms changed his demeanor totally. It was as if day turned to night in a matter of seconds. I would have sworn at that moment that the temperature in the room fell by several very frosty degrees. Siegelman reached for a paper on his desk and produced a poll he had run in my legislative district that showed if I were to vote against his lottery amendment, I would likely be defeated in the next election. He said the scholarship program would be good for Auburn University, which was a significant part of my district, and the students who attended it. To oppose him and his amendment, Siegelman warned, would be a "huge mistake." Before dismissing me, he forcefully said he expected my vote on behalf of his bill. As I left his office, my legs felt as weak as those of a fighter who had just been through a brutal round with a more experienced opponent.

And then the Siegelman intimidation machine went to work.

Suddenly, my phone lit up with friends and supporters calling at the behest of the governor and asking me to support the lottery. Members of the Auburn board of trustees, many of whom had invested heavily in Siegelman's 1998 gubernatorial campaign, echoed the sentiment in calls and letters. Even business associates I depended on to keep my company running sent veiled messages that they could not work with me any longer if I were to cross Siegelman and oppose the lottery.

I had heartfelt talks with Susan and questioned what I had gotten myself into. As always, she offered wise counsel by telling me to search my heart and pray for guidance while reminding me of my campaign promise. In the end, she said, she was confident I would cast the right vote. Never in a million years did I think that one of my first votes as a member of the legislature would be so important or so pressure-packed. While I did not know Siegelman well at the time, I gave him the benefit of the doubt and thought that serious political repercussions would follow if I voted against putting the amendment on the ballot.

But, at the end of the day, I simply could not live with myself if I were to begin my career in the House by betraying my supporters and my own strong feelings on such an important issue. I decided to vote against the lottery despite Siegelman's threats of retribution.

To this day, I vividly remember every detail about casting that vote—who was near me, the tense mood in the air, and the last-minute lobbying I received from those on both sides of the issue. I learned later that several people were watching how I voted so they could judge what kind of legislator I would be—one who based his vote upon personal principles or upon pure politics.

Siegelman needed at least 63 of the 105 House members to support his bill, and because a handful of my Republican colleagues defected to the other side, he captured 70 votes. I was one of only 31 House members to vote against the lottery, which made me question the wisdom of my vote once again.

But the minute I voted "nay" on the lottery bill, some say I began building a reputation as a legislator who would not succumb to pressure or threats or downright bullying. Since that vote, I have never once been the victim of intense lobbying because once I state my position on an issue, most folks understand that my mind is made up. At the time, though, I was sure I had sealed the coffin on my political career.

Once the vote was over, I remember walking down the hallway to my office through what seemed like a gauntlet of lobbyists, staffers and everyday citizens who had gathered for the vote. Some nodded and offered words of encouragement, some offered pats on the back and others shook their heads slowly as if to say I would not be around the Alabama State House for too much longer. When I finally got to my office, I shut my door, sat in the dark all by myself and put my head in my hands in what would be one of the most emotional moments of my political career.

The amendment quickly passed the Senate and was placed on a referendum ballot set for a statewide vote in October. Meanwhile, the wheels began coming off the lottery train. The Associated Press uncovered a widespread ticket-fixing scandal involving high-ranking members of the Siegelman administration, and the public was reminded of all the ethical questions that seemed to follow the governor. In addition, loopholes in the enabling legislation caused editorial writers, several respected African American legislators and others to voice concerns about the potential for cronyism and corruption if the lottery were put in place. The faith-based community joined those who believed that basing education revenues on gambling was simply bad public policy, and, together, the two groups raised money and ran an effective grassroots campaign opposing the proposal.

At the same time, Siegelman was using his political muscle to raise and spend millions of dollars in a pro-lottery effort that rivaled his gubernatorial campaign. Yard signs, billboards, and radio and television ads promoting the lottery as the cure for all ills began to flood the public consciousness, and Siegelman lived up to his reputation as a political dynamo during an aggressive and exhausting schedule of personal appearances that crisscrossed the state several times over. In a last-minute gambit the week before the referendum, Siegelman announced to the press that he had "no Plan B" for public school funding, which could lead to painful cuts and proration in the education budget if his lottery amendment failed. It was obvious that the governor had staked his entire career on this one issue, and had no intention of losing.

I joined voters who streamed to the polls on Election Day and cast my ballot against the plan while hoping that Siegelman's poll that showed my legislative district voting overwhelmingly in favor of the lottery was simply inaccurate.

When the results were announced that night, I was pleased, and more than a little surprised, to see the lottery being defeated by a 54 to 46 percent margin statewide. My home county of Lee narrowly voted in favor of the lottery by a 103-vote margin—12,205 to 12,102—while my House district, nestled within Lee County, had been responsible for most of the opposition and voted it down.

Looking back, I believe the citizens of Alabama strongly opposed the creation of an Alabama lottery and continue to do so today, but they were especially adamant against any lottery that would have been run by Siegelman and his cronies. The questions about cronyism and corruption surrounding the amendment, coupled with Siegelman's own controversial track record, were enough to tip the balance against the proposal. The fact that 37 of the 56 counties Siegelman had carried in 1998 later voted against his lottery in 1999 is evidence of this fact, in my opinion, since he had run as a one-issue candidate. Low turnout, which was less than 50 percent statewide and only 36 percent in Lee County, was another factor contributing to the defeat and further evidence that even his own voters were not enthusiastic about the plan Siegelman presented to them.

Because the lottery was soundly spanked, the political Armageddon that Siegelman promised I would face never came to fruition, and the friends, supporters, and business associates who had pressured me to vote for the lottery never referenced the subject again.

The governor and his aides, however, never forgot my vote against his most important initiative. State Finance Director Henry Mabry, a Siegelman appointee (who now heads the teachers' labor union), was in charge of more than $6 billion in funding earmarked for state agencies and public education. But, as legislators were acutely aware, he also oversaw several million dollars in discretionary money that could be directed toward economic development incentives, school construction, transportation projects, and other needs within our districts. The competition for these funds among lawmakers was fierce and required us to appear before Mabry, hats in hand, to make our case for projects within our districts.

Shortly after the lottery vote, I met with Mabry to request a grant for my district, but before I could begin my pitch, he held up his hand and pointed to a piece of paper under the glass on a table in his office. It was a scorecard, of sorts, that listed the legislators who had crossed Siegelman and were not to receive funding for district projects as our punishment. Mine was among the names prominently highlighted.

That meeting with Mabry could have set a record as the shortest in history, but it had a very important outcome—it redoubled my determination to defeat Don Siegelman at the next election, no matter how hard I had to work or at what personal consequence. My parents had taught me to believe that elected officials should act as leaders and statesmen, but Siegelman and his crew ran the governor's office like thugs and Mafioso. It was clearly time for them to go.

IF THE LOTTERY VOTE provided the biggest challenge of my short legislative career, that first session also produced one of my biggest accomplishments. Even at that early stage, I had no intention of being a backbencher simply content with casting the occasional vote, enjoying the Montgomery social scene, and allowing lobbyists to wine and dine me on their dime.

That just wasn't who I was as a person or as a legislator.

Instead, I wanted to produce results for the voters who elected me, the district I represented, and the state that had adopted me, embraced me, and given me the great wife, family, and career that I enjoyed. My mentor, State Representative Mike Rogers, also encouraged me to find an issue, take possession of it, and sponsor a bill because he thought it might help me jump into the legislative process with both feet. Luckily, Neal Morrison, a Democratic House member from Cullman County who I considered a friend, approached me with a bill he thought I should sponsor, a mandatory automobile liability insurance bill. But he forewarned me it had little chance of passing.

Alabama has historically been a poor state with vast rural areas and a median income that lags behind much of the country. As a result, legislators for decades had avoided passing auto safety initiatives like vehicle inspections because many of their constituents could not afford them or would find their cars black-flagged for violations. Similarly, many lawmakers had resisted bills that required vehicle operators to carry mandatory liability insurance because, they claimed, the working poor could not afford it.

Voters in decidedly middle-class districts like mine, however, literally paid the price because they did carry coverage but found it difficult to collect claims or damages from uninsured motorists who were at fault in auto accidents involving them. I remembered several people had mentioned the issue to me as I campaigned door-to-door, and it was a problem I found intriguing, so I got to work.

To me, it was a simple issue of personal and fiscal responsibility, but I quickly found that several special interests vehemently opposed the bill. Insurance companies, for example, did not want to have to provide coverage to high-risk motorists who were likely to file numerous claims. To be honest, many of the groups opposing the bill had been contributors and supporters of my campaign, so I was going out on a limb to oppose them, especially as a freshman.

During the committee process, I worked with many of the insurance groups to craft a bill that they could live with and one that would be a good first step toward full mandatory insurance.

Once it reached the floor, even though it was my first time at the microphone presenting a bill, I answered every question posed to me. But

I must admit that I was shocked when Representative Alvin Holmes, an African American Democrat representing Montgomery, approached the microphone and began to speak. Holmes, first elected in 1974 and now the longest-serving member in the House, is known for his sometimes humorous and, quite often, over-the-top rhetoric in the well.

At the time, however, I knew none of this.

"Mike Hubbard is the most racist member of the Alabama House and represents the most racist, silk-stocking Republican district in Alabama," Holmes bellowed from across the podium as he ranted against the mandatory automobile insurance bill. He continued in this vein for some minutes. Later, in the hallway outside the chamber, I took him aside and asked if he really believed that I was a racist. "Naw, I think you're a good fella," Holmes chuckled as he turned and walked away.

I quickly figured out his act.

The bill that no one thought I could pass did pass the House, was approved by the Senate, and was signed into law by Governor Siegelman, though not before he added an executive amendment that made it a full-blown mandatory insurance piece of legislation, including a database requirement that drew tremendous opposition from the insurance industry. At this point, I had to make a choice—to kill my own bill or move forward. I chose to move the bill, knowing that it was a great step forward for Alabama and that I could work with it in the next session to correct some of the problems caused by the Siegelman amendment.

It was the first, and remains one of the most satisfying, accomplishments of my legislative career, and it taught me lessons about coalition building, attention to detail, and the art of compromise that continue to serve me well today. In the years that followed, I continued to work to tighten and tweak the law; today, Alabama has one of the strongest mandatory insurance statutes on the books.

In fact, I took the issue very seriously and made myself an expert, even traveling to Illinois, a state that had successfully instituted a mandatory insurance law, so I could study how they did it and adjust ours to make it work better. When I visited the Illinois secretary of state's office, which has responsibility for enforcing the law, I took along the two Alabama state troopers who headed the motor vehicles and licensure divisions for the agency so they, too, could get educated. The receptionist at the front desk got tickled when I presented myself and introduced the two uniformed troopers from Alabama, Bubba Bingham and Roscoe Howell. She smiled and said, "Bubba and Roscoe? You've got to be kidding!" It was one occasion where I fear I unintentionally reinforced the stereotypes many Yankees believe about Alabama.

After the bill first passed in 1999, the *Montgomery Advertiser*, Alabama's capital city newspaper, named me the Freshman Legislator of the Year. On the day they informed me of the honor, I admit that I was feeling pretty good about myself. When I arrived home, Susan was in the kitchen cooking dinner, and I was anxious to share the news with her.

"Honey," I said, "what would you say if you knew that your husband had just been named the most outstanding freshman legislator in the Alabama Legislature?"

Without looking up from what she was cooking, she replied, "Well, I'd say if you're the best we have to look forward to, Alabama's in pretty bad shape."

I can always count on my beautiful and wise bride to keep me grounded.

6

A NEW DAY IN ALABAMA

As his third two-year term representing Alabama's Third Congressional District drew to a close, Bob Riley faced a self-imposed term-limit pledge. Believing the country was in better hands with citizen statesmen rather than career politicians running the show, he promised voters he would serve only six years in Washington and then return to Alabama and his beloved hometown of Ashland.

As a popular congressman who had easily dispatched the opponents the Democrats tossed at him during two reelection campaigns, Riley could have chosen to run for another term. But to a man of his character, a promise made is a promise kept.

His time in office had produced several accomplishments Riley could point to with pride. He and his colleagues helped force President Bill Clinton toward the center of the political spectrum on a handful of issues and became the first Congress in decades to balance the national budget.

As a member of the House Armed Services Committee, Riley became a respected expert on national defense issues and chaired the Subcommittee on Military Readiness. His experience on the committee helped ease the transition when Fort McClellan, located within his district, was ordered closed by the Base Realignment and Closure Commission. Riley had the vision to turn the facility into a training ground for first responders, and today, the Department of Homeland Security's Center for Domestic Preparedness is housed there.

Even parts of his politically split district that African American leaders and Democrats had argued he would ignore while in office had benefited from Riley's years in Congress. For example, he sponsored and unanimously passed legislation that honored the famed Tuskegee Airmen World War II fighter pilots by designating Macon County's Moton Field as a National Historic Site, ensuring it would forever be open to tourists and history buffs.

As he contemplated his future, I, along with a group of other Riley admirers, saw another role in which this brilliant and dynamic leader could continue serving. With members of the Alabama congressional delegation, dozens of Republican state legislators, and grassroots supporters, I helped lead an effort to convince him to run for governor against Don Siegelman.

At the time, Birmingham construction executive Jim Cooper was the only announced Republican gubernatorial candidate. Cooper had led the grassroots group Citizens Against Legalized Lottery in the fight against Siegelman's referendum. He would soon leave the race, though, because of an inability to raise sufficient funds for a serious campaign.

Two other possible candidates had signaled their interest in joining the race. Steve Windom, a long-serving Democratic state senator from Mobile, had switched parties and been elected in 1998 as Alabama's first Republican lieutenant governor since Reconstruction. In the 1999 legislative session, then, he would preside over the legislature's upper chamber, which continued to be dominated by the Democratic majority that had held control for well over a century.

Windom assumed he would wield the considerable power that Alabama's lieutenant governors had traditionally enjoyed, such as assigning legislation to committees, selecting committee chairmen, and generally directing the flow of bills and resolutions. But, when lawmakers gathered for an organizational session at the start of the quadrennium, Windom was given a hard lesson on the transience of power.

As he watched from his chair on the rostrum atop the Senate chamber, the Democratic majority meticulously stripped the lieutenant governor of every power other than gaveling the body into session and adjourning it when work was completed. He put up a tenacious fight and logged long, grueling, and uninterrupted hours presiding over the Senate for fear that he would lose the gavel for good if he handed it off to anyone else. Eventually, nature called. Posed with a difficult choice, Windom stayed in his chair and discreetly relieved himself into a jug underneath his desk. Several Democrats, however, noticed and began shouting to notify the press and members of the gallery of what was taking place. The jug became such a famous symbol of the legislative power struggle that the Alabama state archives made a formal request for Windom to donate it to their collection. He politely notified them the that jug had been discarded.

Yet, he, too, had been a strong and vocal opponent of Siegelman's lottery and justifiably took a share of the credit when the referendum failed. It was obvious there was no love lost between Windom and Siegelman. The governor had played a big role in helping Democrats strip the power that the Senate's presiding officer once held. Windom's willingness to go toe-to-toe with Siegelman on any number of issues and, at least in the case of the lottery, win some battles would help him in a Republican gubernatorial primary. But the jug incident and the adverse national media attention it had brought the state was difficult for many to move past.

The other candidate angling to join the GOP race was a new face in Alabama politics with an old and well-known name. Greenville businessman and toll bridge developer Tim James was the son of Fob James, the governor Siegelman had thumped four years before. Like his father, Tim had been a running back on the Auburn football team. Tim even resembled and sounded like his father with the same speech cadences.

A committed conservative, Tim was more serious and intense than his dad, and he made quality education, especially in the formative primary school years, a cornerstone of his campaign. A line-in-the-sand pledge on no new taxes and a commitment to balance state budgets by trimming the size of government rounded out his agenda. At another time, Tim James could have been an attractive candidate for governor. But just four years after voters had sent Fob packing in a landslide defeat, it appeared that a case of "the sins of the father being visited upon the son" was in the offing.

WITH NO IDEAL REPUBLICAN candidate, especially considering that the governor's office would have to be pried from a desperate Don Siegelman's grip, Riley seemed a perfect savior to take his party to victory. Other than members of his intensely close-knit family, I doubt there was any bigger cheerleader urging Congressman Bob Riley to enter the race for governor than me.

As described earlier, every Riley campaign was a family affair. His eldest daughter, Jenice, was perhaps the most emphatic booster of her father's possible candidacy. She was with him the first time I'd met Bob Riley, and I remember being struck then by the kindness and friendliness that radiated out of her. If any of the children had inherited their father's ability to give the impression of never meeting a stranger, it was Jenice. She also had a deep love for children, evidenced by the passion she brought to her work as a kindergarten teacher and her job as director of development for the Kid One program, which provides rides to children and expectant mothers who need to receive healthcare but have no easy access to transportation.

Despite her enthusiasm for her father's potential candidacy, she also gave him pause to consider the toll it would take on his family. For three years, Jenice had fought a brave battle against cancer. Riley worried about how a long, bruising gubernatorial campaign might affect Jenice and his family.

The Rileys decided to hold a family meeting at which they would discuss—in frank and certain terms—what the race would require from everyone and then hold a group vote to decide if he would run. If even one member of the family vetoed the idea, he would not enter the race for governor but would simply return to private life.

Shortly after the Rileys' family meeting, I saw Jenice at a political fundraiser at a golf course near Montgomery. She summoned me over and said, "Let Dad think he's the one who told you, but you better put your running shoes on because we're in!" I'm sure I could have won an Academy Award when I feigned the same surprise and excitement a little while later when Riley personally told me the news.

While we were all excited about the upcoming campaign, we also realized there was a big mountain before us to climb. Riley was, after all, a somewhat obscure congressman who was better known in D.C. circles than he was within the state, with the exception of his east Alabama district. Early polling showed Riley drawing just over 10 percent of the vote in a Republican primary; the lead was Windom's to lose.

To surmount the obstacles, Riley put on his salesman's hat as he met with various trade associations and lobbying groups in Montgomery. He hoped getting them on board with his campaign would transfer to the thousands of members each organization represented. He also began meeting with Republican leaders and members of the party's executive committee around the state to convince them he was the GOP's best hope of defeating Siegelman. Soon, his efforts began to bear fruit.

Wanting to give his campaign a nontraditional and high-profile kickoff, Riley chose to announce his candidacy on the Fourth of July 2001, almost a full year before the GOP primary, at a hometown rally in Ashland. The town square, which already resembled the mythical and beloved Mayberry of Andy Griffith fame, was transformed into a piece of pure Americana with red, white, and blue bunting hanging everywhere. Carnival rides and games for the children, an old-fashioned barbecue with homemade ice cream, and patriotic music rounded out the scene. Some skeptics thought Riley could not draw a crowd on a holiday with families preferring to spend time at the lake or other activities not involving politics. An oppressive heat wave might also discourage some from wanting to spend the afternoon outside.

As would often be the case, the Riley campaign proved the skeptics wrong. A crowd of more than 800 from across the state gathered for the event. Riley, wearing a tie and a blue dress shirt that quickly became dark with sweat, laid out his campaign platform. His reform-minded agenda included changing the state budget process to lessen the possibility of mid-year proration, roadbuilding based on priorities rather than politics, focusing on economic development, and building a world-class education system.

Riley ended his announcement address by saying in a determined voice, "We're going to take the best of Alabama and make it better, and that mission starts today!" He then jumped from the stage to shake hands with the cheering and excited crowd. His signature quote would be repeated for the next 18 months in commercials, speeches, and rallies.

Because the announcement was made on a holiday and knowing they had a half-hour newscast to fill and little other news occurring, almost every television station sent a satellite truck to cover the event live. It was an early public relations coup for the Riley camp.

Just six weeks after the the kickoff rally, tragedy struck. Jenice, who had fought so bravely in her battle with cancer, suddenly collapsed and passed away. I hurt for the close-knit Riley family and said a prayer for Jenice, who led the kind of full Christian life I know God rewarded. Losing a child is such an unnatural act for a parent that I could only imagine what Bob and Patsy Riley experienced.

Susan and I were scheduled to host a Riley fundraiser at our Auburn home on the day after Jenice's passing. With no way of notifying all of the attendees in time to cancel, Susan and I decided to hold the event even though no members of the Riley family or their campaign team could attend. I am certain it was the most somber campaign fundraiser held in the history of Alabama politics.

The family grieved, and Patsy took the loss particularly hard, but they eventually decided it was time to move ahead with the campaign. Jenice, after all, had been the biggest supporter and strongest advocate of her father running for governor. The family dedicated the race to her memory, which exponentially increased their determination to win.

Once back on the campaign trail, Riley rose in the polls. His television ads highlighted his small-town, rural roots and values and pointed to his core conservative principles. Needless to say, the advertisements featured several shots of cowboy boots, pick-up trucks, and tin-roofed barns.

One project I was assigned to handle produced the iconic photo of Riley's 2002 race. The Alabama Cattlemen's Association had just endorsed the Riley candidacy. We wanted to send a mail piece to its members informing them of the endorsement and promoting Riley's cattle farmer background.

I arranged for a photo shoot with Riley one Sunday afternoon at Dr. Woody Bartlett's cattle ranch in Pike Road, just outside of Montgomery. Knowing Riley had ridden all his life and was an expert equestrian, I put him atop a horse in a pasture with cattle in the background.

When we reviewed the digital images, I knew we had something special. Riley was sitting in the saddle as comfortably as if he'd been born there. His eyes squinted just enough to shield the afternoon sun and his wrists draped across the pommel with reins in hand. Given their natural resemblance and the full head of dark hair that was the signature of both, you would have thought Ronald Reagan was sitting in the saddle rather than Riley.

The mail piece was a big hit among the cattlemen and everyone who saw the photo absolutely loved it. I had a few thousand campaign posters printed with the horse image to distribute statewide. They flew out the door of the Riley campaign headquarters scattered across Alabama. I believe they were especially popular among middle-aged women who sometimes looked at the handsome Riley as a teen idol of their youth.

There was no doubt the sudden jump in Riley's popularity was showed in Windom's polling as clearly as in as ours. If Windom was to remain a viable candidate, he had to go on the attack.

The first volley from his camp involved a Riley campaign commercial featuring the beatific voice of an announcer extolling the congressman's virtues and detailing why he would be the ideal governor. The commercial ended with an in-camera shot of the announcer, identified as the Reverend Ben Rosser of Ashland, who adds the tag line, "I should know. I've known Bob Riley for more than 30 years."

Windom alleged in the media that Riley was intentionally misleading voters by having them assume Rosser was his personal minister when, in fact, the congressman was baptized in and attended another church in Ashland. Riley responded that the ad never specified Rosser as minister of his home church, but, nevertheless, the clergyman appearing in the ad had presided over the marriages of Riley's children, officiated at Jenice's funeral, and served as the family's spiritual counselor in the difficult months after her untimely death. The silly attack went nowhere.

A potentially more serious blow came when Windom aired a commercial accusing Riley of using his congressional office for personal gain. The television ad listed the committees on which Riley served in Congress and scrolled a list of companies that had business before those bodies.

The allegation was that Riley had invested in those companies because of inside information due to his committee membership. Tampering with committee votes to enrich himself was a serious accusation, and, if true, could prove criminal. The problem for Windom, however, was that it was not true.

When he entered Congress, Riley invested in a blind mutual fund to avoid the very improprieties that Windom accused him of violating. An overeager accountant Riley employed to fill out his congressional ethics form had contacted the mutual fund and obtained the list of investments made on his behalf. The list of investments Windom used for the attack was one that Riley's accountant filed with Congress. Riley was just one of several thousand investors in the mutual fund. He had no control over or knowledge of specific investments. The media quickly latched onto Windom's error, and several newspaper editorials chastised his sloppiness. To his credit, the lieutenant governor personally apologized to Riley before the two made a joint campaign appearance at the Alabama Broadcasters Association in Tuscaloosa.

In politics, the primary rule of launching negative attacks is to ensure that your first attack is accurate because you lose all credibility if it is not. Windom violated that rule and paid the price.

Windom's campaign never caught traction again and Riley defeated him in the GOP primary by a 74 to 18 percent shellacking. Tim James ran a distant third but had largely kept his powder dry, apparently content to lay the predicate for a future gubernatorial run (which came in 2010).

If the Windom attacks proved bothersome, they were bean bags compared to the howitzers veteran campaigner Don Siegelman aimed our way. "The Don," as we began to call him internally to highlight the organized crime and corruption we believed he oversaw as governor, quickly tried to grab the offensive. On the night of Riley's primary win, Siegelman used his own victory speech to issue a challenge for the GOP nominee to join him in a series of debates across the state. Thus, the story on Election Night became the incumbent governor's debate challenge rather than Riley's historically large primary win in a multi-candidate field.

Several other attacks were quickly forthcoming. He alleged that Riley was a tax cheat who did not pay thousands of dollars he owed to state and local government entities. The attacks came from every direction in the form of television, radio, and print ads. If the fact that Riley was a fresh but unknown newcomer was a blessing in the primary, it proved to be somewhat of a curse now. General election voters often tend to be a more cynical lot when it comes to "politicians," and many now heard and believed the Siegelman claims.

As with most of Siegelman's accusations, the attack was an overreach and a bastardization of the facts. The truth, unfortunately, was harder to explain than the false claim. Because Riley owned large acreage of timberland, apartments, rental properties, farmland, vacation homes, and other real estate investments, his property tax liability was high and vast. Rather than pay each of his property tax assessments as they arrived, he found it more convenient to let them accumulate and pay them in bulk, even if it meant some were late and carried financial penalties. The taxes Siegelman claimed Riley "cheated" on were the property taxes, all of which were paid, but not all on time. But telling the public that Riley was wealthy enough to pay taxes on his own schedule without worrying about the late fees was not a palatable option for our side, either.

Riley had also owned several businesses over the years, including a car dealership, a trucking company and, of course, his poultry enterprise. Like most business owners in an increasingly litigious world, Riley and his companies had been sued from time to time. Siegelman's crew relished leaking the list to reporters, including the cases Riley had won and those that had been tossed from court.

Perhaps the boldest and most outrageous attack from Siegelman came when he told a crowd at a heavily covered campaign appearance that Riley had sent jobs out of the United States when he voted to support the North American Free Trade Agreement in Congress. The media, to its credit, called Siegelman on the carpet for the claim since NAFTA became law in 1993, three years before Riley was elected to his first term in the House.

Siegelman spewed criticism of Riley's lack of state government experience and the absence of a detailed plan of what he would do as governor. In winning the GOP primary by such a comfortable margin, Riley had been afforded the ability to speak largely in generalities about his vision for Alabama. The general election campaign, however, was another animal altogether, and Siegelman used the lack of specifics to portray Riley as "all hat and no cattle."

Siegelman was also vulnerable to attack from Riley, who simply needed to hold up the newspaper headlines in what we called the "scandal-a-day" campaign. The normal process for choosing vendors to service lucrative state contracts had been tossed out the window by Siegelman and replaced with one that used partisan politics, not pricing, to select the winners.

It's not an exaggeration to say that every day at least one newspaper in the state carried a story or editorial questioning some ethical aspect of Siegelman, his inner circle, and how they conducted state business. He did himself no favors, either, when he ordered his press office to freeze out the reporters responsible for writing the bulk of the stories and refused to cooperate with several open records requests from the media.

Ethics was not the only front on which Siegelman was vulnerable. State finances were at their worst condition in decades under his watch, and the next governor was predicted to inherit a budget deficit of several hundred million dollars. Education was stagnant and, though Siegelman portrayed himself as a prolific industrial recruiter, unemployment had jumped since he took over the governor's chair. Riley noted all of this at every opportunity.

At the same time, Riley utilized one of his greatest assets on the stump— an ability to portray optimism even in the face of terrible adversity. He truly wanted to fundamentally change how state government in Montgomery operated. Several populist candidates in the past had campaigned against the "good old boy" system in the state capital, the most famous among them being Big Jim Folsom, who was elected governor in 1946 and 1954. Riley truly wanted to change the government model and his campaign slogan, "A New Day in Alabama," reflected his reformist desire.

On paper, Siegelman and Riley were evenly matched candidates. Both were capable of raising the millions of dollars needed to run a competitive race. Both were successful veterans of tough campaigns. And both were driven by deep personal reasons for running and winning. By the end of the race, the candidates had raised a combined $24 million, a record amount for a statewide Alabama election that stands to this day.

The general election was a slugfest with both sides experiencing highs and lows. The months of that fall's campaign are a blur in my memory as any given day required me to oversee the drafting, printing, and distribution of tens of thousands of mail pieces to voters across the state on a moment's notice. Radio ads, some planned and some put together in response to Siegelman's attack of the moment, had to be written, voiced, produced and aired. I believe I worked harder on the 2002 Riley campaign than I have worked on any before or since, including my own.

A few memories, however, do stand out.

Siegelman and Riley agreed to participate in a debate to be held in the studios of Alabama Public Television and broadcast statewide. It would be the only joint appearance of the two candidates, and fireworks were assured. The Riley camp held detailed debate prep sessions with podiums set up as they would be on the set. Answer and rebuttal times were exactly as the debate rules would demand. One of these sessions was held in my office at the Auburn Network following an Auburn home football game. Surrogates portrayed Siegelman and came after Riley with a vengeance, just as we expected the governor to do when the camera came on. Riley, as always, was cool, polished, and handled himself well.

We were also preparing a trap we knew Siegelman would fall into head first.

When the night of the debate arrived, we were all confident in Riley and his ability to perform, but Siegelman, who apparently thought of himself as a mind games expert, tried to throw his challenger off even before the event began. The plan was to bring Riley into the studios through a rear parking lot entrance. When the advance staff arrived, they found several Siegelman supporters standing there with a large banner that read "Why don't you pay your taxes?" along with other smaller signs with equally negative messages. This was an obvious effort to divert Riley's concentration from the debate ahead. The campaign staff located another entrance, and Riley did not know until days later that a Siegelman "welcoming committee" had been awaiting him.

What Riley did see was a crowd of supporters being led in cheers by Patsy and Krisalyn, just like a pep rally. The crowd stayed and cheered for their candidate when the debate was over, as well.

When it was Siegelman's turn to appear on camera, he took the exact tack we had anticipated. He accused our candidate of having no real plan other than the broad and general themes he had previously outlined. Siegelman claimed that Riley had no road map for education, no plan to create jobs, and no idea how to accomplish any of the general reforms he had proposed.

Riley then sprang the trap, inviting viewers to visit his website to download *Plan for Change,* a 150-page book his campaign had prepared. In precise detail, it laid out step-by-step plans for accomplishing each of Riley's goals and, conversely, outlined Siegelman's failures to make progress in each area. Bound copies of the book, with the now very popular "horse photo" featured on the cover, were distributed to reporters as soon as the debate was over. We had removed a sharp arrow from Siegelman's quiver.

PERHAPS THE TWO MOST exciting events of the 2002 Riley campaign involved visits by incumbent President George W. Bush. The president was experiencing a strong wave of popularity, especially in Alabama, following his response to the World Trade Center attack. He appeared with Riley at a sold-out luncheon at the Birmingham Civic Center, which set a national fundraising record for a single event. I was given the high honor of introducing the president at the event.

Donors who contributed $10,000 or more to the fundraising luncheon were allowed to have their photo made with President Bush and Riley. Siegelman quickly seized upon the opportunity to portray his opponent as the candidate of the rich and wealthy. He would even carry a disposable camera to his campaign speeches and offer anyone the tongue-in-cheek opportunity to have their photo taken with him for free, as opposed to the thousands of dollars that Riley supposedly charged his supporters.

I was much more hands-on when President Bush offered to return to the state late in the campaign. The president agreed to headline a large, open-to-the-public rally in support of Riley and my other mentor, Mike Rogers, who was campaigning to succeed Riley in Congress.

Given only a few days notice before the massive event was to take place, the Riley campaign and the White House originally scouted locations in Montgomery, but none could be found that provided the tight security and large capacity that was necessary. Seeing an opportunity, I suggested Auburn as an alternative. My arguments included Auburn's proximity to the Montgomery media market, the number of ideal venues available on campus, and the fact that it was located well within the Third Congressional District, whose seat Riley was vacating and Rogers was working so hard to fill. Plus, Auburn University is easily the most politically conservative public college campus in the state.

My efforts worked too well because not only was the Auburn campus chosen as the site but I also had to help organize the event, with my office as the central coordinating site. Few people realize the number of details that go into a presidential visit, just as I didn't until this event. Riley's campaign manager, Toby Roth, and I had only four days to pull this massive undertaking together. Coordinating the ticketing alone was an absolute zoo with demand far exceeding supply. Then, once we had crafted a plan for the event and begun implementing it, the Secret Service got involved and told us we had to toss it out and start from scratch.

We planned to use Auburn University's baseball field, Plainsman Park, as the venue because we could fill the stands while also allowing people to fill the field all the way to the outfield warning track, more than doubling our capacity. Unfortunately, the weather forecast turned nasty. Predicted severe thunderstorms on the day of the scheduled visit meant we had to prepare two venues instead of one. Staging, security, and all other preparations were also made inside the basketball arena in case the event had to be moved indoors. Two hours before the event, the rain stopped and the dark clouds gave way to sunshine. I remember thinking that this was surely a good omen.

The Secret Service made us take several precautions we had not anticipated. The windows in the stadium's press box had to be completely covered, which we accomplished with a custom-made banner welcoming

President Bush to Auburn University. We also had to construct a maze of plywood passageways beneath the stadium seating so the president could be moved unseen. Air Force One, carrying the president, Congressman Riley, Rogers, and the entourage, landed at Montgomery's Maxwell Air Force Base. The party then boarded the presidential helicopter, Marine One, for the short ride to Auburn. ("Marine One" on this day was actually an identical dual-rotor chopper from Fort Rucker, which was painted with insignia to match Marine One, thus sparing the expense of transporting the president's official helicopter to Alabama.)

As the president arrived, his helicopter, along with two identical decoys, did a low pass over the crowd of 14,000. A huge roar of cheers erupted as the three helicopters flew over the baseball park to the landing spot at the nearby intramural fields. The crowd anxiously awaited the first sitting U.S. president to speak in Auburn since Franklin Delano Roosevelt made an appearance in 1939.

I was standing just inside the stadium dugout, holding a microphone as the president arrived. He stood next to me on a piece of white tape on the floor marked "POTUS" (President of the United States), tossed me a wink, and gave a thumbs-up signal. Using the announcer's voice I'd honed during countless hours on the radio, I turned on the PA system and said, "Ladies and gentlemen, the President of the United States, George W. Bush." A tsunami of cheers rose as the Auburn band played "War Eagle." (The band had prepared to perform "Hail to the Chief," but we learned the day before that the song can't be played at campaign events.)

A decade later, I had the opportunity to spend some time with Bush in his post-presidency years and mentioned to him that I was from Auburn. With a sparkle in his eye, he quickly told me that he had once participated in a campaign event at Auburn's baseball stadium and that it had been among the favorites of his time in office.

"I don't remember the speech except that I started it by saying 'War Eagle!,'" Bush said. "The crowd didn't care what else I said after that."

He also said he understood that a video clip of him delivering the university's famed battle cry was played over and over on the Jordan-Hare Stadium video display at football games the next season. I told him it was, indeed, and the crowd reaction was just as enthusiastic as when he had said it in person.

With the Bush event and its wave of publicity occurring just a week before the election, all of us in the campaign felt that everything was peaking at just the right moment. Our internal polls as well as media-sponsored polls conducted the weekend before the election showed Riley leading Siegelman between 9 and 12 points, so we were fairly confident when Tuesday arrived.

Tuesday afternoon, however, we began getting reports that turnout in the African American boxes across the state was extremely high. Knowing Siegelman's popularity among the minority population, our polling had included a much higher sample of African Americans than is typical, just to be safe. Historically, African Americans made up 17 to 22 percent of the vote in a statewide general election, but in 2002, the black turnout spiked to 27 percent. That meant Riley needed 7 out of 10 white voters to defeat a candidate who was hailed by the national media as the next Bill Clinton. The actual turnout exceeded even our inflated expectations, which meant the early night some of us had planned was not going to happen.

Once the polls across the state closed, a wave of severe weather slowed the reporting of returns. Monstrous thunderstorms had even forced the Riley campaign to abandon its plans for an outdoor victory party in Ashland's town square. The event was instead moved to a large auditorium on the grounds of the Talladega Superspeedway. As the returns came in, it became readily apparent that our fears of a massive African American turnout for Siegelman were true, and our easy win promised by the polling data was in jeopardy. The night dragged on and on, and the margin between the candidates got closer and closer.

Two of the most famous and beloved radio personalities in Alabama and the southeast, Rick Burgess and Bill "Bubba" Bussey of *The Rick and Bubba Show* served as emcees at the Riley gathering. They did their best to keep the crowd optimistic and energized, but the large-screen televisions flashing unexpectedly close returns around the room made their job nearly impossible. As late night began turning into early morning, Siegelman appeared before the television cameras and claimed victory, despite the fact that there were returns still to be counted and the margin was razor-thin.

As people stopped me at the Riley event and asked me if the balloting was over and whether we had lost as Siegelman had claimed, I tried to put on a good poker face and offer reassurances, but I feared the sadness in my eyes and my poor acting skills did little to buoy their faith.

At the same time, however, Riley's staff noticed a startling anomaly in the returns. The Republican Party had placed poll watchers in every county courthouse to witness the ballot counting and to phone in returns as they became available. The list showed that Baldwin County had reported Siegelman leading the vote by a surprising margin—surprising because Baldwin is one of the most heavily Republican counties in the entire state. Siegelman's chances of prevailing in Baldwin County were less than zero. Something was obviously wrong.

A call revealed that the same severe weather affecting the rest of the state was bedeviling Baldwin, and power surges and outages resulting from the lightning storms had caused glitches in the devices that electronically read the voting machine returns. When the tapes were reread shortly after midnight, the software corrected itself and gave Riley the win in Baldwin County that everyone had expected and that he had earned.

When all votes had been counted statewide, Riley had won the governor's chair by a bare 3,117 votes out of 1.3 million cast, the closest margin in Alabama history. As I drove back to Auburn after the longest night I could remember, I called my brother-in-arms, Mike Rogers, to congratulate him on his election to Congress, also by the slimmest of margins.

But as Coach Dye had always told me, big or small, landslide or squeaker, a win is a win in the record books.

When dawn broke, Siegelman took little time to cry foul and claim that Republicans were "stealing" the election from him in the dark of night. The Democratic poll watchers in Baldwin had packed it in before the counting was complete and the governor claimed Republican hijinks with the ballots had ensued. Of course, if the shoe were on the other foot and a heavily Democratic county had gone to Riley's column, Siegelman would have noticed the discrepancy, just as our team did, and similarly followed up on it.

Siegelman demanded a statewide recount, which state law at the time did not allow. My personal fear was not that a recount of the ballots cast would go against us. Instead, my fear was that breaking the seals on already tabulated ballot boxes would give Democrats the opportunity to stuff in new ballots, especially in certain Democratic-friendly portions of Alabama where voter fraud and ballot tampering had proliferated for decades. Both the attorney general and the secretary of state held news conferences reiterating the state law against breaking the seals. Siegelman, not surprisingly, claimed they were both partisans working to help Riley. Siegelman prepared to take his case for a recount into court.

While Siegelman was plotting his next move, Riley held a rally in the parking lot of his Birmingham campaign headquarters where hundreds of supporters from across the state had gathered. He gave the victory speech that time and circumstances had denied him the night before and he told the crowd that President Bush had called to congratulate him on his "landslide" victory. With the press present, Riley announced that former Alabama state senator and respected Birmingham businessman Bill Cabaniss (who would later serve as President Bush's ambassador to the Czech Republic) would lead his transition team.

Shortly after, I was announced as chairman of the Inaugural Committee, a daunting job that was made even more so by the uncertainty caused by Siegelman's recount bid.

For thirteen days, Siegelman kept pushing for his recount. His attorneys filed several motions and lost every one. Not a single ballot box was opened even though he was desperate to pop the top on at least one so the others could follow suit. With his case finally before a State Supreme Court that seemed unlikely to hand him a favorable ruling, especially since the law was against him, Siegelman called the media to the capitol and finally conceded the election. My mind wandered back to the threats he had made when I opposed his lottery bill, and I realized that I had kept my pledge to help elect a governor who would bring honesty and integrity to the office.

It was one of the more satisfying moments of my political career, but the clock ticking toward Inauguration Day did not allow me to enjoy the victory for long.

The only part of an Inaugural Day required by the Alabama Constitution is the swearing in of statewide elected officials. The rest is simply a way to show thanks to the supporters who elected them and to publicly celebrate a historic event. Believe me, it is a very expensive, complicated and labor-intensive undertaking. It involves hundreds of volunteers, hours of planning, and more money that has to be raised. There was a great deal of excitement surrounding governor-elect Riley, and it seemed like everyone wanted to be a part of it.

After assembling a staff and coming up with an overall plan and event schedule, I had to quickly raise the funds to carry out the ambitious program. Just as I had done in my sports broadcasting career, I put together various packages that included tickets to the events as well as advertising in the official inaugural program, a bound book that became a collector's item. I was happy to have some eager and accomplished fundraisers assist me with this task and, though it was not required by state law, we publicly disclosed the donors of every dollar that we collected.

Once the money was in the bank, I turned my attention toward the logistical challenge. In addition to the staging, sound, seating, media risers and other details that go into the actual inaugural ceremony, there were other issues.

For example, I worked with officials from the City of Montgomery to arrange the closing of downtown streets to stage the mile-long post-ceremony parade up Dexter Avenue. We had a seemingly endless list of requests by communities, organizations, and marching bands from across the state wanting to participate. In fact, almost every legislator submitted a list of high school and university marching bands in his or her district, which results in a lot of people and a logistical challenge. Seemingly small details end up being big ones, like feeding the parade participants lunch before putting them back in cars and buses to head home. Lunch for that many people ended up costing $15,000.

Other events included a party in the Ashland town square that would allow the folks Riley had laughed, cried, and prayed with throughout his lifetime to give him a proper send-off to Montgomery. In addition to the actual inaugural ceremony and parade, other events our team coordinated included a First Lady's luncheon, a Sunday prayer breakfast, a children's program on the capitol lawn, a legislative reception, and the biggest, most challenging, and most popular event, the Inaugural Ball.

We also put on a brunch at the Governor's Mansion prior to the swearing-in ceremony. This turned out to be a very nice event, but most people don't know that we actually planned it from aerial photos. Siegelman's staff would not allow us access to the Mansion grounds until the Friday before the Monday inauguration, so we had to use aerial photos to determine the size and location of tents and other logistics.

For each event, we produced souvenirs attendees could take home. We produced crystal vases, display plates, paperweights, key chains, cuff links, and ink pens, with each item bearing the Seal of the Governor's Office, the date of the inauguration, and the new governor's signature.

If my job was difficult, there was one that was worse: overseeing the ticketing operations. Riley was now the most popular man in Alabama and Republicans were especially excited to see him become the next governor. Everyone, it seemed, wanted to be a part of the celebration. Many more people wanted tickets than were available. Whoever I put in charge of tickets would need both diplomatic skills and good political instincts. Fortunately, I knew just the guy.

John Ross, still in his twenties and fresh out of college, had worked in the policy shop of the Riley campaign. He had always impressed me with his tact and intellect. Born and raised in Guntersville, Ross earned a bachelor's degree in political science at the University of Richmond and was working toward a master's in Public Administration at Alabama while pulling double duty with the Riley campaign. He had an innate kindness and thoughtfulness about him along with the Job-like patience the ticketing job would require. Most importantly, Ross had the ability to tell someone to go jump off a cliff but to tell them in such a nice manner that they looked forward to the plunge.

His job was made even more difficult because the country group

Alabama had agreed to perform at the Inaugural Ball. When the group separately signaled that its members were about to retire, the hottest ticket in the state became even hotter, but John took it all in stride. He performed the difficult job expertly and protected Riley from the hurt and anger that often follows when a supporter has to be told "no." I filed Ross's organizational skills and uncanny ability to deal with difficult situations away in the back of my mind. I would call on him again a few years later with an even more important task.

At noon on Inauguration Day, thousands in front of the historic Alabama capitol watched as Bob Riley and his childhood sweetheart, Patsy, walked down the impressive marble steps. Then the new First Lady held the official state Bible upon which Confederate President Jefferson Davis and each Alabama governor since has been sworn into office. My political mentor and friend stood with his right hand in the air repeating a sovereign oath. My eyes moved down the row to the Rileys' proud children, each of whom had worked so hard to help their father win, and to the empty chair in the row. Upon the chair, which was saved for Jenice, lay a single rose. It was a lump-in-your-throat moment.

Following the oath of office ending with the words, "so help me, God," it was my great honor to step to the podium and introduce Bob Riley as the 52nd governor of the State of Alabama.

Susan accompanied me to the Inaugural Ball later that evening, and when I saw her in her gown, I was reminded that I had outkicked my coverage when it came to marriage. We enjoyed watching Governor Riley and the First Lady in their first dance in their new roles, to the music of the legendary band, Alabama. Since this was the culmination of a three-day celebration, I was able to relax for what seemed the first time in a year and a half.

When the ball was over, I held Susan's hand and took one last look around the dim and empty Montgomery Civic Center. I thought about the long and bruising campaign that got us here in the first place.

Winning the governor's office had been a tough job for all of us. But I quickly realized the even tougher job was about to begin—governing.

∽ *In Their Own Words* ∽

BOB RILEY
U.S. CONGRESS 1996–2002; GOVERNOR 2003–2011

During my years in Washington, I met some incredible leaders from all over the country. And we, of course, would discuss issues that were facing our respective states. After hearing some of the reforms different states were enacting with remarkable success, I became convinced that Alabama was stuck in the politics of the past and needed a new direction. The same people and special interests had run Montgomery for decades. It was time for a change.

I had told my family that I would serve six years and then come back home. Whether that should be Montgomery or Ashland, I did not know. On Easter Sunday afternoon, 2001, the family took a vote. If anyone thought it would be too much for them, their career, children or family, then I wouldn't run. One "no" vote would have stopped the campaign before it started. It had to be unanimous. And it was. 8-0. Before I knew it, we were off.

Soon after our victory, I asked Mike to serve as the Chairman of our Inauguration. With so many things happening at once—putting a new administration together, fighting the recount nonsense, working on a transition team—I wanted someone I could trust to plan a great celebration. I knew if Mike Hubbard was in charge, it would be done well. And it was. Mike raised all the money, handled the invitations and ticketing for each event, booked the performers, among a million other things. Patsy and I did not even know what it would look like until we arrived. We knew, without a doubt, with Mike Hubbard in control, it would be incredible. We were right.

7

Amendment One

The morning after the Inauguration, the Riley team reported for work eager to get started bringing the change and reform their boss had promised. But their efforts were slowed before they even started. Siegelman's staff had stripped the governor's office of office supplies, leaving the desks empty and bare. Not a pen or a piece of paper or even a paperclip could be found. Some of the computer keyboards were missing the "B" and "R" keys, much like Clinton and Gore staffers had removed the "W" from theirs when President Bush entered office. Worse yet, the computers had not only been cleaned of documents and other files, but the operating systems that ran them had also been removed, along with all of the programs. When the newly appointed Riley crew turned on their computers, all they got was a blinking cursor and a blank screen. The software and operating systems were eventually reloaded at significant expense to taxpayers. Not wanting to begin his administration on a negative note, the new governor instructed his staff to keep the incident quiet. However, a reporter from the *Mobile Press-Register* heard rumors and, upon investigation, wrote a story about the sabotage.

Riley would have been fortunate if pilfered office products had been his biggest problem, but he and his finance director, former Protective Life Insurance Company CEO Drayton Nabers, discovered that the state's budgets were in much worse shape than earlier predicted. Years of passing state spending plans cobbled together with non-recurring revenue and one-time pots of money had finally caught up with the state, and an economic downturn following the 2001 World Trade Center attack only amplified the problem.

The governor had inherited, with no exaggeration, the worst financial crisis in Alabama since the Great Depression.

In four years under Don Siegelman, the state's debt burden had doubled and payments on the debt were expected to balloon by almost $110 million during Riley's first year in office. The "Rainy Day Fund," which was created to protect the state from devastating budget proration, had been depleted. The state's Medicaid Agency, which was already providing only the most basic, bare bones services demanded by federal law, was facing a $110 million shortfall. Our prison system, already operating at more than 200 percent capacity, needed at least $50 million to meet federal court mandates to reduce overcrowding and provide the necessary security. Unsustainable increases in the costs of health insurance benefits to teachers and state employees also had a crippling financial effect.

In short, the state needed almost $700 million in additional revenue just to maintain the status quo. And that was after Riley had already worked to cut more than $230 million in state government waste he found immediately upon taking office.

Riley, for example, dramatically reduced the number of state cars owned by the government. He ordered agencies under his control to turn in unneeded vehicles, and, during a media event at the state surplus property lot, vehicle after vehicle was rounded up for disposal. Almost 600 state cars were sold by Riley, netting the state about $7 million in revenue.

Though unpopular with public employees, merit raises were frozen, saving $30 million. Travel costs for conducting state business were trimmed by $6 million. An across-the-board cut in personnel expenses netted $82 million and, setting an example for others to follow, Riley reduced his own office's budget by about $1 million. Reforming the Medicaid drug program, entering into joint purchasing agreements, and other common sense cost-cutting measures were implemented.

Despite the cuts, the shortfall continued to dwarf the savings.

During the transition period between administrations, Riley had asked me to serve as his floor leader in the House, a position I quickly accepted. As floor leader, it was my duty to help gather the necessary votes to push the governor's legislative initiatives through the House chamber. In some cases, it was relatively easy work, especially when reforms did not ruffle the feathers of special interest groups. In other cases, however, it was among the most frustrating and exasperating tasks I would ever be assigned.

Shortly before the start of the 2003 session, Governor Riley invited me to his office for what he said would be a very important meeting. Entering the governor's office felt very different than it had when Siegelman had summoned me during the lottery debate just a few years before. I was now coming to meet with a valued friend rather than a foe. Sitting me down to relax for a few minutes, Riley asked about Susan and the boys and we briefly discussed the normal political scuttlebutt circulating around the capitol. Then we got down to business.

The governor walked me through the reasons for the shortfall and the reforms he had implemented in response. A dire budget forecast, however, still faced him. Riley had no choice, he explained, other than to ask for a significant tax increase.

Even though he had refused to take a "no new taxes" pledge during the 2002 campaign, I was still surprised and explained that convincing the legislature to support a $700 million tax increase would be difficult. He surprised me even more when he said the tax package would likely total more than $1 billion instead of the $700 million needed to simply fill the hole. I listened intently as he detailed the reasons, which basically were that he wanted to make a bold stroke that would provide tax relief for the working poor and simultaneously lift Alabama from the bottom of national rankings in terms of overall education support.

I must admit that I was torn between loyalty to my governor, friend, and mentor and my adherence to the fiscal conservatism that was then, and remains now, a cornerstone of my political philosophy. The saving grace was that Riley's plan could be implemented only if the people of the state supported it since the 1901 Alabama Constitution prohibits any taxes, other than sales levies, from becoming law without a referendum vote. And, to his credit, Riley said his package would pass or fail in its entirety and on its own merits. Even the few taxes that could be passed without a vote would not be implemented if the citizens disapproved.

To announce his plan, Riley's press office secured time in the evening news block during which the governor would make a rare, live statewide address on the budget crisis. A bust of Ronald Reagan was placed on a credenza just over Riley's shoulder and displayed prominently during the speech. Reagan, too, had been forced to raise taxes during his first term as governor of California as a result of budget shortfalls he inherited from Democrat Pat Brown. Just a few years later, once the economy had improved, Reagan had been able to reverse direction and cut taxes, a fact Riley noted in his remarks.

Like a lawyer making a case before a jury, Riley walked the viewing public through the financial crisis and the reasons Alabama arrived there in the first place. He also explained the consequences if the state did not act. Riley said 6,900 seniors would lose Medicaid coverage and be tossed from nursing homes; 25 of the state's poorest school systems would go bankrupt and affect the education of more than 100,000 children; more than 5,000 prisoners would be released into neighborhoods to reduce overcrowding, and jury trials would be suspended indefinitely.

He concluded by noting that if Alabamians approved the $1 billion-plus in new taxes, the state would still have a lower tax burden than 44 other states and its citizens would continue to pay less taxes than both the southeastern and national averages.

When the speech was concluded, a university political scientist opining on a public television roundtable and in the next day's newspaper noted that the governor's office, from which Riley spoke, was dimly lit. He theorized that the decision was likely made to convey the seriousness of the catastrophic financial situation. In truth, the capitol's aged electrical system could not handle the power needed to run the television lights. In the final seconds before Riley went live, a circuit blew causing half of the lights to go dark.

To SAY THAT THE proposal was not lovingly embraced by Republicans in either the House or Senate would be an understatement. They, like me, were surprised by the scope and size of the tax hike. Most legislators also did not feel the same sense of loyalty toward Bob Riley that I held. Ultimately, most ended up voting for the items in the package and let them go to the ballot.

Democrats, on the other hand, were tickled. If the package was approved by the voters, many of the constituents represented by Democratic lawmakers would receive tremendous tax cuts, if not total relief, from paying taxes. If it failed, the tax package would likely deal a death blow to Riley's political capital and future. It was a no-lose situation for Democrats.

As the various bills within the package were written, Democrats agreed to sponsor some of the tax increases and Republicans stepped up to offer some of the accountability bills. Two bills, however, were treated like Kryptonite—a property tax increase and the actual constitutional amendment that would appear on the ballot. The Riley administration could not find any legislator willing to carry them.

The property tax increase was proving especially bothersome for many. Two of the most influential special interests working the State House—the Alabama Farmers Federation (ALFA) and the Alabama Forestry Association—were dead set against the bill. Both groups had split their support and contributions between Republican and Democratic legislative leaders through the past several election cycles to ensure influence on both sides of the aisle. As a result, when Riley's legislative team went searching for sponsors, the hallways cleared.

In the end, Governor Riley called and asked me to carry the property tax legislation. Although it was the last thing I wanted to do, I understood it was my duty as his floor leader and agreed to sponsor the bills.

In the past, my legislative district in Auburn had approved local property tax increases to fund public education, so I was not terribly worried about repercussions at home. I was, however, concerned about how it would affect many of the relationships I'd forged at the State House and whether they would be lost forever.

As soon as I received the original draft of the property bill, I sat down with representatives of ALFA, the Forestry and Cattlemen's associations, and others. I asked them to share their collective concerns about the details of the bill but not the property tax itself. If the tax measure was approved by the voters, I wanted its implementation to be as fair as possible to the farmers, foresters, and ranchers they represented. Many of their requests were incorporated in my bill, and, I believe, improved it. I am convinced these changes lessened the blow and helped salvage some goodwill both for me, and, more importantly, for Governor Riley.

The final package came to be known simply as Amendment One and contained many much-needed reform measures I believed were long overdue. Strong reforms to control the spiraling costs of public employee health insurance coverage, stricter controls and oversight of education spending and dramatic changes in teacher tenure were just a few of the accountability measures that would go into effect if voters approved the package.

In the eyes of the voters and the media, however, the reforms were overshadowed by the tax increases. Shifting the tax burden from the poorest citizens of our state to the wealthiest proved a bitter pill to swallow by many. Even those who would benefit or be unaffected by the tax reform proposal were convinced they would end up paying more.

In the end, I believe two main factors doomed the Amendment One package to defeat.

First, the sheer size and scope of it made it difficult to explain and even more difficult for voters to digest. When you consider the various tax changes and accountability reforms contained in the package, there were simply too many moving parts for voters to easily follow. They focused on the biggest parts—the income, property, and sales tax increases. I also believe it would have been slightly more palatable had the proposed tax increases totaled in the millions rather than a billion. The mental distinction between an $800 or $900 million package and a $1 billion package would have been considerable and might have allowed the governor to escape the "Billion Dollar Bob" moniker that hounded him throughout the referendum campaign,

The other factor working against the package resulted directly from Riley sticking to his principles and refusing to bend on what he considered an important political point—earmarking.

In Alabama, almost 90 percent of all taxes collected by the state are earmarked for specific purposes. That is the highest percentage in the nation and far ahead of second-place Montana which earmarks a little more than 60 percent of its revenues. The more stable taxes that remain stagnant through good times and bad flow into our General Fund budget, which allocates money to all non-education state agencies. Growth taxes, those that are most likely to increase naturally during good economic times, are earmarked for our Education Trust Fund, which provides moneys to public schools, two-year colleges, and universities. While the earmarked education taxes had traditionally allowed the legislature to spend like drunken sailors when the economy was good, they also bottomed out during economic downturns, requiring devastating cuts and proration in education spending. Taking it a step further, some of our taxes earmarked for education are further earmarked for even more specific purposes, such as the requirement that state income taxes must be spent on teacher salaries.

As a candidate for governor, Riley often railed against earmarking during his speeches. He explained to audiences that such extreme earmarking handcuffed a governor's and legislature's ability to manage the state properly. Riley often used the example of a family specifically earmarking a portion of its income to a family vacation yet refusing to dip into those funds when their mortgage is due. The result, of course, is that the family loses its home but gets to go on a vacation to Disney World.

On the surface it defies logic but the history behind Alabama's extreme earmarking is simple. Years of Democratic rule, shenanigans, and abuse in Montgomery produced a toxic level of cynicism in voters. Asking them to approve ballot initiatives for new taxes based simply upon politicians' promises of how the money might be used proved fruitless on many occasions. Constitutionally earmarking a tax increase for specific outlined purposes, on the other hand, had often resulted in success at the ballot box.

When Riley proposed Amendment One to lawmakers and asked them to approve the $1.2 billion tax package, he had one ironclad, inviolable demand—every dime of the money had to be unearmarked. Doing so, I am convinced, allowed Riley to look at himself in the mirror and know that he stuck to his guns on a policy point that was near and dear to him. It also likely caused him to lose the Amendment One battle before it even got started.

As soon as the legislature approved the package and the referendum election was set for September 9, 2003—just nine months after Riley had taken office—the battle lines were quickly drawn. A group of committed and, in many cases, enraged Amendment One opponents quickly formed the Tax Accountability Coalition Political Action Committee. The PAC's purpose was to raise the money necessary to campaign against Riley's plan, and, in some cases, against the governor, himself. Two of Riley's cabinet members, Labor Commissioner Charles Bishop and Alcoholic Beverage Control Commissioner Guice Slawson, publicly resigned and officially signed on with the anti-Riley effort. Slawson, who had been the single largest individual financial contributor to Riley's gubernatorial campaign just a year before, became the largest contributor to the efforts of the Amendment One opponents.

The opponents produced a series of effective radio ads, television spots, and direct mail pieces. One mailer aimed at Baby Boomers, for instance, carried a photo of schoolchildren crouching under desks with the headline, "Remember Protecting Ourselves from Soviet Attack? That Was a Good Idea. Thinking 'Duck & Cover' Would Keep Us Safe . . . That Was a Bad Plan." The inside of the piece read, "Real Tax Reform for Alabama Is a Good Idea. Governor Riley's $1.2 Billion Tax Hike Is a Bad Plan."

At the same time Amendment One was presented to voters, President George W. Bush convinced Congress to stimulate the economy by providing taxpayers with a special $300 tax rebate for single filers and a $600 return for married couples filing jointly. Bumper stickers could soon be seen across Alabama that read "Bush Giveth . . . Riley Taketh Away."

The governor, meanwhile, reconvened his campaign machine—or at least those who had not defected to the other side—and began pumping out his own material. The Partnership for Progress sent its own mail into boxes across the state and even produced a 15-minute infomercial detailing the complex accountability and revenue package in detail. In the infomercial, Riley looked directly into the camera and presented his case. He crisscrossed the state speaking to every group he could find. Riley answered the same often-hostile questions thousands of times and ran through the same numbers again and again, often to ears that refused to listen.

The friendliest and most receptive groups were found on campuses of the state's public colleges and universities. Tired of competing with Paul

Hubbert and the influence of the teachers' union for a fair share of education funding, most university officials believed passage of Amendment One would expand the size of the funding pie and, thus, provide them a larger piece. Because Auburn University is the cornerstone of the economic base of Lee County, the county's Republican Executive Committee was probably the only GOP-affiliated group to endorse passage of Amendment One. It was also one of the few counties to vote to ratify the plan.

The Partnership PAC was funded through two main and very different sources, supporting the old adage that politics often make strange bedfellows.

The Business Council of Alabama, headed by my good friend and trusted political advisor, Billy Canary, had endorsed the plan and pledged its support. BCA, as it was known around Montgomery, had long championed the call for comprehensive tax reform in Alabama, but only if it were accompanied by similar efficiency and accountability reforms the business community demanded. Riley's 19-point package, while difficult to explain to the public, was just the prescription BCA had ordered and the organization jumped into the referendum campaign with both feet.

On the other end of the political spectrum was the state teachers' union and Republicans' top nemesis, Paul Hubbert. Hubbert, who had long fought pro-business legislation including tax incentives for economic development, signed onto the Amendment One bandwagon early. Hubbert even helped lobby waffling Democratic legislators during the special session. Much like higher education officials, Hubbert believed passage of the tax package would significantly increase funding for the K-12 school system and the thousands of teachers and education support personnel the union represented.

The AEA's A-Vote PAC, funded by the monthly donations of its union members, is one of the largest sources of campaign contributions in Montgomery. The vast majority of the PAC's contributions are made to support Democrats and defeat Republicans. The deep money well in this case, however, was used to support an unpopular, billion-dollar tax package being promoted by a Republican governor whom AEA had vigorously opposed in the election. The fact that AEA and BCA, the proverbial cobra and mongoose of Alabama politics, were on the same side of a controversial issue, made me feel like I was in the Bizarro World of Superman comic books where everything we understand to be one way is actually the other.

Despite his best efforts, thousands of miles on the road and millions of dollars in campaign spending, Riley could not overcome the cynicism and confusion that plagued the electorate. On the evening of September 9, he watched his proposal get crushed under a 67 to 33 percent landslide. Only a handful of Alabama's 67 counties voted to pass the plan. Even lower-middle class and poverty-stricken citizens, who would benefit the most from its passage, voted heavily against Amendment One.

Demonstrating what one state newspaper termed his "trademark optimism," a surprisingly upbeat Riley stood before the television cameras that night and said he had heard the message from voters loud and clear and would provide the lean, trim, and affordable government they wanted. While such a public and lopsided defeat had to sting, the governor handled it with a grace and bravery that is rare among public officials. *Governing Magazine* seemed to agree when Riley was awarded its Public Official of the Year Award in 2003, and *Time Magazine* dubbed him one of the nation's most courageous public figures.

Following instructions given to him by the citizens of Alabama, Riley began a methodical scaling back of state government. State agencies, including the governor's office, were instructed to begin a mandated staff reduction and across-the-board budget cuts.

While the cutbacks were taking place, however, something unexpected was also occurring. Alabama's economy began an unexpected recovery. In 2004, the year after Amendment One failed, the Education Trust Fund budget grew by more than 9 percent and by more than 11 percent the year after. The traditionally stagnant General Fund experienced an uptick as well. While the recovery was good for the state and averted a crisis, it was bad timing for Riley.

Several of his critics and the victorious opponents of Amendment One pointed to the predictions that the elderly would be ripped from nursing home beds and prison doors would be thrown open if the tax increase failed. When the doom-and-gloom scenarios did not materialize, they accused the governor of extreme fear mongering.

In retrospect, I don't believe anyone walking into that job could have looked at the same numbers presented to Riley and not drawn the same nightmarish assumptions, especially without being able to predict that the economy would revive so quickly. He did what he believed to be the right thing and I am comfortable with my decision to support him.

If SERVING AS RILEY'S floor leader during those early days taught me anything, I learned that I enjoyed the give and take negotiation of the legislative process and operating at the highest levels of state government. The fact that Republicans were a minority in the House made legislative victories, no matter how small, even more thrilling and satisfying. The chess game the opposing Republican and Democratic caucuses played in trying to outmaneuver each other was stimulating.

I was no longer content to simply ferry the bills through the chamber as Riley's floor leader. Instead, I wanted to take a more distinct leadership role in working with my fellow Republicans to put us in a position to win during the next election cycle.

As the 2004 session approached, several of my colleagues encouraged me to run for the position of House Minority Leader. Serving as a House member already took a lot of time away from my business interests and my family, and I knew that serving as caucus leader would demand even more. But I also knew the Democrats controlling the House and Senate were not running the state well and something had to be done. We teetered on the edge of insolvency in the budgets because Democrats refused to make the tough choices and stand up to the special interests groups that funded them. They regularly sided against small business owners because the labor unions ordered them to.

Running for minority leader meant taking on Jim Carns, a House member who had represented portions of Jefferson and Shelby counties since 1990 and currently held the job. Carns was a good man and leader and I liked and respected him. But I firmly believed the House GOP caucus could and should be better organized and, as a result, more effective.

I decided to run and went on the road meeting one-on-one with my fellow Republican House members to make my case. With the 2006 election cycle around the corner and Alabama becoming a more and more Republican state, I argued that the caucus needed a leader who could raise the money needed to gain seats. To that end, I pointed to my background in the media and experience in managing high-stakes, combative political campaigns. I also promised to put together a steering committee representative of the caucus and for it to meet regularly to make decisions and set policy rather than running things as a one-man, top-down operation.

A third candidate for caucus chair also emerged as Blaine Galliher, a Republican from Gadsden who had served in the House since 1994, threw his hat into the ring.

I would love to say that my fellow Republicans rallied en masse around my cause and helped me win the race in a landslide, but that wasn't the case. The truth is we had to hold several rounds of voting before a winner emerged. Galliher, recognizing he would not have the votes necessary to win, withdrew his name early in the voting process, but the deadlock still could not be broken. Eventually, I was elected minority leader by one vote.

To their credit, though it was a spirited contest, neither of my opponents let the race adversely affect our relationship. Blaine and I actually became closer friends as I relied on his advice and counsel often during my time as minority leader. Today, he remains one of my strongest allies in his role as chair of the agenda-setting House Rules Committee, one of the most powerful jobs in the legislature. Carns, who left the House to serve on the Jefferson County Commission, has since returned to the legislature, where he remains a Republican stalwart.

Following the advice of Mike Rogers, who had served as minority leader before his election to Congress, I quickly developed the reputation of a stern disciplinarian, often to the chagrin of some caucus members. Because we were in the minority, the only way we could be effective and block bad legislation promoted by the Democrats was to stay united and work together as Republicans. The Democrats recognized this fact and often attempted to lure a handful of our members to vote with them by promising various spoils. Accepting such favors to abandon their fellow

Republicans, especially on issues we had voted as a caucus to take a strong position upon, was akin to changing uniforms in the middle of a battle and fighting with the other side.

From time to time, I called out specific members for abandoning their colleagues and the conservative principles we shared. This was a stark departure from the way things had been run before. On an occasion or two, the steering committee even drafted letters of censure that explicitly spelled out our displeasure when a member went rogue on an issue important to the group. Though the few that too-often sided with the Democrats grumbled under their breath, their forays onto the other side of the aisle became fewer and fewer and morale among the majority of the caucus members increased.

Unfortunately for me, my efforts made me Public Enemy Number One with the Democratic leadership and union boss Paul Hubbert, who was used to bullying legislators into voting his way without opposition. I would find out just how much I had angered Hubbert and the Democrats during the 2006 election when they targeted me for defeat at all costs.

SHORTLY AFTER I BECAME minority leader, we were handed an opportunity to increase our Republican numbers and demonstrate our new political solidarity, though it occurred under tragic circumstances that sadden me to this day. State Representative Jack Venable, a Democrat from Tallassee, was the epitome of a Southern gentleman. As chairman of the House Rules Committee, which set the agenda and determined which bills the body would consider on any given day, he was universally considered fair and even-handed. In the increasingly partisan and political atmosphere prevailing in the legislature, he refused to be drawn into battles between the Democrats and Republicans.

Venable was diagnosed with leukemia in 2004 and began a valiant battle that impressed all of his colleagues. In November of 2005, a year after his cancer was first detected, Venable passed away at the age of 66.

As saddened as we were to lose Venable, his passing opened up an opportunity for Republicans. Since his election in 1974, the counties Venable represented, Elmore and Coosa, had largely become bedroom communities for many Republican families who worked in Montgomery. Venable had not been reelected so many times because he was a Democrat, but, rather despite the fact he was a Democrat. His passing now opened the door for Republicans to capture a House seat we had not held since the days of Reconstruction.

I soon received a call from Barry Mask, the same friend who had sent me a how-to political campaign book during my first race in 1998. He told me he was interested in running for the open seat. Originally, Mask had planned to run against long-time incumbent State Senator Larry Dixon in the next Republican primary, but the open House seat led him to change his focus quickly.

Mask's political interest stretched back to his college days at Auburn where he served as student body president. He made his first run for public office in 1982 while still a college student at the age of 23 when he challenged Lester White for the House seat representing Tallapoosa County. He missed forcing a run-off election by only 31 votes and graduated from college the next year.

Bitten by the political bug, Mask worked for several groups over the years lobbying lawmakers and observing how the process worked in the Alabama State House.

When Mask and I sat down to discuss the race, I laid out the challenge he faced. Venable had been close to Democratic House Speaker Seth Hammett, and I knew that he, along with the rest of the Democratic Party leadership, would fight to keep the seat in their hands. Paul Hubbert and the AEA, too, sensing the momentum a united and cohesive Republican caucus was generating, did not want us adding to our ranks. Barry assured me he was up to the task.

I made Barry an offer the House Republican caucus had never before made to a candidate. I committed that we would help him raise money and, using private dollars, provide a professional consultant and an on-the-ground campaign manager. I told him we would also help produce his mail, radio, and television spots and take care of the other details necessary to run a competitive race. Being so hands-on in a race was unprecedented for the caucus, but it would serve as a template that would be massaged over the years and eventually lead us to capturing the majority.

The Democrats tapped Bobby Payne, the mayor of Tallassee, who had served in that office for about two decades, as their candidate. Payne cast himself as the second coming of Jack Venable—a conservative Democrat you could trust. He ran on a pro-education platform and painted Tallassee as some sort of utopia under his leadership, promising to bring the same successes to state government that he claimed to have produced on the local level.

Funding was not a problem for Payne because Hubbert, liberal special interests, and the Democratic leadership quickly sunk thousands into his race, most of which was spent on negative television and mail pieces attacking Mask. Their polling obviously revealed the same information as ours—that Mask had an instant advantage simply running under the Republican label and Payne's only chance of winning was to tear the GOP standard bearer down.

One commercial aired on Payne's behalf showed a slot machine spinning with the faces of Mask and other Republican leaders eventually appearing in the windows. The commercial claimed that Indian gaming money from Mississippi was funding Mask's effort, a charge that was blatantly dishonest and laughably false. A negative Payne mail piece also focused on Mask's past experience as a lobbyist, equating his candidacy as sending a fox to guard a henhouse.

Mask, meanwhile, worked the grassroots hard. With the help of the campaign manager we provided, Cory Adair, a former caucus intern who happened to live in Tallassee, he put together a massive door-to-door effort. Positive mail flooded boxes and radio ads voiced personally by Mask filled the airwaves and ended with the tag line 'Let's give Montgomery a good dose of our conservative Elmore and Coosa County values.'" His television commercial played off his last name and featured citizens from the community holding up masks bearing his likeness while professing their support.

The caucus funded its own program separate from Mask's and we included at least one piece of "comparative" mail. Featuring the headline "People Judge You by the Company You Keep," the mailer featured a photo of Payne alongside Hubbert, Democratic Party boss Joe Reed, and Don Siegelman. It proved an effective message and a mail piece we would replicate in future races.

We felt confident going into the final days of the race despite the fact that the Democrats had outspent us by $50,000—$150,000 to $100,000. Election Night proved our confidence legitimate. Mask defeated Payne by a 59 to 41 percent margin and was able to join our ranks for most of the 2006 legislative session. No Democrat qualified to run against him a few months later when the window opened, and his election to a full term was quickly sealed without opposition. Payne, incidentally, was defeated in his next race for mayor, due largely to backlash from the campaign he ran against Mask. And by taking Venable's seat, the first domino in what would be a long chain had finally fallen.

∽ *In Their Own Words* ∽

BOB RILEY
U.S. CONGRESS 1996–2002; GOVERNOR 2003–2011

I remember telling Mike that if we continued to play the same political games that Alabama always had, we would continue to rank at the bottom of any list that mattered. But, if you could raise the revenue to truly make strategic investments in the state and, at the same time, bring about reforms in education and economic development that we had needed for decades, then you would see dramatic changes. We would not only be competitive with neighboring states in education and economic development, we would surpass them.

We could begin by making a difference in the lives of working families across the state. At that time, we began taxing a family with an income of just $4,600, which was the lowest in the nation. Mississippi was at $18,000. I thought taxing any family at that level was immoral and said so, during the campaign and the administration. The package would have given the poorest citizens among us some deserved relief while ushering in the toughest accountability reforms in state history, an element often lost in the debate. Of course, the package lost, but it did serve as a new catalyst for change. Eventually, the new plan did exactly what we set out to do. Alabama began to lead the nation in economic development. National education scores moved us from 49th to 25th and continue to rise. For the first time in history, Alabama was above the national average. All in just a little over six years.

MIKE ROGERS
STATE REPRESENTATIVE 1994–2002; U.S. REPRESENTATIVE 2003–

It doesn't matter if you're in politics, selling hamburgers at McDonald's, or a sergeant trying to get your troops to fulfill a mission, you have to have discipline along with a leader willing to enforce that discipline. Take McDonald's, for example. If Ray Kroc and his management team hadn't demanded that every franchise make the hamburgers and fries exactly how they wanted them to, it would have never have become successful because you would have never been able to depend on getting the same product from one restaurant to another. The same thing is true with the military. There is always some slacker in a group of military personnel and that's why they have drill sergeants—to teach them that discipline matters. It's true with any retail business, law firm, or whatever. Mike Hubbard was the leader and it was his job to make people who don't want to go in the direction the team needs them to go, to do it anyway. Let's face it, people naturally don't like to be told what to do—just like kids behaving badly don't like being spanked. But I can tell you that the people who didn't like Mike Hubbard's discipline were the folks who weren't really Republicans and didn't believe in the Party anyway. Mike did exactly what any real leader had to do. You can look at any true leader in history and they all had some folks who didn't like them for being a little too rough. But that's really also why they were successful leaders.

8

JUGGLING CAMPAIGNS
AND DODGING BULLETS

As the 2006 campaign cycle approached, the political prospects for Governor Riley and the Republican Party appeared positive. Great successes in recruiting jobs and industrial prospects to Alabama had helped Riley regain much of the political capital lost during the Amendment One referendum, and his quick and near flawless response to the damage brought to our Gulf Coast by Hurricane Katrina made him one of the few elected officials whose public profile improved after the devastating storm.

In fact, Katrina was the third hurricane to hit Alabama in 11 months on Riley's watch, and his often-innovative response to each had earned the governor high marks. During two of the three hurricanes, for example, Riley ordered southbound lanes on Interstate 65 reversed for the first time in history, so that all of the lanes of this vital artery traveled north and away from the storms, allowing a much quicker evacuation route. Such an unprecedented order requires the coordination of hundreds of transportation and public safety workers, but Riley and his team carried it out impressively.

If there was a misstep during the Katrina crisis, it was Riley's behind-the-scenes attempt to throw a life preserver to beleaguered Federal Emergency Management Agency Director Michael Brown, whose measured response to stranded New Orleans residents and his background as the head of the International Arabian Horse Association led the media to attack his credentials and abilities. While visiting the state and assessing hurricane damage, President George W. Bush privately asked Riley if FEMA and Brown were being responsive to the state's needs. Despite the fact that Alabama's Gulf Coast had been dealt a serious blow, the FEMA efforts in the state appeared to be running more smoothly than those in Mississippi and, especially, Louisiana. The governor assured Bush that Brown had the situation well in hand, at least as far as Alabama was concerned. At a news conference later in the day, Bush, who was known for assigning nicknames to those who worked for him, thought of Riley's measured reassurances and famously announced, "Brownie, you're doing a heck of a job," despite substantial evidence to the contrary in Alabama's neighboring states.

The president's quote was interspersed on the nightly news with footage of hurricane victims trapped on overpasses, at the Superdome, and in the Morial Convention Center in New Orleans. Shortly after, Brown resigned as the FEMA director. Bush would later write in his memoir, *Decision Points*, that Riley was the first to use the phrase "heck of a job" in privately describing Brown's efforts, and the president simply repeated the quote, which quickly became one of the most lambasted of his administration. For years afterward, Bush would tease Riley about the storm of controversy his off-hand remark had generated.

Nevertheless, while Hurricane Katrina had a devastating effect on the entire Gulf Coast region, it provided a national stage upon which Riley's leadership skills could shine.

The state's economy also helped buoy Riley's reelection chances, given the record low unemployment that Alabama was experiencing. With the same salesmanship that he had used to build a fortune in the poultry and egg industry, Riley traveled extensively to pitch Alabama as a prime destination for investment by both foreign and domestic corporations. His efforts in just four short years produced more than 100,000 jobs for the state.

Alabama's workforce training program, which had been extensively restructured under Riley, was ranked the best in the nation, and our state led the Southeast in job growth and development for four consecutive years.

Most impressively, the $675 million budget shortfall he inherited from Siegelman had turned into a surplus and money flowing into the Education Trust Fund budget grew from $4 billion to more than $6 billion, thanks largely to the tax revenues from those jobs Riley had recruited.

Student test scores in public schools soared, and ground-breaking programs like the Alabama Reading Initiative and distance learning, which broadcast advanced placement classes into even the most remote and rural schools, were clearly producing results. While seven out of 10 Alabama schools failed to meet their No Child Left Behind goals under Siegelman, nine out of 10 met or exceeded them under Riley.

DESPITE THIS SOLID RECORD of accomplishment, Riley's reelection campaign drew primary opposition from the right in the form of former Alabama Chief Justice Roy Moore. Moore had shot to prominence as a circuit judge in Gadsden when he hung a wooden plaque of the Ten Commandments behind the bench in his courtroom. A criminal defense attorney, whose clients, a pair of male strippers who performed under the name Silk and Satin, were accused of murder, objected to the plaque's presence and Moore's habit of leading the jury pool in prayer to begin court. The American Civil Liberties Union soon after filed a lawsuit.

When a Montgomery judge ordered Moore to remove the plaque and curtail the prayers, then-Alabama Governor Fob James announced he would call out the National Guard to surround the Etowah County Courthouse and protect the plaque, if necessary. James discussed the issue on the nationally-televised *Today* show on NBC and referred to host Matt Lauer as a "constitutional ignoramus" when Lauer insisted that the words "separation of church and state" appear in the U.S. Constitution—which they do not.

The State Supreme Court issued a stay in the judge's ruling and eventually tossed the case for technical reasons, which allowed Moore to claim victory and later announce his bid for chief justice. Running against a Republican primary opponent who was heavily financed by business interests and used the not-yet-famous Karl Rove as his campaign consultant, Moore easily won the race and then defeated the Democratic nominee in the 2002 general election.

Upon taking office, Moore decided to make an even bolder statement, so he commissioned a granite monument of the Ten Commandments that weighed 5,200 pounds and stood four feet tall, and he had it installed in the lobby of the State Judicial Building. In what I believe was an impolitic attempt to belittle the monument, members of the media described it as the "size of a washing machine" in some of their coverage.

If the plaque in Gadsden gave the ACLU heartburn, then the monument in Montgomery made their heads explode. Joined by the Americans United for the Separation of Church and State and the Southern Poverty Law Center, the monument's opponents collectively filed a federal lawsuit challenging it as an improper acknowledgment of religion in a government facility. Moore countered that the Ten Commandments are the moral foundation for our system of laws and rightly deserved display.

U.S. District Judge Myron Thompson ruled that the monument violated the establishment clause of the First Amendment and, once his decision was upheld by the Eleventh U.S. Circuit Court of Appeals in Atlanta, ordered it removed from the judicial building. Moore publicly announced his decision to defy the court order, which drew individuals from across the nation to Montgomery to support the chief justice's decision. As many as 4,000 people held rallies on the steps of the Judicial Building and several participated in around-the-clock vigils and basically lived on the steps just in case U.S. Marshals attempted to remove the monument.

Obviously remembering the vow that Governor James had made years before, Moore asked Alan Keyes, an African American Republican, radio talk show host, and candidate for U.S. president in 2000, to ask Riley to call out the National Guard in defense of the monument. Keyes, who was a strong supporter of Moore, met with Riley's chief of staff, Toby Roth, and relayed the request, which was denied, citing the authority of the federal court as the reason. Moore and his advisors never got over the rebuff from the Riley administration, but, over time, the crowds dissipated, the monument was removed, and Moore was impeached as chief justice by the Court of the Judiciary, the panel charged with meting out discipline to elected judges in Alabama.

After being removed from office, Moore published an autobiography titled *So Help Me God* and bided his time with a nationwide speaking tour to groups that were receptive to his message. He also flirted with various conservative third party movements that had spun off from the fringes of the Republican Party.

To illustrate how far removed his campaign was from the Republican establishment, former ALGOP Executive Director Tim Howe tells the story that when Moore arrived to file his gubernatorial qualifying papers at the Party's state headquarters in Birmingham, his top aide mistook Party Chair Twinkle Andress for a secretary and asked her to fetch "the Judge" a cup of coffee.

Moore announced his candidacy without mentioning Riley by name, but he did take shots at Amendment One and the taxes it contained. A platform of populist initiatives was announced along with many of the same accountability measures that Riley had campaigned upon in 2002, all of which would serve as the basis of Moore's candidacy. He was also smart enough to announce he would not accept contributions from political action committees, knowing that the major PACs in the state and the groups that funded them would be supporting Riley, thus giving Moore an additional campaign issue.

Shortly after Moore's announcement, Riley scored one of the biggest achievements of his political career and, I believe, one of his greatest legacies. He convened a meeting of his closest advisors prior to the annual legislative session to review the budgets and decide how to best use the substantial revenue surplus his administration had generated. After his aides gathered, Riley reminded them that in 2002, he had campaigned on raising the immorally low tax threshold in the state, a promise that had led, at least in part, to the failed Amendment One effort. Alabama's threshold was, in fact, among the lowest in the nation with a family of four being required to pay state taxes on an income of just $4,600 a year.

Why not, he asked, use the surplus to raise the tax threshold and, at the same time, provide a middle-class tax cut for working families? Riley believed his campaign promise was a moral imperative, and the period of prosperity Alabama was currently enjoying provided a rare opportunity to reduce taxes on a broad cross-section of the state.

Riley used his 2006 State of the State address, a constitutionally required report on the status of Alabama's fiscal and other affairs, to announce his tax cut plan. With his speech broadcast live across the state and a roomful of House and Senate members, not all of whom were friendly, looking on,

Riley always rose to the occasion and thrived in the high-stakes environment the speech provided.

After discussing the great progress Alabama had made under his administration and reviewing his many successes, Riley pirouetted toward discussing the issues of the day, including his proposed tax cut. With a strong voice and the confidence that was his trademark, Riley told the assembled lawmakers:

> So, tonight, I'm proposing a historic tax reduction package for the people of Alabama. I want everybody who pays income taxes in this state to get a tax cut.
>
> Under the plan I'm proposing, every taxpayer will receive a tax cut every year. Over the next five years, taxpayers will keep more than $200 million to meet the needs of their families. It's what our economy needs and, ladies and gentlemen, it is what our families deserve.
>
> There are those who are eager to attack this plan. They'll say, 'More money should be spent on education.'
>
> You know what? We are spending more on education than ever before. $1 billion more with record amounts going into our classrooms.
>
> They'll say, "We should use it to fund other needs like Medicaid and state troopers." But as all of you know, under our Constitution that is not possible. The education surplus can't be used for General Fund programs.
>
> Others will claim the tax cuts won't go to the right people.
>
> Let me say it again: under my plan every taxpayer in Alabama will get a tax cut.
>
> If you approve my plan, we'll increase the tax deduction for dependents for the first time since 1935. We'll increase the personal tax exemption so all taxpayers will see meaningful tax relief year after year—including those on fixed incomes.
>
> We'll also finally make our tax code fairer by increasing the threshold where income is taxed. When fully implemented, a family of four will pay no taxes on the first $15,000 of their income.
>
> And there's one other part of my tax cut plan. As parents and

grandparents buy school supplies, let's ease their tax burden. I ask you to approve a state sales tax holiday to help families with back-to-school expenses.

My enthusiasm for a fairer tax code is nothing new. It's something that I've said we needed to do for years—and it's something I fought very hard for. But this year, in this session—with my budget—we can and we should make it a reality.

If we don't do it now—when we have a record surplus—then when will we ever offer tax relief? You know, and I know, and the people know: if we don't cut their taxes, government will find a way to spend the money. Don't let that happen. Cut their taxes.

Republicans eager for a tax cut of any kind stood up to applaud. Democrats, and especially the African American members of their caucus, stood to applaud the notion of providing tax relief to the poor. And filming all of this were three television cameras, two broadcasting the images live across the state, and a third paid for by the campaign and capturing the footage for a commercial that would soon air.

In his office after the speech, the governor asked me to help pull together the coalition necessary to make his tax cut a reality. We first approached State Representative Jay Love (R-Montgomery) and asked him to carry the House version of the bill because, since his election in 2002, he had proven himself to be an able legislator and one of the top lieutenants to my role as House Minority Leader.

Love agreed, but soon told us he thought chances of passage would dramatically improve if we gave the legislation to Representative John Knight (D-Montgomery). Knight is one of the most respected African American legislators serving in the House and was then the chair of the General Fund Ways and Means Committee, which is responsible for drafting the budgets of all noneducation state agencies in Alabama.

Knight had tried for years to pass a law removing the state sales tax from groceries, but the $325 million price tag required him to make up the revenue in another area. Because Alabama is one of the few states in the nation that allows taxpayers to deduct their federal taxes from their state income tax obligation, Knight proposed repealing that deduction in exchange for the grocery tax ban. Unfortunately for him, we Republicans believed his proposal hit middle-class and upper-middle class Alabamians disproportionately hard, so we worked to block his bill while hoping that a more palatable alternative could be found.

Because of his proven commitment to lessening the tax burden on the poorest Alabamians, Knight was the ideal sponsor, and we would need his support to bring along other Democrats and defeat the 900-pound gorilla of Alabama politics—labor union boss Paul Hubbert.

It did not take long for Hubbert to announce his strong opposition to Riley's tax cut proposal, citing its drain on education funding as the reason. As head of the state teachers' union, Hubbert did not want to set a precedent that would divert money from the members he served.

Knight, however, agreed to sponsor the legislation and members of the black legislative caucus held a joint bipartisan news conference with Riley announcing their support of his tax cut proposal. Other Democrats climbed on the bandwagon, and the battle was on.

Hubbert realized that support for a tax cut of some kind was too strong for him to suppress, but he convinced the Democrats to dramatically scale back the Riley plan. Ultimately, the plan passed by the legislature provided needed tax relief for families making $30,000 and less, and the threshold was raised from the lowest-in-the-nation $4,600 to a more respectable $12,500. Representative Love and I were joined by several Republican colleagues in offering amendments expanding the tax cut to its original proposed levels, but Democrats voted us down each time.

Nevertheless, we had helped Governor Riley pass Alabama's first tax cut in 70 years, we had provided a portion of needed tax relief to the poorest families and those in the lower middle-class, and we had fully funded it with the existing surplus rather than transferring new taxes onto other groups.

Moore put up a good fight and campaigned heavily, but, not wanting to appear as a one-issue candidate, he spoke very little if at all about the Ten Commandments controversy during his public appearances. Instead, he talked about the accountability and ethical issues he had raised during his announcement. But because Riley had supported those same issues his entire time in office, Moore appeared as a "me, too" candidate.

Riley campaigned just as hard, and he traveled the state on grassroots bus tours taking his message of successes in education, ethics, and economic development to as many counties as time would allow. He defeated Moore with 67 percent of the vote, and his campaign slogan of "Alabama is on the right track" caught on to the point that Riley rode into his primary night victory party on a train with the message emblazoned on the side.

Now it was time to take on the Democrats.

Don Siegelman has always reminded me of Jason Voorhees from the Friday the 13th movie series—every time you think he's down for good, he rises up to terrorize the countryside once again—and the former governor proved my comparison right once again in 2006. Since his defeat by Riley in 2002, the ethical issues that had plagued Siegelman's political career, and probably made the difference in the gubernatorial race, continued to follow him.

The federal investigation that had obviously begun during his time in office was closing in on its target, and his long-serving aide, Nick Bailey, would help prosecutors tighten the noose. Bailey began working for Siegelman as his chauffeur during his time in the lieutenant governor's office and had parlayed his close relationship into a cabinet-level position as director of the Alabama Department of Economic and Community Affairs when his boss became governor. Siegelman also awarded Bailey the title of State Budget Officer, which caused many to wonder what qualified a driver and errand boy to hold a job demanding deep knowledge of high finance. Unfortunately for Siegelman, the loyal aide he had trusted with his secrets had been accepting thousands of dollars in bribes throughout his government service, and, when finally confronted with the evidence, Bailey agreed to plead guilty and cooperate with federal prosecutors building the corruption case.

In late 2005, indictments alleging a wide variety of charges, including bribery and obstruction of justice, rained down upon Siegelman and disgraced healthcare executive Richard Scrushy. Two former Siegelman aides were charged on similar counts, but a jury ultimately acquitted them.

Siegelman quickly blamed the allegations not upon his own wrongdoing, but upon an imagined complex conspiracy against him that included the Bush White House, the U.S. Justice Department and the Alabama governor's office. His reasoning was so fantastic, unbelievable, and circuitous that I am surprised he did not include the Dalai Lama and Queen Elizabeth among those conspiring against him.

Never one to shrink from the spotlight, even when his world was crumbling around him, Siegelman declared his candidacy for governor in March 2006. His announcement remarks included an impassioned argument that the charges against him were part of a Republican political machine that, for some unexplained and unacknowledged reason, feared Siegelman and his influence. He also promised to rewrite Alabama's 1901 Constitution if elected and, coming as no surprise to anyone who followed state politics over the past few decades, trotted out his lottery proposal for one last lap around the track.

In a scene reminiscent of flamboyant, yet corrupt, Southern politicians like Louisiana Governor Edwin Edwards—who once said, "People say I've had brushes with the law. That's not true. I've had brushes with overzealous prosecutors"—Siegelman would sit through his corruption trial during the day, exit the federal courthouse when court was adjourned, and jump on a campaign bus to ride to his next political rally.

The day of the Democratic primary arrived before the case went to the jury, and Siegelman pulled just 36 percent of the vote. I found myself wondering which was sadder—the steep freefall that Siegelman had experienced since the height of his power or the fact that more than a third of Democratic voters would support a candidate who spent his days fighting serious corruption charges.

Roughly three weeks after he lost the primary, a jury convicted Siegelman of seven counts, including bribery, honest services fraud, and obstruction of justice for attempting to hide an all-terrain vehicle he accepted from a lobbyist who was doing business with the state. Scrushy, too, was convicted on several charges.

Siegelman began serving his seven-year sentence in the Federal Detention Center in Oakdale, Louisiana, where he became good friends with an aging Edwin Edwards, the incarcerated former governor he had reminded me of so much.

LUCY BAXLEY, THE DEMOCRAT who defeated Siegelman in the primary so handily, was a popular figure in Alabama politics. Though her personality was larger than life, she seemed to have difficulty grasping the complicated public policy issues with which governors are forced to wrestle.

She first became widely known in Alabama in 1986 when her then-husband, Lieutenant Governor Bill Baxley, was running for the Democratic nomination to succeed George Wallace, who was then in what would be his last of four terms as governor. Preceding the Gary Hart scandal by two years, a team of reporters from the *Birmingham News* discovered that Baxley was having an affair with an Associated Press reporter, Marie Prat. Staking out the apartment he used while serving in Montgomery, the journalists found that Baxley had his taxpayer-funded security guard ferry his paramour to a rendezvous in a state car.

A year later, in 1987, Lucy divorced Bill, who eventually married Marie.

Following a successful career in real estate, Lucy then decided to enter public service on her own terms and, in 1994, ran for and won the office of state treasurer. She was reelected in 1998, and while neither of her terms stood out in accomplishments or notable successes, they were without controversy.

In 2002 she ran for lieutenant governor and became the first female in Alabama history to hold that office. Because Senate Democrats had stripped the office of its authority four years earlier when a Republican lieutenant governor held the gavel, Baxley wielded little, if any, power.

By 2006, as a result of the noncontroversial nature of the offices she had held, Baxley was the most popular Democrat in a state that was becoming more and more Republican with each cycle. Her benign nature, large smile, and the "I Love Lucy" slogan she had used in each of her campaigns made her a highly identifiable public figure, and she chased many prominent Democrats, like House Speaker Seth Hammett and former Governor Jim Folsom Jr., out of the race for the Democratic gubernatorial nomination. Only the desperate Don Siegelman was willing to run against her, and, as previously discussed, his reasons had nothing to do with becoming governor.

Baxley's 2006 campaign against Riley focused on two issues—implementing a state minimum wage that was $1 above the federal level, and attacking Bob Riley on whatever ground she could find.

She alleged, for example, that Riley had received $13 million from Indian casino interests in Mississippi during the 2002 campaign in exchange for his promise to prevent casino gambling from taking root in Alabama. Her attack, however, ignored two important facts. First, Riley had raised and spent a grand total of $13 million in his 2002 effort, which, if her allegations were correct, meant that every dime he collected in his campaign chest came from Indian interests and no other source, which was absurd on its face. Secondly, Riley, who is a Southern Baptist, had opposed legalized gambling all of his life and would have fought its implementation or spread within the state in any case.

The governor, meanwhile, was not content to run his general election campaign based upon what he had already accomplished. True to his nature of always moving forward and never resting, Riley produced a new book titled *Plan 2010: Our Vision for Alabama* which listed, in detail, the programs and initiatives he planned to implement if returned to Montgomery for another four-year term. Issues ranging from education to industrial recruitment to conservation and prison overcrowding, among others, were discussed in the most finite terms. Thousands of books were distributed across the state and television commercials presented its plan to viewers.

President Bush traveled to Birmingham to headline a fundraiser for the Riley campaign at which tables in the cavernous civic center cost $10,000 each. It sold out. Vice President Dick Cheney also traveled to Alabama and attended a highly successful fundraiser in Houston County—Baxley's birthplace, a fact that surely made her none too happy.

Not surprisingly, I was intimately involved in every facet of what was likely the last campaign of my political mentor. From working with Dax and Rob on strategy to assisting Minda with the production of television commercials to producing all of the radio spots and overseeing a massive mail program that hit hundreds of thousands of mailboxes across the state, it seemed that most of my waking hours were spent working for Governor Riley's campaign.

THAT WOULD NOT HAVE been a problem except for the fact that I was locked in the most important political battle of my career with two well-funded challengers in my legislative district. I was also overseeing, along with Senator Del Marsh (R-Anniston), the fledgling legislative campaign effort that would teach us many important lessons and serve as the genesis for the successful Campaign 2010 takeover bid.

An old adage says that a son inherits half of his father's friends and all of his enemies. It also holds true in politics, and as Bob Riley's most vocal and loyal supporter, his enemies considered me a target of their enmity. No one painted a bigger bull's eye on my chest than Paul Hubbert.

As Bob Riley's floor leader, it was my job to push the education reform initiatives that the governor wanted to implement, which were the very same issues that Hubbert vehemently opposed because of the accountability and increased demands they placed upon the public education system. And, as leader of the House Republican caucus, it was my job to instill party discipline and keep our members united on the most important policy issues. When one of our members strayed to Hubbert's dark side and voted against the caucus on an issue upon which we had all agreed, it was my job to hand out the punishment and ensure it never happened again.

In short, it was my job to be everything that Paul Hubbert hated.

Though we agree on few if any political and policy issues, I do respect Hubbert and the political organization he has built, and I believe, despite our deep differences, that he respects me, too. He has never lied to me about an issue, nor have I lied to him.

Hubbert has long been considered one of the powerful men in Alabama politics. With each of the Alabama Education Association's 104,000 members donating $3 a month to the A-Vote political action committee, Hubbert controlled one of the largest and most well-funded PACs in the state. He used the money to subsidize the campaigns of public officials and candidates, almost all of whom were Democrats, who, in my opinion, would commit to putting the needs of teachers and their employment benefits ahead of the needs of public school students and classroom essentials.

He took over the reins of the AEA in 1969, when it was a segregated organization separate and distinct from its counterpart that represented African American educators. He combined the two groups into one, doubling its power and influence. Though he refers to it as a "professional development association for teachers," AEA operates, for all intents and purposes, as a labor union complete with local union reps, which he calls "Uniserv directors," who take employee grievances to principals, superintendents, and school board members. If the AEA believes proper relief is not provided, its team of staff attorneys will file lawsuits on behalf of its members.

Over the decades, his political power grew to the point that he was awarded the Democratic Party nomination for governor in 1990, defeating the Energizer Bunny of Alabama politics, Don Siegelman, and four other candidates. Some at the time facetiously questioned why Hubbert would want to give up so much political power to step down and become governor. Incumbent Republican Governor Guy Hunt defeated Hubbert by just over 50,000 votes in the general election, but the loss did nothing to dampen the labor leader's control over the legislature.

Hubbert had butted heads from time to time with Alabama governors during his long tenure at AEA, Wallace and Hunt among them, but he had gotten along well with others, such as Siegelman and Folsom. When Bob Riley captured the governor's office in 2003, Hubbert had clearly met his match. During his time in office, Riley proposed more education reform measures that Hubbert opposed and fought for them more fiercely than any of his predecessors. The proposals ran from charter schools to basing teacher salaries on performance rather than longevity to providing free, taxpayer-funded liability insurance to education employees because many belonged to AEA simply for the low-cost coverage it offered. At times, meetings between the two men resembled a high-stakes confrontation between warring superpowers.

Hubbert spent millions trying to defeat Riley by backing Siegelman and Baxley in their races against him. In years when there were no elections,

Hubbert would run television ads during legislative sessions attacking the proposed education reforms and Riley himself. Despite the millions of dollars Hubbert spent to turn public opinion against the governor, Riley remained immensely popular throughout his two terms with approval ratings well above 50 percent the entire time.

As noted, I did not escape Hubbert's ire. With the 2006 election cycle approaching, Hubbert hired a team to conduct an in-depth investigation into my life, my business, and my finances and report the "findings" to him. His AEA minions would then feed whatever information was gathered to reporters they felt were friendly to them with hopes that scandalous headlines would result. The only problem with their plan is that they found nothing worthy of publishing.

The AEA flunkies oversold the information they had gathered to the journalists they tipped, who then came to me for answers. I sat down or spoke with each one, even inviting some to my office in Auburn for a personal visit, and explained the truth behind everything the investigation alleged. To their credit, not a single member of the capital press corps wrote a story based upon the bogus information they had been fed even though I could tell that at least one reporter, who had an aversion to Republicans and a decidedly liberal bias, was itching to do so.

Anxious to damage me and my reputation in some way, Hubbert printed the material, along with unflattering caricatures portraying me, Riley and others, in the *Alabama School Journal*, a newspaper-style AEA publication that each member receives. Little did I know that he had even bigger plans in store for me.

Having done a good job serving my district, I assumed I would avoid opposition in the 2006 Republican primary, and, quite possibly, in the general election. As a member of the powerful House Education Ways & Means Committee, which writes the budget for all of Alabama's public schools, colleges, and universities, I had ensured that Auburn University received its share of funding. An industrial park and significant road construction projects came to fruition thanks to grants, funding, and accelerated deadlines I had secured. The City of Auburn surprised me by naming the road leading to the new terminal building at Auburn University Regional Airport "Mike Hubbard Boulevard" because of the role I played in securing funding for the improvements.

Yet, at the same time, I had made no secret of my intentions as minority leader to raise money, hire consultants, and make the biggest push to elect Republican legislators in modern history. My plan made a number of Democrats very nervous, especially those who represented increasingly conservative rural and suburban districts, and likely made the target on my own back even bigger.

One day while I was on the House floor, Tim Howe called to inform me that someone named Jim Phillips had just qualified to run against me in the Republican primary. My dentist is named Jim Phillips, as is his father, who had been an All-America receiver at Auburn, co-captained the university's 1957 National Championship team, and later played for the Los Angeles Rams and the Minnesota Vikings. Dr. Phillips quickly assured me that it was not him running against me and that he and his family supported me strongly.

Because they were so well known within the Auburn community, I got permission to print and distribute a campaign mail piece with photos of the father and son Jim Phillips, along with my opponent Jim Phillips and the headline "Two out of three Jim Phillips support Mike Hubbard for the Alabama House." It was a humorous piece that worked to make sure people knew that the Jim Phillips running against me was not the Jim Phillips they knew.

Eventually, I learned that the Jim Phillips running against me was something of a political gadfly who was very involved in the Auburn Trustee Improvement PAC, a political action committee formed to combat Bobby Lowder, the controversial Auburn trustee whose influence over important facets of the university's academic and athletic operations was resented by many.

Phillips had spent much of his working career in Washington, D.C., bouncing from job to job and committee to committee in Congress as a self-professed investigator. Phillips told the press he had worked on the House Committee on Banking and Financial Services during the Whitewater scandal involving Bill and Hillary Clinton. He also claimed to have

worked closely with U.S. Senator Orrin Hatch of Utah during the Iran/
Contra affair hearings.

In truth, Phillips was simply an irritant recruited to run against me by
Hubbert and the AEA in an effort to distract me from working to elect
other Republicans. The vast majority of Phillips's contributions, according
to campaign finance reports, came from Hubbert's A-Vote PAC, political action committees controlled by one of Hubbert's top lieutenants,
Joe Cottle, and other sources led by lobbyists allied with the Democrats.
Tens of thousands of dollars flowed into Phillips's campaign coffers simply
because he was a giant pain in my behind.

Almost from the first moment, Phillips began attacking me with the
same stale, bogus allegations that Hubbert had failed to sell to the capital
press corps members in Montgomery. Only this time, Hubbert simply
contributed the money Phillips needed to spread the falsehoods for him
through direct mail and advertising.

Among the attacks he tossed at me throughout the primary campaign
were:

I did not pay my taxes. *[A company in which I have a 26 percent ownership, Craftmaster Printers, was late paying its property taxes one year. As a
minority owner, I had no control over day-to-day operations and certainly was
not responsible for paying the property taxes. The local tax assessor confirmed
that these charges tossed at me were false.]*

I had run my company into bankruptcy. *[The same company, Craftmaster,
filed bankruptcy papers to bring inherited creditors to the table shortly after
the new ownership team with whom I'd invested took over. The creditors did
agree to negotiate, and the papers were immediately withdrawn.]*

I "stole" millions from Auburn University by passing a bill exempting
my business from having to compete in a bid process to broadcast Auburn
athletic events. *[The bill I sponsored was offered at the request of the university
and applied only to concessions like popcorn, Cokes, and corn dogs, and not the
multi-million dollar media rights that the Auburn Network administered. The
university had always, and continues to, award multi-media rights through
a Request for Proposal, or RFP, process, since it involves professional services
and ensures a hefty measure of quality control.]*

I "conspired" with Bobby Lowder on a number of projects that were detrimental to Auburn University. *[I am friends with Bobby Lowder and have been for years, but my primary dealings with him involved his company's advertising on the Auburn Network and political issues pertaining to Auburn University since he was on the board of trustees. In fact, I did not even bank at Colonial Bank, where Lowder served as CEO, in order to ensure an arm's-length relationship.]*

Wave after wave of political attacks came my way from the Phillips camp on behalf of Hubbert, and it all culminated with an official complaint he filed with the Alabama Ethics Commission that packaged all of the allegations in one document. I was tempted to chuckle at the charge that I had used my office "for personal financial gain" because, if anything, the opposite was true. The Ethics Commission seemed to agree when it dismissed his complaint and called it "baseless"—the only problem is they did it after the primary was already over.

Phillips's mail and radio, produced by Hubbert's vendors, attacked me relentlessly. One radio ad run by Phillips used an announcer impersonating famed sports announcer Howard Cosell and accused me of bringing corruption and no-bid contracts to college athletics. Another ad used a mimic of Paul Harvey and echoed the attacks in a format and distinctive style similar to the popular radio broadcaster. A mailer resembling a book with my photo on the cover and a title that read "How to Raise Taxes on Working People without Paying Your Own Taxes" was widely distributed.

I, on the other hand, kept my campaign mostly positive and chose to focus on my successes as a legislator while highlighting my close working relationship with Governor Riley, who was immensely popular in the Auburn area.

As election day approached, I remained fairly confident, yet something in the back of my head questioned whether Phillips's relentless attacks would have an effect on voters' opinions of me, much like the drip-drip-drip of Chinese water torture. My fears proved unfounded, however, when the polls closed, and I was awarded the Republican nomination by a 73 to 27 percent margin. But, if anyone thought I was cleared for smooth sailing with the irritant of Jim Phillips now out of the way, they were clearly mistaken. Instead, I was about to face the most intense and expensive campaign fight of my political career, thus far.

HUBBERT AND THE DEMOCRATS had recruited a strong and attractive candidate to oppose me in the general election campaign. Carolyn Ellis was a former teacher and active in various community groups, but she was best known as the wife of Cliff Ellis, a former Auburn University basketball coach who led his team to the 1999 Southeastern Conference Championship, the school's first title in 40 years. He had previously served as head basketball coach at the University of South Alabama and at Clemson University in South Carolina.

Ellis wasted no time in beginning her criticism of me and added a new line of attack in her announcement news release, which said "Today we have a representative who seems to spend more time in partisan warfare and building a political machine than serving the needs of District 79." I countered by noting the millions of dollars in university funding, road projects, and other infrastructure needs that I had successfully obtained for my district.

She soon began airing four professionally produced television commercials with a soft focus appeal that looked better than anything aired in the race to that point. The spots were very positive, and they highlighted Ellis's commitment to the elderly and to schoolchildren as well as her civic involvement. The commercials proved very effective because an 18 percent lead I held over her, according to my pollster, quickly fell six points shortly after they aired.

The commitment made by the Alabama Democratic Party to Ellis's effort became even more evident when Wesley Clark, a retired Army general, NATO Supreme Commander, and 2004 presidential candidate, announced he was appearing in Auburn to raise funds for her campaign. Though Clark had won only the Oklahoma primary before endorsing eventual Democratic nominee John Kerry in 2004, having a former presidential candidate stumping in a local House race was big news in the area and more than a little intimidating for me.

Of course, raising money was the last of Ellis's worries given the massive amounts she was receiving from the teachers' labor union, the Democratic Party and their assorted cronies. If Hubbert opened his wallet to help the Jim Phillips campaign, he threw open the back of a Brink's truck to go all out for Ellis.

Her positive campaign proved temporary as she soon began regurgitating the same negative attacks that Hubbert had supplied to Phillips. Because of FCC rules, I even had to run dozens of her negative radio commercials on the local radio station that I owned and operated. Negative mail pieces soon appeared in my mailbox and those of my friends and neighbors, and one mail attack carried a photo of me that was doctored to show a sinister, Richard Nixon-like growth of beard on my face.

I responded as best I could by once again highlighting my close ties with the hugely popular governor and pointing out some public policy positions taken by Ellis that were more liberal than most voters in my conservative legislative district could stand. But for every rebuttal and counterattack I threw toward Ellis, her campaign would go to the next, and much more expensive, level.

The campaign reached critical mass one day when I received a call from my consultant, Dax Swatek, who told me that Ellis had made a $125,000 buy on WSFA-TV in Montgomery. WSFA is one of Alabama's largest and best-known television stations with a broadcast footprint that starts west of Montgomery, travels east to the Chattahoochee River on the Georgia line, and continues down through the southeastern portion of the state into Florida. The massive reach of its broadcast signal makes the station's advertising rates among the most expensive in the state.

My House district, like others in the state, consists of about 40,000 residents. Purchasing commercial time on the Montgomery mega-station to reach the small number of voters in my district was akin to using an atomic bomb to kill a mouse, but Hubbert's dislike of what I stood for, and his endlessly deep campaign pockets, pushed him to that point. Ellis's campaign also bought expensive broadcast time in Columbus, Georgia, to the east of my district, which created a bookend of electronic attacks against me.

Unprepared for the widespread nature of the attacks against me, I had given away much of my own campaign money to other Republican legislative candidates in an effort to increase our numbers. But I had to quickly raise the money to purchase a comparable broadcast buy to counter the Ellis schedule, which were negative spots against me. Fortunately, many of the pro-business groups in Montgomery, along with close friends and supporters, including Congressman Mike Rogers and State Senator Del Marsh, recognized that I was being assailed for simply voicing the conservative views and principles I had always supported, and they rallied to my side. In just a few days, I had raised the $200,000 necessary to compete with Ellis, although I wish that money could have instead gone to other Republican candidates locked in tight contests.

When the election results came in, I had won reelection with 56 percent of the vote, but the campaign left some scars that I still feel today. The lies and distortions tossed at me during the race no doubt hurt my reputation in the eyes of some who do not know me, and I am saddened by that. The sheer cost of that campaign also continues to amaze me.

Shortly after the election was concluded, Bob Johnson of the Associated Press ran a story that tallied the amounts Ellis and I had collectively spent in our contest, and it totaled just under $1 million. With only 12,685 voters going to the polls in my district, it equated to $75.89 per vote.

According to the AP, "Ellis said she went into the race thinking she would have to hold a few fund-raisers and raise about $150,000. She said part of the problem is how expensive it has become to buy television and radio advertising, particularly in her district, where she said she had to buy ads in both the Montgomery and Columbus, Georgia, markets." But the story did not point out that she did not have to buy TV and radio time in Montgomery and Columbus because the cost-to-return ratio made no sense whatsoever. Her mistake was listening to Hubbert and allowing his grudge for me, and his desire to try and distract me from electing more Republicans, to result in the most expensive House race in state history.

9

Getting Aggressive
and Testing a Concept

The Barry Mask victory confirmed that we could win open seats long held by Democrats, but if we were to have any chance of taking the majority, Republicans would also have to take out entrenched incumbents. To put together a plan to do just that, I contacted colleagues in the Georgia House of Representatives. I invited Representative Blaine Galliher, who had become a close friend and ally following our race for minority leader, to join me on the trip to Atlanta for a meeting with legislative leaders as well as members of the campaign team that had put Republicans in control of the Georgia House for the first time since Reconstruction. I was hoping a look at their playbook would provide us with a road map.

Galliher and I spent almost an entire day with the Georgia delegation, which proved to be a critical learning session that would dramatically change the way we would approach future campaigns and our overall strategy to take the majority in Alabama. They made it clear that gaining control would require the caucus to get directly involved in legislative races, providing guidance, advice and consulting to candidates running under the GOP label. Most importantly, since many first-time candidates and non-incumbents have difficulty raising money for their races, they suggested that we follow their plan which called for the Republican incumbents to raise money for them.

Our Georgia colleagues laid out how they had instituted a dues program within their caucus that required each member to raise a specified amount of dollars to be used to fund Republican legislative races. This resulted in their members having actual "skin in the game," encouraged a team spirit, and raised much-needed money for legislative races. If a caucus member in Georgia chose not to participate, they were branded as disloyal and, when Republicans gained control, assigned the worst legislative offices and committee assignments. The more they explained to Galliher and me, the more eager I became to test the same model in Alabama.

At a retreat in Prattville we held soon after the meeting, I stood before our caucus members and proposed a very similar dues program to the one that was successful in Georgia. With a large marker, I wrote out the plan on a flip chart as I spoke to the group. House members who had neither primary or general election opponents would be required to contribute the largest amount of money, those with a Democratic opponent but no Republican a lesser amount, those with a primary challenge but none in the general an even lesser amount, and so on.

Nothing like this had ever been put into place, so Galliher and I had presented it to our steering committee the previous afternoon. The twelve members of the committee liked the plan and voted to present it to the full caucus, but everyone anticipated a certain amount of pushback. Some of our members are contrarian by nature and others consider their campaign chests sacred and are reluctant to open them. A few of our members, quite frankly, had consistently shown allegiance to Paul Hubbert and Democratic House Speaker Seth Hammett. They enjoyed largesse in the form of contributions and committee assignments as a result, so taking on those two was not in their best interest.

When I began to outline the program, however, a sea of heads began nodding around the room and smiles broke out on several faces. It was obvious I had underestimated how sick and tired most of my colleagues had become of being in the minority and having the Democrats call the shots. The reaction was so enthusiastic that even the few who sat stone-faced and unhappy did not raise any objections. Of course, they never paid their dues to the caucus, either.

Between the dues we collected and the money I and several other members raised from groups, individuals and businesses across the state, the funding for our legislative challenge was largely accounted for. Now, we needed a message.

Newt Gingrich and the Congressional Republicans had been successful in capturing the U.S. House in 1994 by unveiling the *Contract with America*, an omnibus campaign platform of social and economic issues that GOP candidates across the country could embrace, campaign upon and promise to enact when elected. The Contract took the guesswork out of where the candidates stood and drew a stark line in the sand between what Republicans believed and where Democrats stood.

I wanted to propose a similar agenda for our candidates to run upon but felt that calling it a "Contract" was not only overused in politics, but also cold and formal, like something you and your attorney would negotiate. Instead, I wanted something that would represent a kind of bond between voters and candidates. In Alabama, giving someone your word and sealing it with a handshake means something, so we decided to call our agenda the *Republican Handshake with Alabama*.

The Handshake included long-held Republican policy initiatives such as extending the Riley income tax cuts to middle-class families, removing the sales tax from over-the-counter medication, small business tax incentives, a measure to limit yearly property tax increases, and a bill to prevent illegal immigrants from utilizing public benefits. Each represented bills that had been previously sponsored by Republicans and subsequently killed by Democrats.

Not to be outdone, the leaders of the House and Senate Democratic Caucus also released an agenda they promised to pass within the first ten days of the quadrennium if allowed to retain power in Montgomery. Called the *Covenant for the Future*, it, too, was comprised of initiatives that Republicans had sponsored and Democrats had killed in previous sessions. I was shocked the Democrats did not giggle and snicker when announcing their agenda because what they said they believed in was a joke.

A constitutional amendment affirming that life begins at conception and should be protected was an item they offered, despite the fact that Democrats routinely filibustered every pro-life bill that Republicans offered. Legislation to combat illegal immigration, a ban on PAC-to-PAC transfers and increased reporting requirements for lobbyists were also included and, again, had been previously killed by the Democrats and their leadership after being proposed by our caucus members.

When the capital press corps asked for my reaction to the Democrats' Covenant, I told them it was "the worst case of political plagiarism in the history of Alabama" and noted, bill-by-bill, the Democrats' hypocrisy. Time, incidentally, would prove me right. Four years later, despite controlling every House and Senate committee, both agenda-setting Rules committees and a having a majority in both houses, only three of the 16 items in the "Covenant" had become law.

NOW THAT WE HAD both money and message covered, we needed to find our targets and the candidates to take them on, so I commissioned an in-depth study of voting patterns in various districts represented by white Democratic legislators across the state. We looked at past results in presidential elections, gubernatorial contests, and other statewide offices and pinpointed the areas that cast the most Republican ballots yet continued to send Democratic lawmakers to Montgomery.

All of the numbers we crunched and all of the data we collected pointed us conclusively to one, most vulnerable target—State Representative Joe Carothers of Houston County.

Elected to the House in 1974, Carothers had held that office for 32 years prior to the 2006 election, yet his influence and power within the body had never matched his longevity of service. Though he chaired the occasional committee, he seemed happy to simply enjoy the camaraderie of the House and leave the heavy lifting of leadership to other Democrats within his caucus.

As a retired public school teacher, Carothers was fiercely loyal to Paul Hubbert and the AEA, but his heavily agricultural district and the fact that he owned a small farm led him to oppose property tax proposals that came before the House, a fact that also earned him support from ALFA and the Alabama Forestry Association. Because he would toss an occasional vote to other business groups when given a wink and a nod by Hubbert, he enjoyed widespread support from various associations whose interests he often opposed. This dichotomy between his perception as a friendly conservative and his often anti-business voting record, which existed both in Montgomery and in his southeast Alabama district, is what helped him achieve reelection for more than three decades.

Though we identified Carothers as a vulnerable Democrat in one of the state's most heavily Republican areas, we also knew that defeating him would be no easy task. Three decades as a lawmaker provided him with several favors he could call in when needed and more pots of money to dip into for campaign contributions than I care to recall. We knew that Speaker Hammett, who lived in a nearby county, would raise money for Carothers and Hubbert would throw the teachers' union resources behind him. In fact, when we surveyed the associations, lobbyists, and political groups operating within the shadow of the Alabama State House, we could not pinpoint even one that was willing to oppose Carothers for reelection. Even the most conservative groups indicated they were firmly in his camp.

But none of that even mattered unless we could find a competitive candidate to run against him. In his ten races for the Alabama House, Carothers had run unopposed three times, won by double-digit margins six times and had only one scare, in 1986, when he claimed a still-healthy 53 percent of the vote. His average victory margin during those ten contests was more than 70 percent, so historical precedent was definitely against us.

A Republican colleague, Representative Greg Albritton, entered the minority leader's office one day with news that he had heard of someone interested in running against Carothers in the upcoming election. I encouraged him to quickly track down the potential candidate and invite him to Montgomery, which would allow us to meet and assess his chances.

Shortly thereafter, I sat down with Representative Steve Clouse, a Republican who represents a district adjoining Carothers's, and members of our political team to meet with Benjamin Lewis. When Lewis entered the room, you could see the same nervous expression that many first-time visitors to the State House share, especially when contemplating such a life-changing step. But there was also a deep determination in him that we could sense. Once introductions had been made, we asked Lewis to tell us about himself.

The oldest of six children, Lewis was born in Dothan and raised on his family's Houston County dairy farm. He began working on the farm at the age of eight, rising at dawn to milk cows with his father before school. He continued to help run the dairy as he completed high school and later graduated from Troy University. After marrying and having four boys, Lewis wanted to continue feeding his thirst for knowledge, so he enrolled in Jones Law School in Montgomery, a five-hour roundtrip from his home. While balancing his farm work and family commitments, Lewis commuted 25 hours a week on a two-lane highway as he obtained his law degree and passed the bar.

When I asked what led him to consider running for the House, Lewis said he had thought about it since he was a boy, and had even personally told Carothers of his interest years ago.

Lewis, a Mormon, explained that he had spoken with a local lawyer at church who happened to know Albritton, also a member of the Latter Day Saints Church. Lewis's long-held desire to run for the legislature and our need for a good candidate had resulted in our meeting that day.

During the course of our conversation, we learned that another Republican candidate was also considering joining the race. I told Lewis that our best scenario was to avoid a bruising and expensive primary so all of our resources could go toward defeating Carothers. If a battle occurred, however, we would have to sit on the sidelines until a nominee was chosen.

Immediately following his trip to Montgomery, Lewis filed his qualification papers to run as a Republican and met with Chuck Harris, the Dothan businessman who was also considering the race. When he saw Lewis's commitment to running, Harris decided that he would bow out.

The fact that Lewis did not have primary opposition probably had as much to do with his eventual victory as anything that happened in the race. We were already starting with a definite fundraising disadvantage, no staff, no support, and a first-time candidate who had a lot to learn in a little amount of time. If we were already behind the eight ball, a primary would have likely taken us entirely off the table.

We immediately paired Lewis with Montgomery political consultant David Azbell, who had an affinity for putting rookie candidates at ease, guiding their efforts, and walking them through the minefield of Alabama politics. Azbell had a political pedigree through his father, Joe, a legendary journalist in the state who had written the first newspaper account of the arrest of Rosa Parks in 1955 and covered the day-to-day events of the resulting bus boycott for the *Montgomery Advertiser*. The elder Azbell eventually left journalism to work as speechwriter and director of communications for Governor George C. Wallace's presidential campaigns in 1968, 1972, and 1976 and operated as a successful political consultant for hundreds of candidates throughout the Southeast until his death in the mid-90s.

David, who learned politics at his father's knee, also spent a few years working for Wallace and served two stints in the capitol as spokesman for Governor Fob James and, later, Governor Bob Riley. Like his dad, Azbell worked on numerous campaigns, including high-level positions on those of the governors he served, and eventually opened a political consulting firm following his near decade of government service.

As minority leader, I worked with Twinkle Cavanaugh, the chairman of the Alabama Republican Party, to put together a network of field operatives to assist our legislative candidates across the state with the day-to-day operations of their campaigns. This effort was headed by our former caucus intern, Cory Adair, who had managed the Mask race for us and would eventually serve as executive director of the Republican Party in both Mississippi and Nevada.

While we divided the state into regions with one field operative assigned to work with several different candidates in each, we knew that Lewis's race would demand a singular focus and searched for a person who could solely concentrate on it.

Jimmy Entrekin was recommended to us by Drayton Nabers, who served as chief justice of the Alabama Supreme Court at the time. Nabers had employed Entrekin as the political director for his successful Republican primary race. A native of heavily Republican Shelby County, Entrekin was a graduate of Samford University and later finished fourth in his class at the University of Alabama Law School. He spent some time working in Governor Riley's policy office and had been employed by Protective Life Corporation before joining the Nabers campaign.

I met with Entrekin and found him to be an impressive young man who was well-spoken, highly organized and, most important to us, politically savvy. To be sure he would mesh with Lewis, I sent him to Dothan for a preliminary visit with the candidate. They hit it off, though Lewis later said he initially worried that the prim, proper, and preppy Entrekin might have been a little too "city-fied" for the rural district in which they were running.

Once the team was in place, they quickly went to work and created Lewis's campaign slogan of "Home Grown Values," which was meant to highlight his deep roots in the district and his socially conservative agenda. Since Dan Quayle first raised the issue of "family values" during his days as vice president, Republicans had often used some version of the phrase to differentiate themselves from the Democrats. In short, the slogan suggested that Carothers had lost touch with his district, sold out to Montgomery insiders, and no longer shared the same concerns as the voters he wished to represent—a big message to deliver in a simple, three-word slogan.

Radio ads were cut and aired, including one in which a voice actor, portraying the House Speaker reading the roll, calls out each member's name followed by other actors responding with "Aye!," as if a voice vote were being taken. The "Speaker" in the ad eventually says, "Mr. Carothers . . . Mr. Carothers . . . Mr. Carothers? Does anyone know where Joe Carothers is?!?" Another announcer then detailed the number of missed votes and absences Carothers had racked up as state representative, which was a hefty amount considering the three decades he had served.

While the consultants were working with Benjamin, I went to work as well, trying to convince our usual allies in Montgomery that they should abandon Carothers for Lewis or, at the least, hold onto their contributions and stay out of the race. My efforts proved unfruitful as group after group told me about their affection for Carothers, even when confronted with his often anti-business, pro-union voting record. In fact, the Carothers campaign mailed a fundraising invitation listing several of the groups I approached as sponsors. The associations for bankers, cattlemen, hospitals, poultry interests, retailers, auto dealers, home builders, insurance providers, and other groups that often worked with me to elect Republican candidates were highlighted prominently on the Carothers invitation.

To say I was frustrated and disappointed would be an understatement.

Eventually, I went to see Billy Canary at the Business Council of Alabama, the state's largest and most influential association representing business interests. Confident that BCA would immediately jump on board our effort, I told Canary about the Lewis campaign and outlined how the House Republican Caucus was involved in the race. Instead of pledging support, Canary indicated that BCA would also likely support Carothers's reelection. I am sure the color drained from my face as he explained that legislative endorsements for the BCA's political action committee, ProgressPAC, are made on the local level by prominent members in each region. The Dothan area meeting had not yet occurred, but it was imminent, and Canary said that Carothers likely had enough votes to secure the endorsement.

I was faced with a dilemma. An unspoken rule in the Alabama House said incumbent members stayed out of each others' elections and did not become involved under any circumstances. An incumbent Republican representative, for example, would never go into another district and campaign directly against an incumbent Democrat. Open seats, like the one Barry Mask captured, were fair game, but incumbent races were off the table.

Of course, this informal edict, supposedly created in the name of civility and camaraderie, had been handed down by the Democratic majority and its leadership. They understood that Republicans were unlikely to ever capture the House if we were not allowed to take on the other party's incumbents or work against them.

Knowing I was crossing the Rubicon, I asked Canary when the endorsement meeting was to be held and whether it would be possible for me to speak to the group before its vote. Turns out the meeting was the next day, and Canary said I would have to contact the local ProgressPAC committee to request permission to address the group in Dothan. I knew an appearance by me at the meeting would infuriate Carothers and send shockwaves through the Democratic side of the House. I also knew, however, that the future of our state was more important than the informal traditions of the Alabama House. I made a call to Charles Nailen, a friend and successful Wiregrass business leader who held a seat on the panel, and secured an invitation.

When I arrived in Dothan, the local ProgressPAC committee was nearing an endorsement for Carothers once again. He had served for 32 years, after all, and had never once had a serious, well-funded challenger or a close election in all that time. Though there were some open to an alternative among the gathered businessmen, the majority of the group seemed to be extending a courteous formality before taking the action everyone knew was coming. I had a tough job ahead of me.

Once the introductions were complete and the group was settled, I began my presentation by detailing the various initiatives that BCA had proposed over the years and the Democratic-controlled legislature routinely killed. Tort reform measures, tax cuts and incentives, reforms to lessen the influence of Hubbert and his union, and systemic changes to make state government more effective, efficient and responsive to the citizens it served were among them.

I then pointed out that Carothers, despite his reputation within his district as a conservative, had voted to oppose almost every one of them. Those examples were quickly followed with a list of various measures that BCA had opposed in the House, and I noted Carothers's votes to support each. Several eyebrows within the room began to rise.

Alabama would never be a truly pro-business state, I told the group, if we keep electing legislators based on longevity and likability rather than accountability. At some point, the Democratic majority would have to answer for the votes they cast, and 2006 was a good year to start holding feet to the fire. The time for Carothers to talk one way in his district while voting another way in Montgomery must come to an end, and Benjamin Lewis was the solid, conservative, business-minded alternative the group needed to support.

I also reviewed the data that showed Carothers was the most vulnerable House Democrat in the state. With BCA's financial help and support along with the assistance provided by the caucus, we could provide Lewis with the resources needed to defeat Carothers and send a shot across the bow of the labor unions, trial lawyers, and liberal special interests.

I concluded my plea by asking a question of the group: "Why do you think Paul Hubbert and the AEA have so much influence in the Alabama Legislature?"

"That's simple," one of the PAC board members quickly replied. "They have millions of dollars to spend in campaigns."

"That's part of it," I said. "But the main reason is because there are consequences for voting against them. Every member of the legislature knows if they vote against the AEA, there is a price to pay. They bad mouth you and spread false information to their membership about you, claiming that you hate teachers and oppose educating kids. Then, they spend money to defeat you in the next election.

"On the other hand, if a member votes against the BCA and other business groups, there are no consequences," I continued. "If you endorse and support Joe Carothers after he has voted against you every time your agenda conflicts with the AEA, you are sending the message loud and clear that he, and other Democrats like him, can continue to vote against business and continue to get your support."

"But Joe's probably going to win, so all we'd be doing is making him mad at us," someone blurted out.

"Well, that may be true," I said. "But at least he, and others, would finally get the message that if they vote against what you stand for, there are consequences. Then, maybe, one day you can get to a point where you don't lose every vote Hubbert doesn't bless."

The room was silent as the regional ProgressPAC members seemed stunned by my response. I wasn't exactly sure if it had made them think or just made them angry. But I was sure that my time was up, so I thanked them for their time and left the room.

On the way back to Auburn, I replayed the meeting in my mind, recounting the points I could have made more strongly and trying to gauge the reaction of each member around the table. My thoughts were interrupted when George Flowers, a Dothan businessman and chairman of the local ProgressPAC board, called to tell me the appearance had done the trick—the group had voted and BCA would support Benjamin Lewis in the general election.

I let out a deep, thankful breath. BCA was the only group in Montgomery that supported the Lewis campaign. Their support, and as a byproduct, Canary's political instincts and experience in the race, would prove vital to its outcome.

AT THE SAME TIME, I was monitoring and, quite honestly, actively participating in several other House races across the state including the contest between 24-year incumbent Frank "Skippy" White, a Democrat, and political newcomer Alan Baker, the Republican nominee.

Baker was a long-time football and track coach at T. R. Miller High School in Brewton, and had amassed ten state championships during his tenure—five for football and five for track. His success and record of excellence made him a living legend in the area and allowed him to run a completely positive campaign. The caucus and the ALGOP did, however, add its own independent mail and radio to supplement the Baker campaign efforts.

I was overseeing several House races, was heavily involved with the Riley reelection campaign, and had a serious challenge from a well-funded Democratic opponent seeking my seat in the legislature. I hardly had time to sleep or eat, and I simply tried to survive during those hectic months.

The Lewis race, however, was the highest priority on my radar screen.

We carpet-bombed Carothers's district with mail pieces highlighting the votes he had cast that did not reflect the conservative nature of his constituents—votes that we termed "liberal." A radio ad began airing that referred to him as "Liberal Joe Carothers." Cavanaugh and the Alabama Republican Party pitched in by recording an automated phone call that went directly into the homes of voters and carried the same message.

Carothers did not respond to the threat to his candidacy happily. He and Lewis were both campaigning and handing out promotional material at a high school football game in Cottonwood one Friday night when Carothers angrily confronted Lewis and had to be pulled away before throwing a punch.

At the time, Carothers was staging his own well-financed effort and was outspending Lewis by a good margin. The forestry and farming interests that supported him created a political action committee named

"Wiregrass Conservatives for Joe Carothers"—a somewhat deceptive name considering most of its funding came from Montgomery and not the Wiregrass—and aired radio and television ads supporting him. The Alabama Education Association was, as expected, pouring resources into his campaign.

By the end of the race, campaign finance records would show that Carothers spent a total of $328,000 with roughly two-thirds of his funding coming from four sources—the Wiregrass Conservatives PAC, AEA, Speaker Seth Hammett, and ALFA. Lewis, on the other hand, would spend just $234,000 with about $115,000 coming directly from the Alabama Republican Party and $57,000 from BCA.

Carothers spent most of his money on advertising that portrayed him as a patriotic, God-fearing conservative who believed in farms, faith, and family as the cornerstones of life. One television ad juxtaposed Carothers in front of a graphic of a waving American flag, much like the opening of the old black-and-white, 1950s Superman television show starring George Reeves.

Because Lewis was a largely blank slate with a squeaky clean background and no political record to attack, Carothers's material said his opponent's youth and lack of experience should disqualify him from office. While the Carothers campaign considered Lewis's lack of political experience a vulnerability, we believed strongly that the attack actually helped our message that Carothers had been in Montgomery too long and that fresh blood and new ideas were badly needed.

As the general election progressed and grew more intense, I arranged for Entrekin, who had been commuting from his home in Birmingham during the week, to move into the district full-time and keep his hand on the campaign rudder.

We polled the race as often as resources would allow and saw that the previously unknown Lewis had eaten into Carothers's initial double-digit lead and pulled within just a few percentage points. But, no matter what we tried, we could not get over that last hurdle and take the lead. At that point, fate intervened.

In mid-October, we learned that a Montgomery-based Democratic consultant working on the Carothers campaign was bragging that they would hold on to the seat because internal polling showed a segment of voters did not believe that Carothers often voted with the liberal Democrats no matter what evidence you presented to them. The conflict between Joe's perception and his actual voting record was hurting us. Immediately, Azbell and Swatek pulled out the latest polling crosstabs, the series of charts that allow political consultants to pinpoint how a certain group of voters view issues, and discovered something very critical.

While it was true that enough voters needed to put us over the top did not believe Carothers was a liberal, the numbers showed we did not have to convince them of that fact. The poll indicated we simply had to point out that Carothers was a pro-union Democrat, not necessarily a liberal one, in a heavily Republican district and would work with other Democrats to defeat Republican proposals if returned to Montgomery. Rather than complicating the race with the conservative versus liberal label, we could simply boil it down to Democrat versus Republican.

The group quickly went to work writing a script for a new television ad that was produced at the Auburn Network. The crux of the ad asked voters, "Which team are you on?" Since the World Series was taking place at the time, they gave it a baseball theme. It asked viewers to decide whether they were rooting for the Republican "baseball team" managed by Bob Riley, who was intensely popular in the Wiregrass at the time, and its star player, Benjamin Lewis, or their Democratic opponents led by Lucy Baxley and tired old veteran Joe Carothers. Once I received the script, I realized that, given the huge volume of political ads airing on television at the time, the concept was just different and unusual enough to stick with viewers and break through the white noise.

Unfortunately, with so little time until the election and under the gun to get the ad on the air, I could not locate any stock vintage baseball footage needed to produce the script. But, since I made my living producing football shows and videos, we had some old football game films from the 1940s already transferred to video. I traded the baseball theme for college football, a passion among Alabamians in the fall, cut the spot, and sent it to the stations in Dothan for airing.

I knew in my heart that it was an effective ad, but with little time to poll before Election Day, there was no way to know whether it would move any numbers until voters actually cast their ballots.

The day of the election is stressful for everyone involved in campaigns—the candidates, the consultants, the volunteers, the contributors, and others. In 2006, it was especially stressful for me because I had broken the rule and gotten involved in other incumbents' races, a decision that could haunt me if we did not win. I also had to worry about my own reelection results, along with those of Governor Riley, but Benjamin Lewis was foremost in my thoughts. The Business Council and my friend Billy Canary had stepped out on a limb by supporting Lewis when every other ally had sided with Carothers. I was afraid of the blowback Canary and the BCA might feel if our insurgent campaign failed.

Fortunately, my election and Governor Riley's were over early as we both won by comfortable margins and I was able to spend most of the night focusing on other races. The popular Alan Baker carried his race easily and sent Skippy White to retirement, but the other campaigns we had supported, funded, and provided staff and consultants for were not faring as well.

The Lewis race, meanwhile, was a see-saw battle with the two candidates trading the lead throughout the night and just a handful of votes separating them. After several hours of waiting for the final results, Lewis had won by 94 votes, a 0.7 percent victory margin that just barely escaped the 0.5 percent needed for a mandatory recount. I exhaled a breath I had been holding all night.

By the end of the night, we would lose four House races by less than 500 votes, a margin that makes any politico's stomach ache. We also received word that two of our Republican seats had been lost that night. Lynn Greer, a Republican legislator who had been elected in a majority Democratic north Alabama district largely by the power of his personality, had chosen not to seek reelection in 2006. We lost that seat in Greer's absence from the race. Nick Williams, another Republican representing a heavily Democratic district, had won his office in a low-turnout special election, but the high-turnout general election allowed the other side to recapture the seat.

After months of campaigning, millions of dollars raised and spent, and countless attacks and counterattacks that have become the norm in modern campaigns, all of our efforts resulted in a simple push—the Democrats picked up two Republican House seats and we picked up two of theirs. The Senate fared a little better with Republicans capturing two previously Democratic-held districts as Arthur Orr won the seat held by retiring Democrat Tommy Ed Roberts in Decatur and Ben Brooks defeated incumbent Gary Tanner in Mobile in a tough contest that was decided by about 500 votes. Despite the seats gained in the Senate, Democrats still counted enough votes in the upper chamber to retain control.

Since I had led the charge to get the caucus actively engaged in an effort to dislodge entrenched Democratic incumbents, my colleagues across the aisle accused me of dialing up the partisanship in the body to an unprecedented level. I believe their outrage was largely a façade because they should expect me, as the Republican leader in the House, to try to elect a Republican majority. In any case, I knew there would be repercussions for my efforts.

That prediction proved prescient when Speaker Hammett asked to meet with me prior to the legislature's organizational session. Hammett informed me that I was losing my seat on the House Ways and Means Education Committee. The state representative from Auburn, and his counterpart from Tuscaloosa, had traditionally been given seats on the committee to ensure that the interests of the state's two largest and most influential universities were represented. Hammett explained, however, that there was a penalty for guerilla campaigns like the ones we ran and my punishment was removal from the budget-writing panel and loss of the prestige that membership on it carried.

Although I was disappointed in his decision, I understood the anger the Democrats felt toward me because of the unprecedented campaign efforts of our caucus. At the same time, I didn't apologize for it. As the leader of the House Republicans, I believed it was my job to try and gain seats in an attempt to increase our influence. Even though the Democrats were upset and mad at the caucus—mostly at me—I believe that deep down they actually respected us more because of it.

As I watched our freshmen Republican members, Lewis and Baker, being sworn into seats the Democrats once considered safe, I knew we were onto something. Though it was the most aggressive and well-funded campaign the House Republicans had ever staged, I knew that 2006 was simply the pilot program for what lay ahead. It gave us the opportunity to kick the tires and take a ride around the block before we dialed in the engine for the next election cycle.

We had learned very valuable lessons. For one, we had put far too much campaign money into races where the poll numbers showed we could not win. We had let our emotions and affinity for the Republican candidate get the best of us and we funded the races in spite of the evidence. In other words, we had made decisions based on our hearts instead of our heads. If that money had gone into the four razor-thin-margin races, the story on the 2006 election night might have been very different. I made a note to approach future campaigns like a business by removing emotion and focusing simply upon the numbers.

The most important lesson learned, however, was that we had to be much more involved on the front end of the campaign. The recruitment of candidates was of paramount importance. Rather than hoping quality people would decide to qualify to run for the legislature as Republicans, we would have to put time, energy, and resources into recruiting the type of candidates we needed.

We had learned what messages worked, and which ones did not. We saw which groups stood by us and which were summertime soldiers and sunshine patriots. We were taught valuable lessons that could be examined, reexamined and refined. We discovered that we could raise campaign funds as a group and that a coordinated campaign could defeat an entrenched Democrat.

The 2006 campaign obviously did not yield the overall result we had hoped for, but without those experiences, I am not too sure we could have enjoyed the success we would achieve four years in the future.

Of course, I did not know that at the time.

~ In Their Own Words ~

BENJAMIN LEWIS
STATE REPRESENTATIVE 2006–2010;
HOUSTON COUNTY DISTRICT JUDGE 2010–

I always had an interest in going into politics, and that's actually the reason I went to law school. When I was a teenager my dad had an issue about dairy farms and he called Joe Carothers for help in the legislature. When he called Daddy back, I told 'Mr. Joe' that one day I was going to run for his seat. And Joe Carothers said 'Maybe by the time you get old enough to run, I'll be ready to retire.' Well, I was finally old enough and he hadn't retired, so if I was going to run, it would have to be against him.

Immediately after I filed, but before I met with Chuck Harris, I called Joe Carothers to tell him I was in the race. I really didn't know him very well. Joe had actually been a teacher at the high school I had attended in Ashford. I never had his class even though he told everybody he had taught me. Anyway, I called him and told him that I'm hearing this guy, Chuck Harris, is going to run, and I've always told you that I wanted to run for this seat, too. I let him know that I had already qualified and said, 'Chuck Harris is going to have to beat me before he can beat you.' Carothers tried to talk me out of running and encouraged me to get my qualification money back and withdraw. I told him it was too late. At that point, Carothers confided that he didn't think Chuck Harris lived in the district, and was planning to have him disqualified so he would be elected without opposition. That was Carothers's plan, but I guess I put a big kink in that plan.

He just wouldn't give up, though. One of my sons, Weston, had been injured and while we were in the hospital Carothers called to ask how he was and suggest again that I drop out. He said he would retire after that term and support me to take his place if I would just drop out this time. I explained that I'd made a commitment to people and told him as firmly as I could, 'Joe, I'm running.'

But he still called me, and the last time was at my daddy's farm. He was all kind and friendly explaining why I was making a mistake and asking me to wait just four years to run. When I refused, he said, 'I guess you're my damn opponent then,' and he wasn't so nice to me after that.

Mike Hubbard lined me up with some consultants, and I tried to do everything they told me to do. I had no political experience, and I considered them the experts. All I knew to do was go out, be myself and work hard. They advised me on what kind of stuff I needed to be doing on the ground to work the grassroots. They told me, 'We need you out here fighting the ground war, and we'll fight the air war for you.' And so that's what I focused on. My consultants were good guys, honest guys, and I knew they had my best interests at heart. In fact, the first time I heard several of the ads they produced for my campaign was when they aired on the radio or the television. That's the level of trust we had in each other.

I think Mike Hubbard is the most committed, hard-working, focused individual I've ever met. He's successful at what he does because he just works harder than anyone I know. I can honestly say I am where I am, as far as my political career is concerned, because of Mike Hubbard. If it wasn't for him I would be practicing law somewhere or milking cows in a barn. There's nothing wrong with that, I've done that before, but I prefer where I am now much more. I did my part, too, but without Mike Hubbard, there's no way I could have won my 94-vote landslide. There were a lot of people involved both here, locally, and my consultants, but Mike Hubbard is the one that organized it all.

JIMMY ENTREKIN
Benjamin Lewis Campaign Field Operative 2006

Mike Hubbard was instrumental in getting me a place to stay—a first-floor business suite at the Dothan Holiday Inn. I had moved there because Saturdays became the days to get out and meet the people at their homes and at events like the Peanut Festival in Dothan. I also got to spend a lot of time with Benjamin and his family and got to know them well, which was nice. On most mornings I would work on door lists, letter lists and such while he would try to visit a senior center, a Rotary Club and other group meetings. We usually met for lunch and went over what needed to be done the rest of the day, plus the next day's activities. After lunch I took care of the business side of things so he could meet with potential donors or knock on doors. Benjamin still had to spend a lot of time working on his family farm. And usually, at some point, both of us would be knocking on doors and asking for votes before the day was over.

"We won by 94 votes. I wasn't able to go the victory party because I was sitting at the probate judge's office counting and recounting and counting again. The thought was that we might have to have a recount, but when it was all said and done, there was no recount. Benjamin's lead only increased after they counted the absentee ballots. That was the biggest memory for me, sitting in that office checking every box and totaling everything. It was close the entire time. We won Joe Carothers's own box and probably would have lost without it. Politics is funny that way."

Left: High school senior Mike Hubbard wins the state VFW "Voice of Democracy" public speaking competition, Albany, Georgia, 1980. His parents are pictured at left.

Below: In 1979, Hubbard (right) defeated future Christian Coalition head Ralph Reed (left) in district American Legion oratorical contest in Athens, Georgia. Hubbard went on to win the state title.

Hubbard worked on two successful Heisman Trophy campaigns, for Georgia's *Herschel Walker, above, in 1982, and Auburn's Bo Jackson, below, in 1985. At Georgia, Hubbard also spearheaded a 1983 Heisman campaign for his roommate, Terry Hoage. Hoage, a future member of the College Football Hall of Fame, finished fifth in the Heisman balloting, the highest ever for a defensive back.*

Mike
HUBBARD
STATE REPRESENTATIVE

Conservative
Republican

"I'm a Conservative Republican who believes in limited government, free enterprise and individual freedom. I will fight for pro-family values and will be an advocate for a healthy business climate in Alabama."

Hubbard and wife Susan were featured on a push card for his first campaign, 1998.

Right: Then-Congressman Bob Riley, holding newborn Riley Hubbard, 2000. Below: Riley and big brother Clayte were included in a 2006 Hubbard mailer refuting charges that he didn't support public education.

Two Very Important Reasons
Mike Hubbard Supports Education

Reason #1

Reason #2

Top: *The Hubbard family at Jordan-Hare Stadium. Hubbard founded Auburn's radio and television sports network in 1990. Above: Mike and Susan flank Auburn Network associate Chris Hines, wife Karla, and son Harris. Below: In the governor's office with Governor Riley just before his 2003 inauguration.*

Top: Governor Riley and Congressman Mike Rogers help kick off the 2006 Hubbard reelection campaign at Johnston's Farm in Auburn, Alabama. Below: Victory night, 2006.

Left: Greeting President Bush at Maxwell AFB in Montgomery.

Below: As chairman of the Alabama delegation to the Republican National Convention in St. Paul in 2008. To Hubbard's left is U.S. Representative Robert Aderholt; to his right are U.S. Representatives Spencer Bachus and Jo Bonner.

Above, top: Hubbard and Governor Riley fly on the Alabama state jet to meet with an economic development prospect in north Alabama.

Above: Hubbard arranged for a portion of U.S. Highway 280 to be named for Lieutenant General Hal Moore of Auburn.

Opposite, top: At the U.S. Capitol with friend and political ally U.S. Representative Mike Rogers, who first predicted Hubbard would become the first Republican Speaker of the Alabama House since Reconstruction.

Opposite, bottom: Benjamin Lewis visits with Governor Riley during the 2006 campaign. Electing Lewis to the House from Houston County was a huge victory and the campaign served as a valuable learning experience in planning Campaign 2010.

Above: Announcing "Republican Handshake with Alabama," an agenda of specific, issue-oriented bills, August 2010.

Below: These yard signs were a popular part of the Republican campaign in the summer and fall of 2010.

Hubbard glancing toward the House gallery after his election as Speaker during the December 2010 special session.

Below: Exhausted but happy Republican Party staff following returns for Campaign 2010.

Hubbard being sworn in as Speaker of the House, December 8, 2010, as Susan, Riley, and Clayte look on.

Presiding in the House chamber over the Special Session on Ethics.

Above: Del Marsh and Hubbard look on as Governor Riley addresses the legislature at the start of the 2010 special session for ethics reform.

Below: Joking around with former U.S. Rep. J. C. Watts and Business Council of Alabama President Billy Canary prior to a BCA dinner in Birmingham.

Above: Having a tort reform discussion in the Speaker's office in the Alabama State House with Business Council of Alabama Chairman Will Brooke.

Below: With Senate President Pro Tempore Del Marsh (R-Anniston).

Left: With Auburn Head Football Coach Gene Chizik following Auburn's win in the 2011 BCS National Championship game in Glendale, Arizona.

Below: With Governor Robert Bentley as he signs his first bill into law. The Responsible Budgeting and Spending Act, sponsored by Representative Greg Canfield (R-Vestavia), left, was part of the "Republican Handshake with Alabama." At right, Senator Bryan Taylor (R-Prattville).

The new Republican legislative leadership, March 2011. From left: Senator Arthur Orr of Decatur, chairman, Senate Ways and Means General Fund Committee; Senator Del Marsh of Anniston, President Pro Tempore; Senator Trip Pittman of Daphne, chairman, Senate Ways and Means Education Fund Committee; Representative Mike Hubbard of Auburn, the Speaker of the House; Representative Micky Hammon of Decatur, House Majority Leader; Senator Jabo Waggoner of Vestavia, Senate Majority Leader; Lieutenant Governor Kay Ivey, President of the Senate; and Representative Jay Love of Montgomery, chairman, House Ways and Means Education Fund. Representative Jim Barton of Mobile, chairman, House Ways and Means General Fund, is not pictured.

10

AN UNEXPECTED CHALLENGE
AND THE BIRTH OF A BIG IDEA

J ust a week or two after the 2006 elections, Governor Riley asked me
to stop by his office for a visit. He said he had something important
to discuss. Since I had agreed to head his inaugural committee again,
I assumed he wanted to give me his thoughts on some of the upcoming
events already being planned. Or perhaps he wanted to review the make-
up of the new legislature and discuss his upcoming agenda. Had I known
what awaited me at the time, I might have declined the invitation and
gone into hiding.

After the usual pleasantries and a recap of the recent campaign, the
governor revealed the purpose of my summons. Twinkle Andress Cavanaugh, who served as chair of the Alabama Republican Party, had decided
not to run for another term as the ALGOP leader and would soon join
Riley's gubernatorial staff in a cabinet position. Her absence would leave a
void at the top of the party structure, he explained, and it was important
that Riley have someone he could trust and rely upon take over the reins.
I assumed he was going to let me know his chosen successor's name and
request my support for his choice, which I was happily prepared to give.

"Mike, I have something I want you to do for me," the governor said
in a tone resembling a father asking his son for help.

"Governor, I'll do anything for you," I answered without thinking
twice. After all, this is the man I had patterned myself after, politically
and otherwise. My youngest son was named Riley after him, so surely
there was nothing he could ask of me that I would not do.

"I want you to run for party chairman," the governor replied.

The statement was met with stunned silence. I know the expression
on my face had to be one of pure horror. I could feel the blood rushing

from my face and I got a sick feeling in my stomach as the request sunk in.

The governor was asking me, as his ally, friend, and loyal supporter, to run for the party chairman post. It was a job I had never considered and did not want.

After what seemed like a full minute, I was able to regain my composure and get some words of protest out of my mouth.

"Governor, I can't think of anything in the world that I want to do less than be party chairman," I said. "Susan will definitely divorce me if I do that."

My activities on the Riley campaign, my own reelection effort, and the various House races in which I was involved around the state had taken me away from home for much of 2006. Susan had made it clear she was ready for me to spend more time with our boys who were growing up fast, and return to the life we had enjoyed before the election cycle started.

I was also fully aware that serving as state chairman of the Alabama Republican Party could be one of the more thankless jobs in the state. It required constant travel to every city, town and bump in the road that had an organized Republican group, each of which expected the chairman to appear regularly and rally the troops. The job also demanded a relentless fundraiser who could keep money flowing in to keep the lights on and to make political campaigns competitive. Literally thousands of hours of my time would have to be devoted to the chairman's duties, time that I could instead commit to my business, my family, and other activities of my choosing. Worse yet, the post was and is completely voluntary. That meant it would be a money-losing proposition for me.

"Governor, I can't do it, but I will help you find someone else," I said. "I'll work with whoever is elected chairman and you know I'll do whatever I can do to help you. I'm still the minority leader and I can do more to help you through that position."

Governor Riley looked at me and nodded as I spoke. He listened to my arguments but had a smile on his face, a smile I'd seen many times before. It meant he was listening but wasn't convinced.

About 10 minutes later, I walked out of the governor's office a candidate for chairman of the Alabama Republican Party. I had gotten the governor's firm commitment to help me raise money throughout my tenure if I won, but my biggest concern was how to break the news to Susan.

Having just decompressed from the "campaign mode" that politicos go into each election year, it was difficult to immediately and abruptly change course. It didn't take long, however, for my competitive juices to take over and my team and I jumped into action. I had to convince a majority of the 380-member State Republican Executive Committee that I was the right choice to lead the party for the next two years, the length of the ALGOP chairman's term.

There was only one other announced candidate, Scott Beason of Gardendale, who had just been elected to the State Senate after serving with me for eight years in the House. Around the time I announced my entrance into the chairman's race, Beason and his supporters had put out the word that my candidacy was for naught because he had already secured nearly enough commitments to be elected chairman. His friends filled the comment section of a popular political gossip blog at the time, *Doc's Political Parlor*, with posts scoffing at my efforts and claims that they would embarrass the governor by defeating his hand-picked choice. To say his crowd was no fan of Bob Riley or, by association, me, would be an understatement.

I sent a letter to each member of the executive committee, began making personal phone calls, and held as many one-on-one meetings as possible to make a case for my election. Despite the boastful claims by the other side, I could not find a single member who had committed to support Beason. I suppose they thought if everyone else got scared out of the race, their candidate could win by acclamation. Now that I was in the race, though, I was committed to not let Bob Riley down. I was not going anywhere.

In fact, I was beginning to rack up the solid commitments and votes needed to win. Having the support of the very popular sitting Republican governor did not hurt, but I did not intend to balance my entire candidacy on that crutch. Instead, I outlined to committee members my plans to aggressively raise the funds and build the resources necessary to finally wrest control of state government from the Democrats. In essence,

I was planting the seeds that would eventually grow into our 2010 effort.

OUR PITCH WAS APPARENTLY convincing because just three days before Christmas, Beason called my home and told me he had decided not to seek the party chairmanship. With Beason dispatched, I was able to focus my full attention and energies on the inaugural festivities that Riley had asked me to coordinate. Just as it had four years earlier, this required us to raise more than $1.5 million, stage numerous supporting events, organize the inaugural parade, produce the actual swearing-in ceremony and put together the inaugural ball. This time, the ball had to be held in Birmingham because Montgomery's Civic Center was being renovated and there were no other suitable venues there.

Fortunately, I had saved all of the plans, outlines, and names of vendors we had used in 2003 in meticulously organized three-ring binders. The information, including invitations, layouts and diagrams of events, financial records, and other details, was invaluable in recreating the inaugural. It was still a gargantuan task that required a quality staff, hundreds of volunteers, countless man-hours and military-like precision, but having done it before made the second time easier. One of our bigger decisions was whom to hire to perform at the inaugural ball. Everyone had a favorite—the governor liked the Oak Ridge Boys—but we ultimately decided upon multiplatinum-selling singer Sara Evans, who had just been selected as Female Vocalist of the Year during the nationally televised awards shows of both the Country Music Association and the Academy of County Music. Evans would soon have deeper Alabama ties as she began dating, and would later marry, Jay Barker, the former University of Alabama quarterback who led his team to a national championship in 1992.

Security is always a big concern at events like the inauguration, and it seemed even more imperative at that year's event because of an important guest—U.S. Senator John McCain of Arizona had come to Alabama for the Riley inaugural in hopes of wooing the popular governor to endorse his presidential campaign. McCain, at the time, was the front-runner for the Republican presidential nomination and was in the state as a direct result of a bill I was sponsoring with an unlikely ally.

Representative Ken Guin from Carbon Hill was the leader of the House Democratic Caucus and was also chairman of the body's Rules Committee. As the head of the Democratic Caucus, his job was to be the bad cop to Speaker Seth Hammett's good cop. Any crumb that got tossed to Republicans was attributed to Hammett's generous heart and sense of fair play while any unfair ruling, broken promise, or painful defeat was blamed on Guin's partisan nature and ruthlessness. H. R. Haldeman, who had served as chief of staff to former President Richard Nixon, was once famously quoted as saying, "Every president needs a son of a bitch, and I'm Nixon's." I suppose Guin played that role for Hammett.

Because of our battles on the House floor and our constant jousting as leaders of the majority and minority caucuses, many were surprised when Guin and I not only supported the same high-profile bill, but even served as its principal sponsors in the House. For years, Alabama had been an also-ran when it came to presidential politics. Because our primary was always held in June, the nominations for both parties had long been decided by states that voted earlier in the election cycle. Our early-summer primaries had been a long-standing tradition dating back to the days when Alabama was a one-party state and capturing the Democratic nod in June was tantamount to election in the fall.

As 2008 approached, several states were working to move their presidential preference primaries to the front of the calendar, a process commonly known as frontloading. Some even wanted to infringe upon the sacred dates held by Iowa, New Hampshire, and South Carolina, the states that have long held the first three selection contests. The desire to rush to the top of the calendar became so prevalent that the Republican and Democratic national committees threatened to remove all or most of the convention delegates from any state that held a primary prior to February.

Guin and I both understood that if Alabama was going to receive any attention from either the Democratic or Republican presidential candidates, we, too, would have to join the race to the front. Twenty-three other states were looking to hold primaries or caucuses for one or both parties on February 5, 2008, a date that became known as Super Tuesday. We decided to jointly sponsor legislation moving our party's primaries to that date as well. Ours was a symbolic gesture highlighting that both Democrats and Republicans in Alabama supported the move. Our bill became law and our presidential primary set turnout records that year as Alabamians went to the polls to let their voices be heard. The primary for state offices, mostly appellate judgeships and other traditionally down-ballot races, was still held in June, and its turnout was, conversely, anemic.

Alabama's jump from June to February also resulted in several candidates visiting the state who would have otherwise ignored us for delegate-rich early-voting states. Both Senators Barack Obama and Hillary Clinton made appearances before Democratic groups. In addition to McCain, former Massachusetts Governor Mitt Romney, Congressman Duncan Hunter of California, former New York Mayor Rudy Guiliani, former U.S. Senator Fred Thompson of Tennessee, and former Arkansas Governor Mike Huckabee, who campaigned with action movie star Chuck Norris, also made appearances in the state.

McCain probably made the most pilgrimages to Alabama and he committed full-bore to the state once we moved the primary. He hired a team of Alabama-based consultants, set up a grassroots structure, and committed significant resources. During the majority of his visits, McCain would meet with Riley and try to earn his endorsement. But the governor ultimately remained neutral in the 2008 presidential primary.

The trip to Riley's second inaugural was among McCain's first visits to the state, and I must admit I was impressed with his lack of pretense. Rather than having an entourage trail him, as so many candidates do, McCain traveled with a single aide. Though he was the Republican presidential frontrunner at the time, the senator brought no security with him and moved easily through the crowd, shaking hands, and greeting well-wishers.

Of course, the two-block radius around the Capitol during the swearing-in ceremony was probably the safest place in Alabama. We had teams of state security, both uniformed and plainclothes, scattered throughout the crowd and SWAT snipers stationed on the roofs of government buildings. Despite the secure bubble we had prepared, Attorney General Troy King, whose sense of self-importance often exceeded that of the office he held, insisted upon wearing a bulletproof vest throughout the ceremony. He was the only person on the inaugural stand or in the audience who wore one.

McCain would later be forced to abandon his foothold in Alabama when his national campaign committee ran out of money and experienced a precipitous decline. Most political prognosticators wrote off his chances of gaining the nomination, but a big McCain win in New Hampshire, followed by a victory in South Carolina, renewed his momentum. Though Huckabee would ultimately win the most primary delegate votes in Alabama, McCain would capture the GOP nomination. I did not know at the time that I would soon be caught in the middle of a contentious dispute between the McCain and Huckabee supporters.

THE REPUBLICAN STATE EXECUTIVE Committee meeting took place in Montgomery on February 10, 2007, the day before my forty-sixth birthday. As the only declared candidate for chairman, I felt pretty confident in my chances. Emory Folmar, the legendary former mayor of Montgomery and long-time Republican who helped build the party brick by brick, nominated me for the post. Twinkle Cavanaugh, the outgoing chair who had made calls and written letters on my behalf, seconded the motion. Before I knew it, the committee had unanimously elected me as the new leader of the ALGOP.

In my remarks that followed the election, I unveiled an idea that had been germinating since we had completed our embryonic pilot program to elect Republican legislators just a few months before. Rather than waiting until the 2010 election cycle to begin raising money for legislative races, I had determined that we should start immediately—a full four years before the first ballot would be cast—and earmark the money for those efforts. We could begin recruiting the pollsters, mail houses, opposition researchers, strategy consultants, and other vendors needed for the effort.

We could also begin to track the politically damaging legislative votes of Democrats as they cast them. In my mind, our campaign to take over the legislature would commence before the smoke had cleared from the last election.

"As Republicans, we have made great strides in Alabama," I said to the crowd following my election as the party's new chairman. "We hold a majority of all of the constitutional offices, a majority of the congressional delegation, and every seat on all three statewide appellate courts. We have had tremendous success, but our work is not done. The Alabama Legislature continues to be solidly controlled by Democrats.

"That's why today, I am proud to announce the formation of Campaign 2010," I continued, publicly uttering the phrase for the first time. "Campaign 2010 will be a comprehensive and unprecedented campaign that will take our party to the next level and finally put Republicans in charge of the legislative branch of government in Alabama. Details of this ambitious effort will be announced soon, but know that, as your chairman, I pledge to work every day to put Republicans in a position to win in 2008 and make history in 2010."

It was the moment Campaign 2010 became official. On behalf of the Republican party, I had drawn a line in the sand, and now we had to back it up.

The prediction that my new responsibilities would take me away from home and away from my business more often than Susan or I preferred turned out to be extremely accurate. With the ALGOP headquarters located in Birmingham, a two-hour drive each way on heavily trafficked Highway 280 from Auburn, I was forced to lose entire work days going there to conduct the simplest party business a few times each week. Speaking and fundraising engagements in far corners of the state ate up much more of my time. Addressing gatherings like the massive Madison County Men's Republican Club Saturday breakfast meeting in Huntsville demanded that I spend the night before away from home. Missing too many of the boys' ballgames and spending time away from my wife was not my idea of fun, but I was totally committed to an important mission that sometimes required me to wear blinders.

There were perks to the job. As chairman, I was automatically a member of the Republican National Committee. The RNC consists of three members from each state—the chairman, the national committeeman, and the national committeewoman. The RNC meetings allowed me to network with some of the best-known political leaders in our country and help set the policy and direction for my party. I also fostered several close friendships, including one with Katon Dawson, the head of the South Carolina Republican Party who would later run unsuccessfully for chairman of the RNC, and with Mississippi national committeeman Henry Barbour, the nephew of former RNC chairman and Mississippi Governor Haley Barbour.

Each December, Susan and I were invited to attend a Christmas party at the White House, and we always enjoyed visiting our nation's capital at this special time of the year. Susan always looked elegant in her holiday gown during these very special occasions and there are certainly worse ways to spend the holidays than hobnobbing with President George W. Bush, his wife, Laura, and countless other recognizable faces. Catching up with close friends Mike and Beth Rogers was an added plus.

Being chairman also came with great responsibilities that often brought their own logistical nightmares. The 2008 Republican National Convention in Minneapolis/St. Paul, was one example.

Following the Alabama presidential primary, we gathered everyone who had been elected as GOP presidential delegates in Montgomery to discuss our plans for the convention and to conduct some required business. Even though Huckabee had finished first in our primary, our delegation was almost evenly split between delegates pledged to him and those committed to McCain. Our state party bylaws mandated that delegates could only be awarded to candidates that captured at least 20 percent of the vote, and since Romney, Paul, and Guiliani fell below that threshold, they exited Alabama empty-handed. That left our delegation closely divided on a proportional basis between Huckabee, who had won 41 percent of the vote, and McCain, who was not far behind with 37 percent.

During the organizational meeting, held in the first-floor meeting room of the Business Center of Alabama in Montgomery, the elected delegates had to elect a delegation chairman. This would be the person who would officially lead the delegation to Minneapolis/St. Paul, formulate the logistics for the group's daily agenda for the week-long affair and, most of all, serve as the official liaison between the visitors from Alabama and the RNC convention coordinators on site.

Attorney General King, who had chaired the McCain campaign in

Alabama and even traveled to other southeastern states to support his candidacy, believed he should lead the delegation, citing his position as an elected constitutional officer as the reason. His stance did not sit well with the Huckabee delegates, who noted that King's candidate had lost Alabama, and allowing his campaign chairman to fill such a high-profile role would send a wrong message about how our state had voted.

Arguments flew back and forth with King bloviating about his importance and Huckabee's crowd not backing down. A true standoff was in the offing until Alabama's longtime and highly-respected national committeeman Edgar Welden took the floor. As committeeman, Welden had an automatic delegate slot and thus was not committed to either candidate. He also held a seat on the RNC's committee on arrangements, one of the more prestigious convention committees that provided him with significant authority to ensure our delegates would be treated well while in Minnesota.

Welden pointed out the plan my staff and I had already put into action to ensure the needs of the delegation would be met and highlighted that I, as state party chair, was also an automatic, yet uncommitted, delegate to the convention. He stated that he believed I was the logical choice to lead the delegation because of the staff's comfort with me and the fact that I had remained neutral in the primary. He then nominated me for the position. Weldon's reasoning and nomination angered King and his backers, but after some debate, with Welden and King's name also placed into nomination, the question came to a vote. Though I had not said one word during the meeting, the delegation overwhelmingly voted me as its chairman.

When the vote was taken, it was obvious that most of the McCain delegates had voted for me over King, a move that both my staff and I deeply appreciated. The staff and I went to work coordinating the housing, food, transportation, and entertainment of the more than 150 people who were part of the Alabama delegation. We also had to raise the money to fund the receptions, delegation breakfasts, and other events, which was no small task. And, of course, to try out best to keep everyone happy, a daunting challenge in itself.

The convention was a whirlwind of receptions, parties, delegation meetings, platform discussions, and, of course, historic speeches and nominations. In fact, one of my duties as delegation chair was to join Congressman Spencer Bachus of Birmingham on national television as we pledged all 48 Alabama delegates to John McCain. Within seconds I began receiving texts and e-mails from friends across the country who had been watching the convention coverage. Having grown up watching the televised nominating conventions with my parents, being able to participate in the pomp and circumstance of the roll call vote is a memory I will take to my grave.

In addition to the national convention, my staff and I were also tasked with putting together two meetings of the almost 400-member State Republican Executive Committee each year, one in the summer and another during the winter months. These gatherings were basically mini-conventions held at various locations throughout the state; they allowed the executive committee to debate resolutions, elect party officers, and have direct input into ALGOP operations. These meetings were often staid and routine, but sometimes a controversial resolution or unexpected motion from the floor would liven things up. As the meetings' presiding officer, I had to stay on guard for any surprises that might arise from factions within the party.

Because any gathering of several hundred Republicans offered a prime fundraising opportunity, we always staged a dinner the night before the executive committee meeting. Nationally known elected officials ranging from McCain and Minnesota Governor Tim Pawlenty to Republican strategists Mary Matalin and Dick Morris to conservative columnists Cal Thomas and Fred Barnes would speak to the attendees. We would sell tickets at $150 a pop and offer VIP sponsorships with proceeds used to fund the party's overhead and other noncampaign expenses.

One year, our desperation to find a speaker led us to unknowing involvement in a scandal that would soon make national headlines. Getting commitments from speakers, especially those at the top of the political stratosphere, was often a nail-biting process as many waited until the last minute to finalize their plans. In the winter of 2009, we had just such an occurrence when former U.S. Congressman J. C. Watts notified us with little time before the event that he would be unable to appear.

Looking for a suitable replacement, I remembered that Mark Sanford, the incumbent two-term governor of South Carolina, was being touted as a possible candidate for the Republican presidential or vice presidential nomination. He had a reputation as a dynamic public speaker and I knew he was friends with Governor Riley dating back to the days when both served in Congress. I reached out to a friend in South Carolina, Katon Dawson, and asked for his help to secure Sanford's appearance, which he did by calling in a favor.

We had originally arranged with Sanford's scheduler to send a private plane to Columbia to transport him to Alabama for his appearance and return him to South Carolina immediately afterward. At the last minute, Sanford's assistant called to tell me that there would be an unexpected change. The governor would be flying to Alabama from New York, not South Carolina, and had asked that we provide him with a ticket on a commercial flight from LaGuardia to Atlanta. I offered to purchase a first-class fare, but the assistant explained that Sanford had simple tastes and insisted on traveling only in coach.

When Sanford's flight touched down in Atlanta, we had ground transportation ready to bring him to Montgomery. I was waiting to greet him in the lobby of the Renaissance Hotel when he walked through the front door, carrying his own bag and with no security detail. He was pleasant and personable as we made small talk, discussing our mutual friends in Riley and Dawson, the fact that I grew up on the Georgia-South Carolina line, and I reminded him that I had actually met him once before at the governor's mansion in Columbia during an RNC chairmen's meeting.

Since there was lag time between his arrival and the dinner, I told him that we had arranged for him to have use of a room in the hotel to relax, return calls, read, or prepare for the night's speech. John Ross and I escorted him to his room, the hotel's Governor's Suite, but when we opened the door and Sanford stepped in, he protested that the suite was too extravagant. When we explained that it was being provided to us as part of our package with the hotel as thanks for holding the dinner there, he relented.

My staff, meanwhile, wanted to see the opulent suite, so when it came time for Sanford to come downstairs for the VIP reception and photos with donors, Ross and Philip Bryan went up to get him and used the opportunity to take a look inside. Upon entering the room, they found the cushions had been removed from the furniture and scattered around the room, some as if thrown and others as if arranged methodically. Other pieces of furniture had been placed on the hotel's balcony. Sanford was in the room alone the whole time. Though I did not witness it myself, the word most often used by Ross and Bryan to describe the scene was "strange."

Sanford did a great job greeting and chatting with our guests as hundreds went through the photo line. Many of us did think it a bit odd when he wandered off by himself throughout the night to talk on his cell phone, but we just figured he was conducting state business.

Sanford's keynote speech lived up to its billing and was intellectual, thought-provoking, and exceptionally well-delivered. I know more than a few of my fellow Republicans left that dinner intrigued by the thought of a Sanford presidential candidacy, especially since he was from a sister southeastern state. The reaction indicated that his hastily arranged appearance had been a great success for us, financially and otherwise.

I thanked the governor for taking the time to visit Alabama, and he thanked my staff and me again for rearranging his travel out of New York City. As Candice Clark, the legislative director for the House Republican Caucus, left the hotel to drive Sanford to the Montgomery airport to board the private plane we had secured for his return to South Carolina, I assumed that might be the last time Sanford and I would speak.

Just over three months later, in early June 2009, I was disturbed to learn that Sanford was reported missing in South Carolina. Neither his wife, his state security detail, nor his chief of staff knew his whereabouts. Calls to his cell phone went unreturned, and the media reported he had made a vague reference to hiking the Appalachian Trail prior to his disappearance.

Four days later, I was working in my Auburn office when I received an e-mail from Minda Campbell suggesting that I turn on the television. I was dumbfounded to see what was taking place. A reporter had spotted Sanford in the Atlanta airport arriving on an international flight from Argentina, and just as had been the case on his flight from New York, with no security. When confronted with questions, the governor returned to South Carolina and called an emergency news conference in which he admitted to an extramarital affair. That first televised news conference and a series of media interviews in the days that followed contained revelations and statements more appropriate for an episode of Jerry Springer than for the corridors of the South Carolina capitol.

Referring to her as his "soul mate," Sanford told the Associated Press and other outlets that he and Maria Belen Chapur, a 43-year-old Argentine journalist and divorced mother of two living in Buenos Aires, had carried on a torrid year-long affair after having met in Uruguay several years prior. He further admitted that Chapur was simply the latest in a string of women with whom he had "crossed the line" during his marriage, but said the relationship with her was, by far, the most serious. In fact, he said, his wife had learned of the affair around the time of our ALGOP dinner and, unbeknownst to the citizens of South Carolina, he and the first lady had been separated for a few months. In less than a year, they would be divorced.

Legislative leaders of both parties in South Carolina called upon Sanford to resign. Those pleas only intensified when it was revealed that he had used taxpayer money to visit his mistress. The governor refused, and articles of impeachment, along with several charges of ethics violations, were introduced against him, but did not pass. Though the legislature did officially censure him, Sanford served out the rest of his controversial term.

Just a few days after the scandal broke, I was vacationing in Destin, Florida, with my family when my cell phone rang. The caller ID displayed a number with an 803 area code. Not knowing who it was, I answered the phone with a generic greeting, "Mike Hubbard."

"Hello, Mike. This is Mark," the caller announced.

For the life of me, I didn't recognize the voice. Instead of admitting I didn't know who was on the other end of the line, I gave a generic response. "Hello, Mark. How are you?" I asked, in hopes of gleaning a clue as to the mystery caller's identity.

"Well, I guess I'm fine except for a self-inflected bullet hole in my head," was the response.

I knew immediately that it was Governor Sanford. He explained that he was calling to apologize for embarrassment he might have brought our party as a result of the scandal that followed his appearance. He also offered to reimburse us for the cost of his flight from New York City, indicating that he had flown there after a tryst with his mistress.

I assured him that there was no need for any reimbursement since the commercial ticket was less expensive than a private charter from South Carolina would have cost. I also pointed out that he had done a wonderful job for us that night, helping us raise almost $50,000 for the ALGOP. He continued to apologize to me, someone he had only met twice before, but I told him that no apology was necessary.

It was difficult to watch such a public self-destruction of an elected official with so much potential. The Mark Sanford story should be a warning tale to every officeholder in the nation.

～ *In Their Own Words* ～

BOB RILEY
U.S. Congress 1996–2002; Governor 2003–2011

I knew when I asked Mike to be party chairman that I was facing an uphill battle. That's putting it mildly. He had a business to run, a district to serve and a family to take care of. But, he was also the only person I believed could do for the Alabama Republican Party what we had begun to do for the state: throw out the old models, devise an entirely new strategy and then execute a plan. The old ways had kept us the minority party in the legislature for over a century. I was absolutely convinced, with the right party leader and the right committed team, we would change that too.

I knew what I was asking…unprecedented travel and time away from home and work, fundraising like never before, multiple events every week and all completely voluntary. But, I also knew no one could close a deal or inspire people to believe in this mission like Mike Hubbard. And there was no substitute for that.

11

BUILDING A TEAM

I have had the great fortune of spending most of my professional life witnessing iconic football coaches and visionary business and political leaders assemble winning teams. By watching them, I learned that recruiting and bringing the wrong person on board can ruin the chemistry of the team and cause it to collapse. As the newly elected chairman of the Alabama Republican Party, I knew that assembling the members of the team to help me run the organization was absolutely critical.

For me, the foundation of any successful team must be built on trust and loyalty. Using this as my compass, I set out to assemble a group of individuals who believed we could make history and were willing to sacrifice to do it. I was fortunate to identify some of the most dynamic and impressive people I have ever known, which has given me faith that our state will be in good hands when the time comes for my generation of leaders to step aside.

God blessed me with two wonderful sons who are the joy of my life. If he had chosen to bless me with daughters, it would have been my prayer for them to be like Kate McCormick and Sidney Rue. I first got to know Kate and Sidney while working with them on Governor Riley's 2006 reelection campaign, where both served as staffers. Despite their youth, both only in their early 20s, they had a knack for working as a team to accomplish whatever project they were assigned—from planning small or large events, to direct mail projects. Just as important, their attention to detail was uncanny and their maturity far surpassed their ages.

When Governor Riley asked me to serve again as chairman of his inauguration, I immediately asked Kate and Sidney to come on board. As expected, they surpassed my expectations in every area of planning and carrying out the multiple inaugural events they were assigned.

My decision to seek the ALGOP party chairmanship, at Riley's urging, overlapped with the inaugural project. So when the inaugural ball wrapped up and the crews began dismantling what had taken weeks to put together, I already knew I wanted Rue and McCormick on my team with the party. I had no doubt they were up to the task of coordinating the fundraising efforts of Campaign 2010, which I often described as the most comprehensive, aggressive, and ambitious plan in the history of the Alabama Republican Party.

Fundraising—asking strangers or mere acquaintances to open their wallets and donate hard-earned money—is by far the most difficult job in politics. It's also absolutely critical if you are to have any chance of being successful. Finding someone with the talent, ability, intelligence, and motivation to succeed in this field is a rarity. Fortunately for me, I knew two who excelled at it. I was elected as chairman of the Alabama Republican Party on a Saturday and Kate and Sidney were my first two hires, starting work first thing on Monday morning. Both were eager to get started even after I explained the unbelievable challenge ahead.

Prior to my becoming chairman, the party had never had a full-time fund-raiser. Now suddenly we had two. Hiring them as the first two members of the staff sent a strong message that my top priority was going to be ensuring we had the resources to mount aggressive campaigns, elect Republicans up and down the ballot, and flip control of the Alabama Legislature for the first time in more than a century.

McCormick made her way from her hometown of Jacksonville, Florida, to attend Birmingham's Samford University. A native of Mobile, Rue graduated from the University of the South—Sewanee—and then earned a master's degree from the University of Alabama. The pair first teamed up at the Birmingham Chamber of Commerce where they worked in member relations. After learning that a position on the 2006 Riley campaign had opened up, Rue interviewed with the governor's son, Rob, and was offered a job in fundraising and event planning. When told there was another position available in the fundraising shop, Sidney knew the perfect person for the job—Kate.

After getting my fundraising team in place, I quickly turned my attention to finding someone to captain the ship—an executive director who could run the day-to-day operations of the party. For this key job, I had John Ross, the talented ticket manager from the first Riley inaugural in 2002, in mind from the outset. Ross's ability to deal with and diffuse difficult situations had made a lasting impression on me, and I knew he was a loyal, level-headed and intelligent young man. I had stayed in touch with him off and on over the past four years, so I was anxious to gauge his interest in the job.

Following the 2002 inaugural, he had traveled to Argentina and lived for several months as a last hurrah before entering the workforce full time. On his return, he became a district aide to U.S. Representative Robert Aderholt; married Allison, a native of Pascagoula whom he had met while a graduate student at Alabama; and relocated with her to Decatur, which served as the home base for his activities on Aderholt's behalf. He had worked with Aderholt for just over three years.

Before contacting John, I felt it important to seek Aderholt's blessing. The congressman and I had known each other for years, and I wanted to make sure he was amicable to my hiring away one of his top staffers. In a telephone call with Aderholt, I learned that the Rosses had just purchased a new home in Decatur. It was apparent that John and Allison, who was vice president of the Morgan County Economic Development Authority, were putting down roots. However, Aderholt gave me his blessing and, undeterred, I gave John a call.

I knew he wasn't going to be completely caught off guard because I had asked my longtime friend and trusted political advisor, Dax Swatek, to tip him off that I would be calling. After exchanging pleasantries, I went right into my pitch. I outlined my plan in as much detail as possible and asked if he wanted to join me in making history. It was evident that Ross was immediately interested. The issues Aderholt had mentioned, along with some uncertainly about leaving his current role, were naturally weighing on John, so we agreed to meet at the party headquarters in Birmingham later that week for further discussion.

The meeting in Birmingham proved extremely helpful for John and me. I had asked the outgoing executive director, Tim Howe, to sit in on our meeting. Howe, who had been in the trenches as we implemented our legislative campaign effort in 2006, answered John's questions and put him at ease about assuming what is truly a unique role.

A couple of days after our meeting, to my delight, Ross accepted my offer to become executive director of the Alabama Republican Party. But we had one last hurdle to overcome.

THE BYLAWS OF THE ALGOP allow the chairman to select an executive director, but the selection must be approved by the State Steering Committee, a small group of prominent Republicans who help set policy and direction. Prior to the vote, I set up meetings with two of the most prominent steering committee members at the time—national committeeman Edgar Welden and national committeewoman Bettye Fine Collins. Ross and Welden immediately hit it off. Interestingly, Welden had been named executive director of the ALGOP in the 1960s at the young age of 28— the same age as Ross. This further strengthened their bond, and Welden proved to be one of my strongest allies throughout my time as chairman.

Collins always made time to serve the Republican party even though she was constantly saddled with tough issues stemming from her other job as president of the Jefferson County Commission. After careful questioning and learning about Ross's background, she smiled and said he had her full support. Elated and relieved, we left the Jefferson County Courthouse and prepared for the steering committee meeting.

Since I was anxious to get Ross on board and to start kicking off Campaign 2010, I decided to hold the steering committee meeting via teleconference. I'd asked John to join the call at a specific time after the committee had conducted some other business. That way, I would have a chance to discuss exactly why I wanted him to lead the organization. After Ross dialed in, he outlined his background and why he felt he could excel at the position. After taking a couple of questions, he hung up, we had some further discussion among the steering committee members, and he was unanimously approved. After the meeting, I called Ross to give him the official news and asked him to get started as soon as possible.

Two weeks later, he was on the job. He had put his new house in Decatur on the market, his wife had quit her job with no current prospects in Birmingham, and they had moved into an apartment just south of downtown. It was obvious then, and even more so now that I look back on it, that they had totally bought into the plan and were taking a leap of faith with me for the opportunity to change the political landscape of Alabama for years to come.

THE FIRST SEVERAL MONTHS of my chairmanship were difficult. There is no other way to put it. Our biggest impediment was the outstanding debt, which totaled just under $180,000. Election years are expensive for political parties because they typically spend every dime on hand and borrow even more in support of their candidates. The worst nightmare of any politico is to lose an election by a handful of votes with piles of money still in the bank. The ALGOP had jumped into the 2006 election with a determination to win as many offices as possible, and the debt it incurred was evidence of that fact.

My plan to dig us out of the hole and get us in a position to move forward was simple: significantly cut costs and begin raising as much money as possible. To implement the cost-cutting portion of the plan, I began by trying to find an experienced bookkeeper who, with the help of longtime party treasurer Homer Jackson, could make sense of our current financial situation. We needed help in identifying areas where we could scale back and assistance with the tedious reporting requirements mandated by the state and the Federal Elections Commission.

At the suggestion of Rob Riley, I reached out to Birmingham CPA Matt Turpin who said he had worked with an experienced bookkeeper who had a forensic accounting background. He also believed she would be a quick study on the reporting requirements.

Kasie Nimm proved to be an invaluable asset to us climbing out of our financial hole all the way through the 2010 election cycle. Nimm worked with Ross over the next three months organizing the party's finances. They spent a great deal of time cutting any expense we could identify as not absolutely essential—copier and phone leases were renegotiated, travel expenses were slashed, office supplies were conserved, and old computers were brought back to life. We also tapped a supply of interns from Samford University and Birmingham-Southern College, and students from non-local schools were utilized during the summer. They received school credit and worked for us without salary. During that first year, it was common to see up to five interns at the office on any given day. Free, capable labor was something we simply couldn't pass up, but I do believe we provided students with real-world experiences. They were performing jobs that full-time, salaried employees would have been doing anywhere else.

The major expense we were forced to live with was the office lease. It had been signed years before and was a triple net lease on a balloon payment schedule. The last year of the lease, which was my first year as chairman, an office containing four staffers and the interns was costing the party $6,000 a month, plus utilities, cleaning, and maintenance. There was more empty space than occupied space and the headquarters was a financial burden too difficult for us to carry on a monthly basis. On top of that, the neighborhood wasn't the safest place to be after dark. In fact, Ross's first task every morning was to clean the beer bottles off the front steps that had been left by the patrons of the bar next door. I often wondered what our committee members would think if someone happened to drive by one morning and report they'd seen our executive director holding a beer bottle on the front steps of the headquarters. Fortunately, it never happened. Even worse, the Girls Gone Wild bus parked in front of the ALGOP headquarters while doing a promotion at the neighboring bar, and I am forever glad that the Democrats did not get a picture of that.

The instant the lease expired, we moved to office space in Homewood. Our costs went down to $3,500 a month, which included utilities, cleaning, and maintenance. Even though we were in a much better financial position by then, it was satisfying to remove this albatross from our neck.

Fundraising had started to take off by the summer of 2007. Our goal had been to pay off the debt and be in the black by the end of the year. By June, we were ahead of schedule which was the result of nothing more than hard work. Rue, McCormick, finance chairman Senator Del Marsh, and I were tirelessly exploring ways to increase revenue. We held in-home fundraising events with Governor Riley, attracted more low-level donors through direct mail letters, and expanded our donor clubs ranging from $500 to $5,000 per year.

We were saving the larger donors for the program we were launching as part of the overall Campaign 2010 effort—the Governor's Circle. As we began ramping up Campaign 2010, it was important for us to have someone to focus solely on this donor group, corresponding and interacting with them on a regular basis. Our fundraisers were focused on bringing in the contributions we were using for operating expenses and to pay down debt. They were also spending a good deal of time prospecting for larger donors and then scheduling Del and me to meet with each one individually.

I decided to bring Minda Riley Campbell on board to coordinate the Governor's Circle and assist in other areas of fundraising. A Vanderbilt law graduate, Campbell was overqualified for the job and, when her daycare expenses were figured in, likely lost money on the salary we paid her. But, always the team player, she believed in the effort and sacrificed to help us succeed. She was a surrogate of sorts for her father and had built strong relationships with large donors around the state during her work on both of his gubernatorial campaigns. I enjoyed having her on our team because of my close association with the Riley family and the many hours we'd spent together on congressional and gubernatorial campaigns. I knew she was talented, loyal, intelligent, and understood politics. She was a great fit for our team. While there is no full accounting of how much money she raised on her own, it would certainly exceed 10 times what we paid her during her four years in the office.

IN THE FALL OF 2007, the Siegelman conspiracy theorists were ramping up their efforts and, incredibly, were having some success in shopping a totally fabricated story to national media outlets. The story claimed the White House, and specifically Karl Rove, was involved in the former governor's indictment on bribery and other charges. My plan all along had been to hire a full-time communications director but I had wanted to wait until our financial situation was more stable and able to support another salary. With bullets now flying at Governor Riley on a daily basis, however, Ross and I sped up our timeline on finding the right person for the job.

My first priority, as always, was to find someone I could trust. A good communications director understands he or she is the first line of defense when shots are being fired; having someone who will stand in the line of fire is a prerequisite. I also wanted to find a "bulldog" of sorts whose sole mission was to wake up every day with a mission of causing the Democrats discomfort by forcing them to answer questions about issues they were accustomed to having swept under the rug.

My goal was to begin softening up the opposition early and often and to begin developing a stark contrast between Democrats and Republicans in Alabama. For too long, so-called conservative Democrats had been talking the talk back home in their district, but walking a much different walk when they were in Montgomery. That would have to be made known to the average voter if we were going to flip the Alabama Legislature. Finding the right person to lead the effort was key.

With our search just getting off the ground, Dave Stewart, Governor Riley's chief of staff, called and said he might know someone worth interviewing. "He's a great guy, his dad is the senior minister of the First United Methodist Church in Montgomery and he has a strong background in communications," Stewart told me. "He's an Auburn graduate, so you'll like that, but here's the bad news—he's never worked in politics."

When I heard the part about no political experience, I immediately thought that Dave was wasting my time. We didn't have time for on-the-job training. But because of my respect for Dave and his insistence that I at least interview the candidate, I agreed.

A couple of days later, Philip Bryan was sitting in my office in Auburn to convince me he was the best choice to be the communications director for the Alabama Republican Party. All I knew is that he had worked for an ad agency in Chattanooga, done some free-lance corporate communications consulting, and most recently been the spokesman for a construction firm that had gone bankrupt. I admit that I was wary.

It was during this meeting that I began to get a good deal of insight into Bryan as a person. I learned that he'd grown up a preacher's son and an only child. He spent his childhood in Montgomery, Dothan, and Mobile as his father, Dr. Lawson Bryan, was moved to different churches. Philip was confident but not cocky, and he said all the right things to alleviate my concerns about his lack of political experience. I really liked him, especially his eagerness, enthusiasm, and determination to succeed. Even when I explained that the salary would be less than he had been making in his past jobs, he continued to throw out ideas of how he could build a top-quality communications shop that would be required for Campaign 2010 to succeed.

Following the interview, I was convinced Philip Bryan was the man for the job. But I had a test for him before I made a final decision.

It was very important to both Ross and me from the outset that we go to painstaking lengths to ensure the chemistry of the staff remained intact. The staff to this point had been exceeding my expectations, not only because of their talents and the commitment to the lofty goals I'd set for them, but because of their innate ability to work flawlessly as a team. My executive director had done a good job delegating tasks and responsibilities and our small group was hitting on all cylinders. Our biggest fear was disrupting the chemistry.

So Philip's final hurdle would be how he was seen by his potential co-workers, Ross, Rue, and McCormick. I suspect Philip thought he was just meeting the staff at a "get to know you better" lunch. The fact is, I'd given careful instructions that every staff member was to provide me with honest feedback and if any of them had any hesitations, we would go a different direction.

After a long group discussion covering a myriad of topics over lunch at Newk's in downtown Birmingham and then a one-on-one meeting with Ross back at the party headquarters, Bryan's interview process was complete. Ross called my office as soon as he walked out the door.

"We all think he's great,' Ross said. "Kate and Sidney really like him and believe he will fit in well. All three of us have a feeling that Philip is exactly who we need. We all think you should hire him."

It was music to my ears and I quickly brought Philip on board to begin learning the political communications landscape, with guidance from former Riley press secretary David Azbell.

After a tough first year of trying to keep our heads above water financially, Bryan's sense of humor and energy provided much-needed comic relief for the rest of the staff. I also believe the level of trust he quickly established with the media was a key in the 2010 campaign along with other issues we had to deal with along the way. The media knew he would always shoot straight with them and never lie to them. His reputation as a trusted source of information played a vital role in ensuring our message was delivered properly and truthfully.

With our communications shop now in place, my next goal was to begin building a top-notch political organization. Ross and I gathered details about a unique Get Out the Vote (GOTV) program the Republican National Committee had developed in George W. Bush's 2000 presidential campaign. Called simply "Victory," this program was implemented in targeted swing states and was credited as a major factor in President Bush's win over Vice President Al Gore. In the spring of 2008, with our fundraising in full stride, we felt comfortable bringing on a full-time political director. I believed it was important to have someone in place in time for the 2008 primary election so we could implement at least a part of the "Victory" structure and use the 2008 general election as a dry run. Thus we could get a better understanding of its strengths and weaknesses.

As in any election year, the party received a pile of resumes from across the country. We could cull the majority because we knew we wanted someone with enough "Victory" experience to come in and build our program from the ground up. Tyler O'Conner, a young man I got to know while he was a student at Auburn and later as a staffer for Congressman Mike Rogers, was now serving as the southeast regional political director for Rudy Giuliani's presidential campaign. We had stayed in touch and reconnected now that I was party chairman. O'Conner and Ross had also become friends after an introduction from Edgar Welden.

Ross and I knew O'Connor had a great deal of RNC "Victory" experience and we began asking him for potential prospects for our soon-to-be-created political director position.

"Michael Joffrion is your man, no doubt," Tyler said without hesitation. "But you'd better get him now before someone else does."

Joffrion was serving as one of O'Connor's deputies in Missouri, but the Giuliani campaign was winding down after a poor showing in Florida and we knew Michael would soon be available. His talents were well-known in those circles and O'Connor told us he was certain Joffrion would be asked by the RNC to run a GOTV.

As it turned out, "Joff," as we all would later call him, was indeed offered the opportunity to run a Victory program in a swing state. But our little start-up political shop had one major thing going for it that the RNC couldn't offer—location. After receiving his master's degree from Auburn, Joff married Jennifer, his high school sweetheart from Hoover, and moved back to Birmingham. While his political job kept him on the road for many months out of the year, his home was in Chelsea, Alabama, and Joff and Jennifer were ready for him to be at home on a more regular basis. That turned out to be our win and the RNC's loss.

After Ross had an initial meeting with Joff in Birmingham, the three of us met in Montgomery for a formal interview. I was impressed with Joff's depth of knowledge and meticulously laid-out plan on how to put together a top-notch GOTV program. I was very clear that I expected whoever was in this position to make the number-crunching and grassroots-turnout plan his baby. I also promised that he would be provided the tools, resources, and flexibility to build it as he saw fit. I could tell by the twinkle in his eyes that Joff was excited about this challenge and opportunity.

I'm a firm believer in not stymieing the creativity of talented people by micromanaging their every move. It was my job as chairman to map the course and provide guidance, but it was our staff's job to implement and carry out the plan. Unfortunately, most political organizations are run in a dictatorial manner with staffers constantly living in fear of doing something wrong and being fired. I was determined to do it differently and I believe this was another of the keys to our success in 2010.

After determining Joff was the man for the job, he, like Bryan, was given the ALGOP chemistry test. He passed with flying colors and the core staff that would carry us through the historic 2010 Election Cycle was then in place.

We added other great staff members as the 2010 election drew closer, including Blakely Logan, Meg Eldridge, Ryan Adams, and Ryan Cantrell. A seven-member field staff, under the direction of Joff and the political shop, grew our total team to eighteen members at the height of the campaign in the fall of 2010.

Though he was not on the payroll, political consultant Dax Swatek was a much-needed presence and offered his valuable advice, insight, ideas, and suggestions without asking for a penny in return. Swatek, a confidant, friend, and advisor since my first race in 1998, was born and raised in Shelby County, long considered among the most heavily Republican regions in Alabama. His sister Barret chose acting as her profession and has appeared in several Hollywood movies, with a recurring role on the popular teen drama *7th Heaven*, but Dax selected a decidedly different career path. Though he remains a self-professed University of Alabama football fan, Swatek graduated from Auburn University and later obtained a law degree from the Mississippi College of Law. After a stint with the national Republican senatorial committee, he began his quick rise in Alabama politics by working closely with Billy Canary, another friend whose advice I often sought. Swatek would later serve as general consultant and strategist for yet another mentor of mine, Congressman Mike Rogers, along with numerous Republican candidates and public officials across the state. I came to depend on Swatek for guidance and counsel throughout the highs and lows of my political career and continue to do so. He would play a large part in the creation of our plan to take the legislature from the Democrats and was instrumental in its success.

In retrospect, I still find it hard to believe I was fortunate enough to find and place the right people for each role during our quest to make history. Anyone who has ever been associated with political campaigns understands that egos often get in the way of productivity and teamwork. Many people in the political campaign business are more worried about who gets the credit rather than abiding by the words made famous by President Ronald Reagan—"There is no limit to what a man can do or where he can go if he doesn't mind who gets the credit."

I'm proud to say that our team put Reagan's words into practice.

This group of talented young people had an uncanny ability to understand their individual strengths and weaknesses and utilize the talents of those around them to create an unbeatable team. Failure was never an option, even as doubters vigorously worked to discourage them.

The creativity, intelligence, commitment to success, teamwork, and endless energy were keys to the success of Campaign 2010. And, by the end of the campaign, our team was more like a family than a staff. We shared each other's engagements, weddings and the births of babies. We were like foxhole friends, and those ties never break. There was no jealously, no competition, and no rivalry among the group, just mutual respect, admiration, support, and unabashed friendship. In politics, I think that may have been the rarest accomplishment of it all.

12

DEVELOPING THE TAKEOVER PLAN

A n important and until now unacknowledged member of our team to overturn the Democrats' control of the Alabama Legislature was Rahm Emanuel. A former political advisor to President Bill Clinton, Emanuel had served as a Democratic congressman and as President Obama's chief of staff and is currently the mayor of Chicago. Of course, Emanuel was, and remains, totally clueless about the role he played in our efforts, but he actually provided the blueprint for the development of Campaign 2010. His assistance arrived on my doorstep in a gift-wrapped package.

Alison Wingate, vice president and governmental affairs director for the Alabama Retail Association in Montgomery, had long been a supporter and ally in our efforts to elect a pro-business, Republican legislative majority. Though she and her group had strongly supported Joe Carothers against Benjamin Lewis during the 2006 cycle, Wingate and her boss, Rick Brown, were otherwise almost universally supportive of our Republican candidates.

Nevertheless, I was surprised when a package from Wingate arrived at my Auburn office shortly after my election as chairman of the Alabama Republican Party. When I opened it, I found a book along with a note that read: "Mike, this is your guide to taking over the House and Senate. Read it as soon as you can, follow what it says, and I am sure you will be successful—Alison."

The book was titled, *The Thumpin': How Rahm Emanuel and the Democrats Learned To Be Ruthless and Ended the Republican Revolution* by Naftali Bendavid. It detailed how Emanuel, then a second-term congressman from Illinois, took the reins of the Democratic Congressional Campaign Committee during the 2006 election cycle and captured the U.S. House from Republicans by using unconventional methods.

The title of the book referred to President George W. Bush's reaction to the 2006 mid-term election results when he said, ""As the head of the Republican party, I share a large part of the responsibility [for the Democrats' landslide]. You look at it race by race, it was close. The cumulative effect, however, was not too close. It was a thumpin'.""

I later learned that Mike Rogers recommended the book to Wingate, who is somewhat of a political junkie. She had devoured every word and developed a fascination with Emanuel after reading about the charismatic, often profane, and always ruthless political consultant.

As I read the book, I recognized many of the same lessons we had learned following our own nascent efforts to win the legislature in 2006. It was actually reassuring to have our own observations confirmed in print. Emanuel had used the same basic model we employed in 2006, but his plan was significantly expanded and differed slightly from our version.

I read, for example, that Emanuel believed simply waiting to see which stereotypical Democrat would walk in the door and decide to run for Congress would be a recipe for a string of lopsided losses. Instead, he aggressively recruited Democrats who fit a particular profile he needed for a specific race. He actively recruited candidates with extensive military backgrounds to blunt the usual Republican attack that Democrats were soft on defense. In more conservative areas of the country, he found pro-life, pro-gun Democrats who did not toe the typical left-wing party line on social issues, thus blocking the "liberal" label. In other words, rather than waiting for the "perfect candidate" to stumble in the door, Emanuel listed the attributes of what he considered the perfect candidate to be and combed the country actively seeking those who fit his model. Some in his own party disagreed with Emanuel's efforts and claimed he was diluting the ideological purity of the Congressional Democrats, but he simply tossed their concerns aside and focused on winning a majority.

Even though I differed with Emanuel politically, I admired what he had accomplished in spearheading the Democratic takeover of Congress. Even before reading his book, I had come to the same conclusion about the absolute necessity of recruiting good candidates.

I was convinced that Republicans could have captured even more House seats in 2006, especially those we lost by fewer than 500 votes, if some of our candidates had been better. Heading into the 2010 election, I was determined to avoid another round of underperformance at the ballot box because of the candidate. We, too, had to find and recruit candidates to run under our party label; many whom we identified had never considered for a moment seeking elected office.

For Campaign 2010 to have a chance, we needed a recruiter of candidates. I knew just the person for the job.

Tim Howe had moved from his native South Carolina to Birmingham to attend Cumberland School of Law at Samford University. Upon admission to the Alabama bar in 2002, he went to work as deputy campaign manager for Supreme Court Justice Harold See's successful reelection effort and later managed Jefferson County Probate Judge Mike Bolin's successful bid for the high court. ALGOP Chair Twinkle Cavanaugh hired Howe to serve as executive director of the party, the same role John Ross would later fill for me during my two terms as chairman.

Because the executive director serves as the chairman's buffer, often making or taking phone calls that his boss wishes to avoid, and dealing directly with Republicans at the grassroots, he gets to know the inner workings of the party intimately. Given the number of Republicans he had met and the contacts he had made as executive director, I was certain Howe could bird-dog ideal potential legislative candidates. Once he identified prospects, he would make an initial visit, cull down the list, and then call in the governor and me to close the deal and convince them to run.

The Thumpin' also detailed how Emanuel insisted that each campaign be run on its own merits rather than relying on a cookie-cutter, one-size-fits-all model. He recognized that campaigns have their own ebb and flow and their own particular sets of issues. For instance, using the same direct mail piece in several different districts would not be as effective as tailoring specific mailings to fit each one. We had learned this lesson in 2006, as well, and luckily in time to narrowly defeat Joe Carothers by abandoning the assembly-line campaign and trying something different. In 2010, we would be prepared to follow whichever trails the campaigns took us down rather than trying to crowbar in a model that simply did not fit.

Emanuel, according to the book, was an effective leader who could rally his staff with simple force of will, a titanic temper, and a demonstrated willingness to work harder than anyone around him. He pushed those who worked for him to the brink, but he also inspired them and made them perform to his standards.

I, too, drove myself so hard that Susan often got angry when she thought I did not sleep enough, eat well enough, or relax enough. The mission of flipping the legislature was always foremost on my mind. The ALGOP staff, though they had the energy of youth on their side, worked equally long hours, lost quite a bit of sleep, and also spent considerable time away from family, friends, and other pursuits. An election cycle is like a marathon, but my staff treated it like a sprint. I was afraid that they would burn out before we reached the finish line. I needed to make sure they had enough reserves to run through the tape, not to the tape. Working with Del Marsh, I created an incentive plan for them.

As a Republican lawmaker, I had long supported the concept of performance-based pay for teachers and public employees. Now, I was going to put the idea into action with my own party staff. From the day I hired each one, I knew I couldn't afford to pay them nearly what they were worth, especially given the long hours required. Instead of large salaries, I wanted our money to go toward defeating Democrats in the upcoming campaigns. Plus, I had promised all of our Governor's Circle members who had embraced the Campaign 2010 formula that none of their $40,000 investment would go to overhead.

I drove to the Birmingham headquarters one day in early 2009, gathered the senior ALGOP staff in the conference room, and laid out my plan for them. For every legislative seat in the House and Senate that changed from Democratic to Republican hands, I would pay each staffer a bonus of $1,200. An additional $2,500 would be awarded if we captured a majority in one of the legislative chambers. If we took both chambers, the bounty would be an additional $6,000 each. Each one of them was working desperately hard before I outlined the incentive package, but they really kicked it into high gear afterwards.

In addition to their regular job duties, they stayed at night to make phone calls identifying potential voters, gave up their weekends to go door-to-door in competitive legislative districts, and crisscrossed the state making speeches and appearances to keep our base enthused. I'm not sure if my incentive plan was unique in the political party world, but it worked in our case. Actually, it was a very simple concept used every day in the business world—the harder you work and succeed, the more you are rewarded.

Marsh and I raised the money to pay the earned incentives following the election so no one could claim we had diverted any campaign resources. We also raised the money privately and totally independent of the ALGOP and its accounts to avoid appearances of draining party resources.

I will always remember the looks on the staff members' faces when I passed out the checks a few weeks after the election. It's amazing what you can accomplish by offering a talented and motivated team of people an extra incentive for achieving desired results.

Just as Emanuel had done in his congressional takeover effort, maximizing the dollars we raised for our campaigns was always at the top of my priority list. We sought vendors who would be willing to work for a little less if we allowed them to service all of our campaigns. Because fees charged by political consultants can vary widely, we chose a handful we trusted and asked them to work for a modest flat monthly rate. In return, we would pair them with our top-tier, high-priority candidates and pay for half their consulting fee, with the candidate required to carry the other half. That way, the consultants were guaranteed business, each had quality candidates with which to work, and they knew they would be paid in a timely, steady manner—not always common in the political world.

For our pollster, we decided to hire McLaughlin & Associates, a highly respected Republican polling and research firm located in New Jersey. We had learned another valuable lesson in the 2006 campaigns. We discovered that simply having polling numbers without personalized one-on-one analysis of demographics, message, ideology, and other variables did not provide enough intelligence to tailor a race. In 2006, we didn't have much money so we went with the cheapest option we could find. Now, in 2010, we were still watching our costs, but we weren't going to be penny wise and pound foolish. We needed a pollster who could balance the dozens of surveys required throughout the campaign, be available around-the-clock to interpret polling results, personally review the messaging in our ads and cross-check it with the survey data, and basically provide much-needed counsel.

Jimmy McLaughlin was the perfect pollster for Campaign 2010. McLaughlin had polled nationally for a Who's Who of Republican politics including former President George W. Bush, California Governor Arnold Schwarzenegger, former U.S. House Speaker Dennis Hastert of Illinois, and the late Jesse Helms, a legendary U.S. senator from North Carolina, just to name a few. When billionaire businessman Donald Trump was considering a run for president against Barack Obama, he hired McLaughlin to poll his chances before deciding to take a pass.

Many of our Alabama legislative candidates were visibly taken aback when they first met with McLaughlin or talked to him over the phone about their survey results. He has a thick New Jersey accent more suited for a member of Tony Soprano's mafia crew than a nationally known political pollster. His accent and the fact that his polling firm is headquartered near New York belie the fact that McLaughlin had done considerable work in Alabama for well over a decade and understood the state very well. His clients included former Governor Fob James, former Attorney General Bill Pryor, Congressmen Mike Rogers and Robert Aderholt, and Governor Bob Riley, whose 2006 reelection effort was strongly influenced by McLaughlin's advice.

Billy Canary introduced me to McLaughlin during my first race in 1998 and he had handled my own campaign surveys ever since, so I knew he could be trusted. I always found his polling data to be extremely accurate and an excellent barometer of how the public was digesting our Campaign 2010 efforts.

I have long believed that the effectiveness of a direct mail effort can make or break a political campaign, so choosing our mail vendor was very important. Unlike television or radio advertising, which cannot guarantee that a voter will see an ad, sending mail to someone's box ensures that they will at least glance at your message, and, if it is effective, read it more closely. We needed a firm that could react quickly to developments in a campaign while avoiding the cookie-cutter approach we were forced to use in 2006 and that Emanuel had railed against in *The Thumpin'*. With so many targeted races and several thousand pieces of mail to be distributed in each district, whoever we chose had to handle the massive capacity we demanded, provide quick turnaround, and be willing to have conference calls with a combination of John Ross, Dax Swatek, McLaughlin, Marsh, and me to tailor the message to the survey data.

We settled upon Majority Strategies, a Florida-based direct mail firm whose promotional material boasted that they were responsible for creating, printing, and sending a half-billion political mail pieces since its founding in 1996. We had worked with Randy Kammerdiener, a senior consultant with the firm, on our 2006 legislative efforts and found him to be both creative and reliable. I personally liked the fact that Majority Strategies tried to include a certain amount of humor in some of the mail they produced, which made it more memorable and helped deliver a strong dose of political attack without leaving voters with a bitter taste. In 2006, due to budget constraints, we forced Kammerdiener to use the same designs and message in multiple races. This time, we would be smarter and better-funded.

Another important item gleaned from *The Thumpin'* as well as from our 2006 experience was the need to prioritize and carefully target districts. We had to have the discipline to compete only in races that offered a reasonable chance of victory. Spreading ourselves too thin and spending money based on affection for a candidate rather than their probability of victory was a costly and painful lesson we had learned, a mistake that would not be repeated in 2010.

To BEGIN RANKING DISTRICTS and determining which districts to target, the party hired consultant Scott Stone to conduct an infinitely more in-depth analysis than the one produced four years earlier. John Ross and I had interviewed Stone for the party's political director position before settling on Michael Joffrion for that job. Stone had been memorably cordial and impressive during his interview and when told that the party job was going elsewhere. Ross and I remembered him and reached out a few weeks later to hire him to conduct the painstaking study.

Stone developed a formula based on historical election results, district demographics, and numerous other factors and ranked each House and Senate district. The most vulnerable Democrats were obvious, but his report was extremely helpful in developing the second- and third-tier targets that we would eventually fund. Stone's study also included the population centers of each district so we knew where to focus our recruitment efforts to increase the potential for votes.

One reason Emanuel and the Democrats had gained control of the U.S. House by taking 29 seats held by the GOP lay with their success in tarnishing the Republican brand, according to *The Thumpin'*. Of course, President Bush and Congressional Republicans had basically given Democrats the bullets to load their guns in the first place. A general feeling among Americans that the war in Iraq was going poorly, the botched response to Hurricane Katrina, and a growing series of Republican ethics scandals were being exploited by Democratic candidates nationwide in 2006. When it became known that Congressman Mark Foley, a Republican from Florida, had sent sexually suggestive and inappropriate instant messages to underage male congressional pages, the final nails went in the coffin, especially when it was revealed that Speaker Hastert knew of the actions but did little to stop them.

By highlighting specific incidents and painting Republicans with a broad brush, the Democrats made their opponents' political affiliation simply unacceptable in a number of swing districts. We knew we could do the exact same thing to the Democrats in Alabama.

Several Democratic public officials in the state had recently been convicted of felonies and removed from office as the result of ethical violations.

Representative Sue Schmitz, a Democrat from Toney, had been given a job created specifically for her within the state's two-year college system. She rarely, if ever, showed up for work despite collecting roughly $177,000 in taxpayer-funded salary over three-and-a-half years. Schmitz was convicted on mail fraud and program theft charges and sentenced to a federal prison term.

State Senator E. B. McClain, a prominent African American lawmaker from Birmingham, was caught funneling more than $750,000 in taxpayer grants to a community program housed within his district and run by a local minister. Federal authorities found that McClain had personally received about 40 percent of the money in kickbacks from the program. He and the Rev. Samuel Pettagrue were convicted of 48 counts of money laundering, mail fraud, bribery, and conspiracy.

State Representative Bryant Melton pled guilty to providing $85,000 of legislative discretionary money to the Alabama Fire College and later receiving a kickback of $65,000, which he used to pay off gambling debts. Melton was sentenced to 15 months in prison on theft and money-laundering charges.

Jefferson County provided Republicans with the trifecta of corruption scandals when former Alabama Democratic Party chairman Bill Blount and former executive director Al LaPierre both pled guilty to bribing Birmingham Mayor Larry Langford in exchange for bond business. Blount, who provided Langford with $235,000 in bribes, including Rolex watches and expensive clothing, was sentenced to 52 months in prison followed by 36 months of supervised release. LaPierre, who ferried the bribes, was given 48 months of incarceration and 36 months of supervised release. Langford, the former Democratic president of the Jefferson County Commission, was convicted in a federal trial and handed a 15-year sentence.

And, of course, a jury had convicted former Governor Don Siegelman on charges related to bribery, conspiracy to commit honest services fraud, mail fraud, honest services mail fraud and obstruction of justice, though some of the convictions would later be overturned on appeal.

There was no doubt the Democrats' long history of corruption and the fact that their legislative leadership consistently killed Republican-sponsored ethics reform proposals would be a central focus during Campaign 2010.

The corruption angle actually became part of a larger messaging effort that emerged after McLaughlin conducted a statewide poll to gauge voter awareness prior to the 2010 election. A question in the survey asked which political party controlled the state legislature. Despite the fact that Democrats had held both the House and Senate continuously since the days of Reconstruction, respondents answered that Republicans were in power. I credited this perception to the fact that only one Democrat, Don Siegelman, had won election as governor since 1986, so voters therefore assumed Republicans must control the legislature as well. It is very difficult to run on a platform of change and reform when voters think you are the party in power. We obviously had to do a better job of educating the public about which party held the reins of legislative power in Montgomery.

In the conference room of Rob Riley's law office in Homewood, McLaughlin presented the statewide survey results to our staff. When McLaughlin informed us that a majority of the voters incorrectly believed that Republicans were in charge of the legislature, party spokesman Philip Bryan did some quick math and concluded that Democrats had controlled the legislature for 136 consecutive years. This long of a streak shocked even those of us who knew it had been a very long time.

Minda Campbell, always quick to come up with a snappy line as a result of her experience writing and producing television and radio commercials for her father's campaigns, had an idea pop into her head.

"We just need to say '136 years is long enough,'" Campbell offered to the group. "Then, when people see it, they'll wonder what in the world has taken place for 136 straight years. Then, we'll let 'em know."

Everyone loved Campbell's idea. We brainstormed and laid out all kinds of ways to push the *136 Years* message, which would eventually appear on yard signs, billboards, bumper stickers, and television commercials.

To make sure we were right in our message, McLaughlin asked the following question in another survey: *If you knew Democrats had been in charge of the Alabama Legislature for 136 straight years, would you agree or disagree that it's time for Republicans to have a chance to lead?*

The response was overwhelming. After 136 years, Republicans deserved to be in charge.

Communications Director Philip Bryan, political consultant David Azbell, and our team searched for even more ways to drive the point home and soon found an effective one. A few minutes of research revealed the obvious—that the United States of 1874 was vastly different than the one we lived in during 2010. Taking this information, Bryan and our social media director, Meg Eldridge, produced an in-house video that would soon go viral on the internet.

The 90-second video script read :

> The year was 1874. Hawaii still had a king. Jesse James and his gang of thieves were robbing trains. Grant was president. And Levi jeans were $13 a dozen.
>
> Yes, 136 years ago, things were a little different than they are now. But one thing has remained the same since 1874—Democrat control of the Alabama Legislature.
>
> After 136 years of control, Democrats care more about the liberal special interest groups than the people's interest.
>
> After 136 years in power, Democrats refuse to pass legislation to curb corruption.
>
> After 136 years, Democrats felt they owned Alabama, so they voted themselves a 62 percent pay raise . . . with our money.
>
> After 136 years, the Democrats have brought us Obama, Pelosi, government healthcare, liberal policies, higher taxes and wasteful spending.
>
> But, after 136 years, it's time for a revolution in Alabama.
>
> On November 2, 2010, let's send Obama, Pelosi and the corrupt Democrats a message—a message that says *136 years is long enough*.

The accompanying images ranged from sepia-toned images from the 1870s to grainy, foreboding photos of Obama and Pelosi to our "136 Years Is Long Enough" logo as well as another slogan that would become very familiar to Alabama voters in 2010—"Fight Back—Vote Republican!"

Once we began the "136 Years" campaign, which would run concurrent with our Campaign 2010 efforts, we soon learned it would have a second advantageous effect. In addition to educating general election voters about the need for change in state government, it also energized our base voters, which is vital to any successful election. Showing the video to the endless Republican groups I spoke before was tantamount to waving a red cape in front of a charging bull. Whoops of delight and handclapping followed its every showing. Our "136 Years Is Long Enough" yard signs flew out the door and billboards in targeted districts were prominently displayed.

As eager as our Republican voters were for a victory, I saw very little enthusiasm among Democrats in my travels across the state or even during my few joint appearances with Democratic Party Chairman Joe Turnham. The African American community, which comprises the majority of the Democratic vote statewide, was similarly blasé despite the fact that Congressman Artur Davis was running for governor. Davis was the first black candidate with a serious chance to win the state's top office in modern times. Most of the black political leadership across the state, however, endorsed Davis's opponent, Agriculture and Industries Commissioner Ron Sparks, who was running on a decidedly pro-gambling platform.

WHEN I FINISHED READING it, my dog-eared and heavily annotated copy of *The Thumpin'* would prove invaluable as my team and I developed and refined our Campaign 2010 plan. The book quite accurately confirmed our experiences from 2006 and showed us how to benefit from our mistakes. With financing for our priority legislative races already drawing interest in the bank, our vendors and local consultants now signed up, critical data being collected in the field through polling, and a plan to educate voters about more than a century of Democratic power abuses in place, we were finally ready to put Campaign 2010 into action. The only ingredient missing was the actual candidates, and Howe was rounding them up for us.

Rahm Emanuel is obviously a smart guy, a brilliant political tactician, and an inveterate campaigner. I would not vote for him in a million years, but I do appreciate the advice he indirectly provided us in the months leading up to 2010. I view it as akin to General George Patton reading Field Marshal Erwin Rommel's book on tank warfare to devise a plan to defeat Rommel's forces in North Africa during World War II. I recall the line in the movie *Patton* when George C. Scott, portraying the general, shouts toward the retreating German tank corps, "Rommel, you magnificent bastard! I read your book!"

Perhaps one day I will have the opportunity to personally thank Emanuel for helping me devise the plan to elect our historic Republican legislative majority.

I'm sure it will make him proud.

⌒ In Their Own Words ⌒

JOE TURNHAM
ALABAMA DEMOCRATIC PARTY THREE-TERM CHAIRMAN

While I certainly did not agree with it, I think the message that Democrats had been in office too long was an effective one. We were seeing the Democratic Party ID, essentially among white voters, began to erode every cycle. While a lot of those voters don't say they are independent or vote the person not the party, we were always able to get them to split their ticket. We got involved in a lot of the campaigns in 2010 and tried to help pull them out of the fire, but it was just a historic time. The Republicans were able to have a central theme to rally around and unite against President Obama and make the issue of corruption a partisan issue, which I felt was unfair. Voters were very angry about the economy and direction of the country. But I've given Mike Hubbard a lot of credit. He's extremely disciplined and works very hard. He's a very good fundraiser. He knows how to build organizations. He's not afraid to take heat from his own party. He had Governor Riley helping him with fundraising. Add all that up, and you get the result we got in the 2010 elections. It's as simple as that.

13

FUNDRAISER-IN-CHIEF

A s much as we might wish the old saying "money is the lifeblood of politics" were not true, the simple fact is that it's probably the most accurate statement I have ever heard. Some campaigns try to win elections on shoestring budgets, but they typically come up short. Whether this is a testament to the current state of politics in our country, I don't know, but I do know that raising money is the worst part of running a campaign. It is also an absolute necessity if you want to win.

Developing an ability to raise money came via a variety of different life experiences for me and is a craft I continue to refine. My experience selling advertising for my company, running my own campaigns, and raising funds to cover the cost of two gubernatorial inaugurations all helped prepare me to be a decent political fundraiser. To raise the money required to fund a historic campaign to change the state forever, however, would require me to take fundraising up several levels.

Prior to 2010, the teacher's union, the Alabama Education Association, had dominated legislative campaigns in Alabama. With a large membership pumping over $270,000 a month into its political action committee, the organization had evolved into a one-stop shop for candidates it endorsed, almost all of whom were Democrats. It also provided mountains of campaign funds to candidates, many times totaling over $100,000 per race. As the largest contributor to its endorsed candidates, the AEA reaped the dividends once these individuals were elected, giving the union a literal stranglehold over state government. A study conducted by some Republican consultants showed that in 2006 alone, AEA had spent $5.1 million supporting Democrat legislative candidates through its own A-Vote PAC and others.

Because the AEA was such a dominant force, I knew we would need an unprecedented amount of campaign money along with a first-class organization to give us a chance to be successful in 2010. For too long, Republicans were at an extreme disadvantage from the outset of a campaign because of a lack of funding, organization, and an effective means of delivering their message. My goal was to change that.

I was convinced the Alabama Republican Party could be the perfect vehicle to operate this first-ever coordinated campaign effort for Republican legislative candidates. The infrastructure was already there and so was the credibility of being the top Republican organization in the state.

Now that we had our team in place and were bringing in enough money to keep the lights on and pay the rent, I set out to put together the most aggressive and comprehensive fundraising plan in the history of the Alabama Republican Party—Campaign 2010. The centerpiece of this plan, where we would raise the majority of the funds needed, was to be a donor club we named the "Governor's Circle." The level of contribution required to be a member of the Governor's Circle would be $40,000—$10,000 a year for four years.

Implementing such an aggressive fundraising plan was going to be difficult, but having a sitting Governor with a desire to see the plan succeed and a willingness to help made all the difference. Despite his successes, he realized the only way to make sweeping and lasting change was to flip control of the legislature. In my opinion, he was the most successful governor in our state's history in spite of the fact that each year much of his legislative agenda was immediately sentenced to death by the Democrats in charge of the legislative branch. For his final four years in office, he made it his mission to be an integral part of Campaign 2010.

The position of finance chairman for the Alabama Republican Party was also extremely important. This position is appointed by the party chairman and for Campaign 2010 to be successful, I knew my choice would have to be my partner, believe in the cause just as Governor Riley and I both did, and be willing to spend the time necessary to raise the unprecedented amount of money required.

Shortly after I decided to run for party chairman, I reached out to Senator Del Marsh of Anniston and asked if he would serve in this role. I knew that Marsh shared the desire of flipping the legislature and believed, like me, that it was an obtainable goal. We had worked together in 2006 to raise money and run campaigns for House and Senate races. As I have noted, the 2006 effort was a scaled down version of what would become Campaign 2010, but Marsh and I knew from it that the concept of co-ordinated campaigns would work. We also knew what mistakes had been made in 2006 and were eager to avoid repeating them.

Marsh was a well-respected member of the Senate Republican Caucus and was known as a coalition builder. He was also a successful business-man. We were both elected to the legislature in 1998 and had followed similar paths into politics. I liked and trusted him and was convinced that he and I, along with Governor Riley, would be a great fund-raising team.

Del Marsh is a true success story who epitomizes the American Dream.

Born in West Virginia and raised in Birmingham, Marsh graduated from Banks High School and Auburn University. His entrepreneurial talents were evident when he started a business while in college in the late 1970s applying decorative striping to automobiles. Soon, he had contracts with all of the area car dealerships and had a dozen employees, all while he was going to school to earn a business degree. He had such a thriving business, in fact, that when he graduated and took a job at a manufacturing facility in Anniston, he took a pay cut. He married his college sweetheart, Ginger—an Auburn University cheerleader—and started his post-college business career.

Marsh eventually became the owner of that manufacturing facility and would start another successful aerospace manufacturing business in Anniston. Like me, he was totally committed to running his business and never even thought about politics. But in 1998 he decided to run because he didn't like the direction he saw things going in Montgomery. He vowed to be a part of the solution and Alabama is better because of his decision.

MARSH AND I WORKED with John Ross to fine-tune Campaign 2010. We knew the overall concept would be to recruit quality, pro-business candidates, then make certain each of their campaigns was run profes-sionally with our oversight and direction, employing economies of scale whenever possible by pooling services like polling, opposition research, media production, and creative production. But our biggest and most pressing obstacle during the implementation process in the spring of 2007 was how to raise the money to pay for it all.

I set a goal of raising $4 million for Campaign 2010, an audacious amount that caused many critics and even some supporters to snicker and shake their heads in disbelief. No one is going to give the party $10,000, much less $40,000, they said. But that was the amount I determined we needed to have a chance of success. After all, the folks we were trying to unseat would likely have twice that amount at their disposal. Because of the monumental task we faced, I knew we had to think outside the box. Doing things the way they'd always been done wouldn't cut it.

Raising money for a state political party is not easy because individuals and organizations like to give their contributions directly to candidates. Giving money to pay rent, salaries, and other overhead is not very exciting to most major donors. Our job was to convince people that contributing to Campaign 2010, through the Alabama Republican Party, was the best way to make sure their dollars were spent effectively and efficiently in the upcoming cycle. We would have to make sure donors knew their money would elect Republicans in a well-planned manner, not pay the light bill at the party headquarters.

Four million dollars is a lot of money, especially when you consider that the most the party had previously raised for an election cycle was a fraction of that. I knew we had to consider different techniques so I called a friend named Jerry Smith.

Smith had been the executive director of the Auburn Alumni Association during my time working for the Auburn Athletic Department. He was a prolific fundraiser and, during the late 1970s had put together Auburn's first major capital campaign, which was an incredible success. In 1991, he formed the JF Smith Group to assist colleges, universities, and nonprofit entities implement capital campaigns. Over time, his company became one of the premier such firms in the country.

Jerry is so in demand as a fundraising consultant that he travels five days a week and is home in Auburn only on the weekends. I reached him by phone one afternoon as he was rushing through some faraway airport and briefly told him that I was now the chairman of the Alabama Republican Party and had a plan to change the direction of our state but needed to raise an unprecedented amount of money to do it. He explained that he had never done any political work but would meet me at his office that Sunday afternoon.

It had occurred to me that the same principles used in capital campaigns for universities and nonprofits should apply to political fundraising. After all, the foundation of fundraising is convincing people to invest in a cause. Fortunately for us, we had a great cause—completely changing the landscape of Alabama politics and creating a pro-business legislature for the first time in more than a century.

I had never had a political conversation with Smith, but he and his wife had contributed to my past legislative races so I assumed he was a Republican. Or maybe he just liked Susan and me. But when I walked into Jerry's office, my eyes were drawn to a Republican National Committee calendar hanging on his wall. I knew that was a good sign. We visited for a couple of hours and I laid out my plans in detail. I asked how he raised money for capital campaigns and if we could employ the same concept in the political arena. He again warned me that his firm had never been involved in political fundraising but that he thought they could help us.

With the approval of the party's steering committee, I hired the JF Smith Group to help us hit our $4 million goal. It was a departure from what the party had ever done, but I was convinced it was a good move and appreciated the committee's confidence.

NEWS OF THE DECISION to hire a company that specialized in capital campaigns made its way to Washington and the Republican National Committee. To say they thought it was it was a terrible idea would be a colossal understatement.

The fundraising leaders of the RNC believed there was no correlation between traditional capital campaigns and political fundraising. They also didn't like part of the pitch we planned to make to our potential Governor's Circle donors—we would be pledging not to ask them for an additional penny for four years after they made their commitment. The RNC's philosophy was to find a willing donor and bleed them for as much money as possible as often as possible. I didn't like this approach and didn't agree with the traditional fundraising practices they were preaching. I wanted us to develop partnerships with our investors, keep them posted on our progress, and invite them to all of our functions for free.

We were committed to doing things differently, which caused a strained relationship with the RNC during the first two years of my chairmanship. The RNC had regional political and finance directors who in theory were on staff to assist state parties and provide them with guidance. We discovered very quickly, however, that their "assistance" amounted to little more than attempts to control our operations. For instance, they required us to send them weekly finance reports so they could track our progress. When these reports didn't reflect what they wanted to see, they reprimanded our staff.

This practice of oversight and second-guessing with no assistance didn't sit well with me, so when I was told I was making a huge mistake by hiring a firm to assist us with our fundraising, it only motivated me to prove them wrong. I also instructed our staff to cease sharing information with the RNC. If they weren't going to be supportive, then we weren't going to waste our time complying with their requests, especially since they delivered no money.

This further convinced the RNC that we were going to fail. And they told us so. (Just a couple of years later, of course, the RNC would hold up the Alabama Republican Party as a model for political fundraising. I was even asked to speak at their national meeting in Albuquerque, New Mexico on how to implement an aggressive fundraising plan. I received calls from state GOP chairmen around the country seeking advice and guidance, which was very gratifying.)

After several meetings with our fundraising duo of Kate McCormick and Sidney Rue, Smith developed a plan of action for us to follow. We collected fundraising lists from every Republican elected official who was willing to share them, as well as any other fundraising list we could get our hands on. Many of our federal elected officials chipped in along with, of course, Governor Riley. These donor lists combined with the ALGOP's existing list provided plenty of prospects. Our next step would be to determine which ones were candidates for the Governor's Circle and which ones should be approached for lesser contributions.

The JF Smith Group employed a useful piece of technology, a computer software program they called the Wealth Engine. It was a tool used in the capital campaign world to identify prospects. By tapping into a variety of public sources, the software created a comprehensive wealth profile on an individual. That information allowed us to separate our prospects into potential donor groups based on their ability to give. You wouldn't want to ask someone to contribute $1,000 a year if he or she had the ability to give $10,000 a year. Conversely, you would not want to ask someone to contribute $10,000 a year if they could afford only $1,000.

This tool allowed us to confirm our Governor's Circle and lower level donor prospects. It also ensured we were using our time as efficiently and effectively as possible as we weren't asking too much or too little of a potential donor. The Wealth Engine was the first of many items I'd never seen used in the political arena. Another was asking for multi-year financial pledges and getting pledge cards signed by contributors. This way, you don't have to retrace your steps each year and you can calculate how much money you should have at the end of the fundraising drive. All of this strengthened my belief that bringing the JF Smith Group on board was the right move.

The next task was to define our donor groups. The ALGOP had traditionally had its own donor levels, but we revamped them. We kept the traditional Capitol Club level, a $180-per-year commitment. We created other levels including the Chairman's Club at $500 per year, three different Ivory Club levels at $1,000, $2,500, and $5,000 each per year, and the now well-known Governor's Circle at $10,000 per year. We created logos and a professional customized and bound proposal that we presented to prospects in personal meetings.

To hit the fundraising goals, Rue and McCormick focused on the lower-level clubs, utilizing in-home events, phone calls, and direct mail. Marsh and I focused on presentations to prospects for the Governor's Circle.

We also decided to put a major effort into increasing the number of donors at the Capitol Club level. At the time, operational costs for the ALGOP were approximately $400,000 per year. Our goal was to find enough Capitol Club members to cover these costs on an annual basis so the vast majority of other funds could be spent solely on electing Republicans. We sought advice from national committeeman Edgar Welden, who had a successful Capitol Club campaign during his tenure as chairman. We also tapped different executive committee members to assist with these efforts. Rue and McCormick came up with the idea to offer prime seating at dinners, tickets to Alabama and Auburn football games, and I even threw in a weekend trip to our townhome in Destin, Florida. These incentives allowed us to greatly expand our membership at this level.

The other effective program we initiated to expand not only membership in the Capitol Club but our donor base as a whole was a calculated direct mail program. Rue and McCormick found a direct mail firm in Florida to partner with us to mail to the donors on our master list who had given $180 or less to the ALGOP. We began mailing this group at the beginning of every year and would send subsequent mailers to the entire group minus the ones who had contributed. We also partnered with a telemarketing firm that would follow up receipt of a letter with a personal phone call. As we perfected it, this program began to net us approximately $40,000 per year. It wasn't a lot of money, but it helped pay the bills.

In the end, the expansion of the Capitol Club, the direct mail and telemarketing program, and the winter and spring dinners paid 100 percent of our overhead, even after we expanded our staff closer to the 2010 election. This meant that all of the other contributions being received from the other donor groups were being set aside for elections and every penny of the Governor's Circle funds was earmarked for the 2010 legislative races.

THE MOST CRITICAL COMPONENT of the Campaign 2010 effort was the success of the Governor's Circle. Marsh and I began traveling the state, sometimes in tandem but mostly separately, to pitch the $40,000 package. The Smith Group worked closely with Rue and McCormick to schedule meetings with people identified as prospects. They provided Marsh and me with biographies on each prospect, and someone from the Smith Group even attended the initial meetings to give feedback for refining our presentations.

Marsh, Minda Campbell, and I quickly perfected our pitch. The most important part was convincing the potential donors that we had a plan and that we weren't just asking them to give us money and hope for the best. We pledged to recruit quality candidates, provide assistance with the day-to-day operations of the campaign, and, rather than handing out campaign cash, provide in-kind services via mail, media, polling, opposition research, and grassroots organization to put them in position to be successful.

Part of the plan that donors seemed to understand and embrace was the fact that we were going to utilize economies of scale with our vendors. Because we were going to be involved in so many races, we negotiated vigorously with potential vendors to get the best pricing. The cost savings allowed us to do more with our funds. This made sense to the business people we were pitching and further convinced them we had a well thought out plan.

Over the next several months, Marsh and I spent a great deal of time on the road. We strongly believed that to ask people for a $40,000 commitment, we needed to sit down with them face-to-face. I traveled the state meeting with prospects. I remained encouraged, despite being away from my family and my business for extended periods of time, because of the success I was having. Someone actually turning me down was a rarity. It was at this point that I began to realize just how much the people of Alabama wanted to see the change we were pushing and how they were willing to invest in a solid plan to make it happen.

From the very start, my friend and former colleague Mike Rogers was a believer. I spent a great deal of time reviewing the plan with him and giving him my sales pitch. When I finished, he immediately told me to sign him up. He also encouraged me to come to Washington to give an overview of the Campaign 2010 plan to each Republican member of Alabama's congressional delegation. At the end of the day, Senators Richard Shelby and Jeff Sessions along with incumbent Representatives Spencer

Bachus, Jo Bonner, Robert Aderholt, and Rogers all became members of the Governor's Circle. Our entire GOP congressional delegation had stepped up to the plate in a big way and it did not hurt my future fundraising when I mentioned that fact to potential donors.

A key ally throughout Campaign 2010 was Phil Musser. I met Musser in March 2007 at the St. Regis Hotel in Washington while I was in town for a National Conference of State Legislatures conference. Governor Riley suggested we meet, and Musser took the time to sit down with me on the day after his daughter was born.

Musser had been the executive director of the Republican Governor's Association under Massachusetts Governor Mitt Romney. I explained to him my goal of flipping the Alabama Legislature and how we planned to do things differently. He liked the concept and agreed to help by opening doors, making introductions, and steering me to people outside of Alabama who would like what we were doing. Looking back, this proved to be one of my most successful fundraising meetings. Using his contacts throughout the country, Musser helped me raise more than $300,000 for Campaign 2010.

OUR HARD WORK THROUGHOUT the summer, fall and winter of 2007 paid off. In January 2008, at the Alabama Republican Party's winter dinner and state executive committee meeting, I proudly announced that we had secured 67 members of the Governor's Circle, which put us two-thirds of the way toward our goal. To have made this much progress in less than a year was astounding not only to the members of the party, but to the news media and Montgomery insiders as well.

In the spring of 2008, reporters began questioning our efforts. Stories by Brian Lyman with the *Mobile Press-Register* and Sebastian Kitchen with the *Montgomery Advertiser* implied that the Alabama Republican Party and I were selling access to the governor. This could not have been further from the truth. In fact, Governor Riley simply made thank-you calls to donors after they had committed to the $40,000 contribution, and he attended some of our meetings. He guided us in the right direction and, on rare occasions, made a follow-up call to encourage someone to sign up, but anyone who knows Governor Riley knows that access to him because of a campaign contribution is not a possibility. He is too ethical and honest for that.

The media was also demanding we provide a list of the Governor's Circle members as a show of transparency. Their line of questioning on this matter always baffled me. The party filed its reports in a timely manner and never missed a deadline, so we were disclosing our donors just like everyone else was. The news media had never demanded to see the AEA's donors or the Alabama Democratic Party's donors prior to a reporting deadline, so I couldn't understand why we were being held to a different standard. I believe the Democrats were quietly pushing these stories behind the scenes because our success was making them nervous. As it turned out, they had every reason to be.

By the summer meeting of the State Republican Executive Committee, just over a year after we initiated Campaign 2010, I was able to announce that we'd hit our goal of 100 members of the Governor's Circle with commitments totaling $4 million. At the dinner the night before, Governor Riley surprised the staff and me when he announced that we would be raising our goal to $5 million because of the unprecedented success of the program.

The plan had worked. It had worked so well, in fact, that after a year the JF Smith Group told us we didn't need their further help and guidance and voluntarily stopped the future contracted consulting payments. They were of the opinion that they had shown us the path and provided guidance, but that we'd done most of the heavy lifting. I attribute this not only to the hard work and dedication of Rue and McCormick, who were relentless in keeping us on task and on schedule, as well as to Minda, who carried out an unprecedented program to stay in touch with the members of the Governor's Circle to update them on our progress. It was a true team effort.

The fundraising success also gave our plan to flip the legislature a tremendous amount of credibility. Some of the most influential business leaders and organizations in the state had bought into our plan, despite the fact that we were in the minority in the legislature; if we had failed they would have been targets of the Democrats. This resulted in a snowball effect because in fundraising, success begets success. The more individuals bought into the plan, the more the word spread and the easier it became to raise money.

In the end, we raised just over $5.5 million for Campaign 2010. Of the 104 members of the Governor's Circle, it is important to note that 78 had never before contributed a penny to the Alabama Republican Party.

We had a solid plan in which many people were willing to invest. Now, with the resources in place, it was time to begin implementing it.

∼ In Their Own Words ∼

BOB RILEY
U.S. Congress 1996–2002
Governor of Alabama 2003–2011

After the second gubernatorial race, and working with a Democrat legislature for the first term, it became evident that the best way to change the state fundamentally was to change the legislature. The Alabama Republican Party, with the leadership and team it had in place, was the perfect vehicle to make that happen. In the past, second-term governors had never fully engaged in fundraising for the party. Realizing that the only way we would be able to make the systemic changes we wanted, however, required that I did. As anticipated, people from across the state were willing to step up and help. Even though we received some negative press and editorials by saying very early in the second term that our goal was to remove the Democratic members of the House and Senate, there were still committed individuals who saw the wisdom in Campaign 2010, in going after the legislature, early and relentlessly. They saw a plan that was well-thought-out, a talented team to execute it and the leadership to see it through. People who had never given to the party before were now engaged participants in the success of Campaign 2010. And, as we would later realize, the Governor's Circle was a crucial element in our success. Our goal was 100 members. By 2010, we hit 105.

DEL MARSH
ALABAMA SENATE PRESIDENT PRO TEMPORE, 2010– ; ALABAMA SENATE 1998– ; FORMER ALGOP FINANCE CHAIRMAN

I can't overemphasize the importance of having a plan. When you go to talk to people and ask them for $40,000, you want to go in with a very organized plan that is convincing and realistic. Mike and I had to convince these people that this could be done after all these years of talking about taking control. I believe the fact that Mike and I both put in $40,000 of our personal money—not money we raised for a campaign, but our own money—made a big difference. We would always close out a meeting by explaining that we believe in this so much that we are each Governor's Circle members ourselves. That was very effective.

It's almost a miracle that it all came together because we were walking into an office where, in most cases, people didn't know Mike or me. We would introduce ourselves, talk about the problems in the legislature and explain why the legislature would never pass what we considered pro-business reforms as long as the Democrats were in control. Our whole angle was that we wanted to make Alabama into a pro-business state with the best business climate possible. To do this, we had to elect conservative, business-minded Republicans. If they wanted to see true change, this is what we needed to do. We told them our goal was to raise $4 million and with that money we would go across the state, recruit candidates, and run their campaigns.

JO BONNER
U.S. REPRESENTATIVE, ALABAMA 1ST DISTRICT, 2002–

I was fully committed to helping Mike with Campaign 2010, and in addition to giving personal money, I helped him raise money by introducing him to my friends and supporters so he could share the vision. Mike Hubbard was very successful in selling the vision. To convince people what they thought was impossible could be possible isn't easy, but Mike made the case that we could make a fundamental difference in Montgomery.

If anything, Mike has a great work ethic. Knowing how hectic my schedule can be, I was so impressed with his willingness to travel around the state at a moment's notice. I would introduce him to friends and he would drive all the way to the Gulf Coast from Auburn to meet with just one or two people. There were times when we had larger crowds and he would tell the story to the people there. He got turned down so many more times, especially in the beginning, but Mike was so determined and willing to listen to people. People would call me and say "this guy is different." If Mike Hubbard was the strategist, then Governor Bob Riley was the "head coach," and people saw that he was truly trying to change the state.

14

Peaks & Valleys

Over the course of my four-year tenure as chairman of the Alabama Republican Party, we experienced highs and lows. Fortunately for us, at the end of the day we ended up with more highs. But the manner in which we dealt with the peaks and valleys of the political world is what truly defined our commitment to making history.

The highs were treated as milestones and served as both motivation and confirmation that we were striving for an obtainable goal. The lows, while disappointing, were viewed not so much as setbacks but as learning experiences to help us refine our plan. By learning from our mistakes, we were able to develop a stronger feel for things once we got to the big test—the 2010 election cycle.

In retrospect, the many special elections we were involved in, both successful and unsuccessful, leading up to 2010 were a blessing. These skirmishes held before the end of the quadrennium helped us learn what tactics worked and which didn't. Each of these elections played a major role in our later success. I would even argue that the losses taught us more than the victories.

In late 2007, longtime Democratic Senator Jimmy Holley of Enterprise contacted Senate Minority Leader Jabo Waggoner and me to tell us he was prepared to switch parties. Holley was one of three dissident Democratic senators who had been caucusing with the Republicans in the Senate. The reasons could be attributed to a variety of factors, but the major one was that the Democratic leadership, namely Senator Lowell Barron of Fyffe, had declared war on the Alabama Farmers Federation. Holley, along with Senator Tom Butler of Madison and Senator Jim Preuitt of Talladega, were strong supporters of ALFA and Barron's blatant disdain for the organization didn't sit well with them.

Then, during the 2007 session, members of the Senate Democratic leadership attempted to punish Holley for caucusing with the Republicans. They could not have picked a worse way to play politics. The Democrats attempted to withhold some of the funding to reconstruct Enterprise High School, located in Holley's district, following a devastating tornado that had destroyed the school. At that point, Holley decided he had had enough of the Democrats.

Once Holley committed to formally switch parties, I rolled out the red carpet for him. I knew it would have a tremendous impact on the dynamics of the Alabama Senate and send a message to other Democrats around the state.

My staff and I began coordinating with local party members during the Christmas and New Year's holidays, specifically with Sue Neuwein of Enterprise, ALGOP chairwoman for the Second Congressional District. She reserved the Enterprise Civic Center and a date was set for the formal announcement in early January 2008. Neuwein assured me we would have a big turnout of locals and we began working to get leaders from around the state to attend.

Neuwein more than delivered on her promise as 200-plus people packed the venue for the announcement. Governor Riley made the trip as did Attorney General Troy King, who, interestingly, again felt it necessary to wear a bulletproof flak jacket, this time to an event in his home county.

Flanked by Riley, King, several Republican senators and me, Holley made the announcement that he was becoming a Republican to loud cheers from the audience. He outlined his reasons for switching parties and told the group the Democratic Party had left him, not vice versa. This would become a common theme as 2010 got closer.

Holley's switch was the first major victory of Campaign 2010. Now, there was one less Senate seat we would have to target.

At the same time as the Holley switch, an important special election was called in Cullman County's in House District 12 to replace Representative Neal Morrison, who had resigned to become president of Bevill State Community College.

This race was of particular interest because it was viewed as a strong pickup opportunity for Republicans. Morrison was a conservative Democrat in what had become a Republican-leaning district. If we could win this race, Republicans would be one seat closer to a majority in the House. As a result, the campaign was being closely monitored by Montgomery insiders and politicos from around state. It was widely viewed as the first major test for Campaign 2010 and for our team.

After a tough Republican primary and runoff, county commissioner Wayne Willingham emerged as our nominee. ALFA had endorsed Willingham early in the process and provided enough resources for him to inch out a runoff victory against longtime Republican leader and local State Farm agent Bill Floyd.

The runoff had caused a fracture in the local Republican Party because Floyd had served as chairman of the organization and had been a mainstay at the state executive committee level for years. Conversely, Willingham had only recently been elected to his post as county commissioner and wasn't as well known in party circles. So, right out of the gate, our team began working with the local party officials to create a united effort in the general election, which proved to be difficult.

On the other side of the aisle, in typical fashion, the Democrats had cleared the field for their nominee, a well-respected member of the community named James Fields, a former minister and an unemployment fraud investigator at the Alabama Department of Industrial Relations for three decades. Fields was an interesting choice because the district was close to 98 percent white but Fields is African American.

Cullman County had long been known around the state for a history of racial discrimination. A *New York Times* reporter who wrote a profile of Fields noted, "Versions of Cullman's old sundown sign hung beside county roads well into the 1970s, and all of them repeated the message that the travel writer Carl Carmer saw when he visited Cullman in the late 1920s: 'Nigger Don't Let the Sun Go Down on You in This Town.' The sign was notorious all over Alabama, and coupled with Cullman's powerful Ku Klux Klan, it created a racial deterrent so effective that even today, Cullman's are exits off the Interstate that most African-Americans avoid."

For many Cullman County residents, this dark and difficult history was a blight on the community.

The racial undertones surrounding the campaign for House District 12 began immediately. Rumors swirled about members of Willingham's family being a part of the KKK. A relative of his who owned a local junkyard proudly flew a Confederate flag in front of his place of business. Some even claimed Willingham had been a member of a little-known political party built on a platform of the South re-seceding from the union. We knew right out of the gate this was going to be a difficult race.

Based on our polling, we knew that making issues the centerpiece of the campaign would give us our best shot of winning. The people of Cullman County were overwhelmingly conservative and wanted to vote for a conservative candidate. In our communications with voters, the goal was to develop a contrast between the two candidates by defining Willingham as the conservative and Fields as the liberal supported by the left-wing special interests in Montgomery. Fields was a popular candidate, but we knew that outlining these key differences was the path to victory for us.

Willingham's political consultant was Chris Brown, a former executive director of the Alabama Republican Party. After leaving ALGOP upon Twinkle Cavanaugh's election as chairman, Brown and a partner opened up a political consulting and campaign firm. The duo had some early successes, most notably Scott Beason's improbable victory over incumbent State Senator Jack Biddle. They also ran Trip Pittman's successful campaign in the special election to fill the State Senate seat vacated by Bradley Byrne after he stepped down to become chancellor of the state community college system.

Because of Brown's recent successes, we took more of a secondary role on the strategic decisions. Our plan was to provide financial support and assist in other areas on an as-needed basis. The other reason for taking a backseat was that we were in a Catch-22. Brown was a member of a small, but vocal faction of the party that had openly disliked Governor Riley since the internal fight within the ALGOP during the Amendment One campaign.

Naturally, their dislike of Riley spilled over to me. If we attempted to push Brown aside per our Campaign 2010 plan, blame would be placed solely at my feet in the event of a loss. If we took on a secondary role and ended up victorious, however, Brown and company would get the majority of the credit but I would still be in good shape because we would be one seat closer to a majority in the House, which was my ultimate goal anyway.

That arrangement was working out fine until a couple of weeks were left in the race. Then a miscalculation, while downplayed by Brown, proved to be the proverbial nail in the coffin for Willingham's campaign. In sticking with the theme of the campaign, a mail piece was produced that highlighted the fact that Fields was attempting to distance himself from the national Democratic Party and its liberal leaders. On the front side of the piece, the graphics showed a pack of hunting dogs with the headline "There are only certain dogs that will hunt . . . ," intended as a reference to our argument that Fields's claims to be distanced from the liberal policies of the Democratic Party weren't believable.

The mail piece was produced by Brown and, to be fair, reviewed by our team. The fact that the mail piece could be misconstrued as racist never occurred to any of them. Once it hit mailboxes in the district, however, a firestorm erupted. The Fields campaign and the State Democratic Party cried foul and the already-sensitive voters in the district became irate. This proved to be the beginning of the end for Willingham.

A couple of weeks later, the race was over and James Fields had won by almost 60 percent of the vote. Shortly thereafter, the *New York Times* ran its story entitled "Race Matters Less in Politics of South." In the article, it became apparent that the people in the community were embarrassed by their past and saw the election of Fields as a way to prove they had put it behind them. This sentiment, coupled with the Democrats running a great race with a solid candidate, had simply been too much for Willingham to overcome.

Since this was a race that should have been a pickup for Republicans, the Democrats and our rivals within the Republican party immediately began predicting that Campaign 2010 was going to be a colossal failure. While I was disappointed by the outcome of the House District 12 race and our staff was discouraged, we quickly moved on and chalked it up to a good learning experience. It was one of the low points for me as chairman, but I refused to allow it to deter my focus. I also noted that having the party serve in a support role did not work well.

THE NEXT MAJOR MILESTONE for me as party chairman would be the 2008 general election. This election cycle would be remembered not for what Republicans accomplished, but rather for missed opportunities.

Despite winning every statewide race but one, including Greg Shaw's victory over Debra Bell Paseur for the Alabama Supreme Court, Alabama Republicans lost a congressional seat that we had held since 1964 and another U.S. House race that, at least on paper, we should have won.

Wayne Parker, in his third attempt to become the congressman from north Alabama's fifth district, lost to Democratic State Senator Parker Griffith by a margin of 51 to 49 percent. Party leaders from that region were devastated. We had devoted a fulltime staffer to the campaign, Ryan Adams, who would later serve as a deputy political director in 2010. Adams had done an outstanding job of embedding himself in the campaign, the state party had spent funds on a non-allocable direct mail program, and we had provided ballot security in the district.

Adams's job, under political director Michael Joffrion's supervision, was to put together a Victory program in the district in hopes of stimulating turnout enough to put Parker over the top. I also knew that our legislative takeover efforts in 2010 would hinge on the outcome of a handful of races in north Alabama, so a secondary purpose of Ryan's presence in the district was to begin developing an organization that could be utilized in the next cycle. While we came up short in this race, I knew the decision to have a staffer there would pay off in the long run.

While the congressional loss in North Alabama stung, the one that hurt the most was in the Second Congressional District where my friend, State Representative Jay Love, lost to Montgomery Mayor Bobby Bright, a Democrat. This loss meant that Republicans went backward in numbers in the federal delegation. We had placed a field representative in the race just as we had done in the fifth district. His name was Ryan Cantrell, and he would also later serve as a deputy political director in 2010. We also paid for a direct mail program and ballot security in the race.

For me, though, the race became an issue shortly after the primary. Love and State Senator Harri Anne Smith had emerged from a crowded primary to face off in a GOP runoff. Smith dumped her consultant from the primary and brought Senator Scott Beason and Chris Brown on board to run her campaign during the short six-week runoff.

This race was of particular interest to the National Republican Congressional Committee (NRCC) because it was deemed a priority "hold" district. Since it was an open seat, due to the retirement of Republican Congressman Terry Everett who had represented the district since 1992, and because of the national climate, they wanted to make certain the best candidate emerged from the runoff.

Whether it was based on polling or the results of the primary, the NRCC decided Love was the candidate in the ideal position to win the general election over Bright. They essentially endorsed Love in the runoff and began providing his campaign with resources. Republicans in the Wiregrass, Smith's home region, went ballistic. To make matters worse, the Smith campaign began accusing me of orchestrating the endorsement because of my close friendship with Love.

While I personally wanted to see Love win, I knew better than to involve myself in any primary, especially one as heated as this one had become. A party chairman must remain neutral in primaries or risk losing credibility with party leaders and primary voters. Love understood this and never once asked me to do anything that would jeopardize my position. I can say unequivocally that I had absolutely nothing to do with the NRCC endorsement of Love. This decision was made in Washington and I found out about it in the news just like everyone else.

Despite my assurances to the contrary, the Smith campaign would not let it rest. I dispatched our executive director, John Ross, to the Wiregrass to calm the fears of party leaders in the area and to express my disappointment in the NRCC involving itself in our primary. Most of the southeast Alabama Republicans came around, but I believe there are still a handful of Smith loyalists who think I told the NRCC what to do.

The NRCC's actions also backfired among voters, a number of whom didn't like the fact that a group from outside the state was attempting to affect their election. After enjoying a relatively large margin over Smith in the primary, Love's race tightened in the runoff.

Not only had the NRCC issue played a role in shrinking Love's lead, but the campaign also turned into one of the most negative races ever run in a Republican runoff. The now infamous and failed developer Ronnie Gilley, who was attempting to build a controversial country music-themed gambling hall in Dothan, and his band of supporters had declared war on Love. Most notably, Gilley talked one of his investors, country music legend George Jones, into cutting a radio ad attacking Love. The ad closed with Jones emphatically stating, "Jay Love is a liar." Naturally, this had a significant impact on the race.

After a hard fought runoff, Love beat Smith by a 54 to 46 percent margin and claimed the Republican nomination. Smith, still fuming from the negative campaign and the NRCC endorsement of Love, refused to support the GOP nominee or just ride off into the sunset.

Shortly after the runoff, we began receiving information at ALGOP headquarters that Smith was considering an endorsement of the Democratic nominee, Bobby Bright. While Love had attempted to make amends with her, Smith was determined to do all she could to see he would never serve a day in Congress.

While much of Smith's efforts to undermine Love were done behind the scenes throughout the rest of the summer and into the fall, it all came to a head in early October when Ross received a frantic phone call from Bill Harris, a previous executive director of the ALGOP. Harris had served on the Smith campaign and was calling Ross to let him know the Democrats were offering Smith money to retire her campaign debt in return for an endorsement of Bright. As it turned out, Smith had accepted a loan from her mother and was desperately looking for a way to pay it off. Harris told Ross that if we could come up with $150,000, then Smith would hold off on the endorsement. Ross conferred with me and then informed Harris that the Alabama Republican Party would not be blackmailed.

After further investigation, it was discovered that Harris had offered the same deal to national committeeman Paul Reynolds, who met with Smith and told her the party would look for an opportunity to hold a fundraiser to assist with debt retirement, but that there was no way the ALGOP would be willing to cut her a check simply for her not endorsing Bright.

A couple of weeks prior to the 2008 general election, Smith held a press conference alongside Bright and announced her formal endorsement of the Democrat. The endorsement sent shockwaves throughout the congressional district and Republicans across the state. A sitting Republican state senator publically endorsing a Democratic nominee over a Republican nominee was unimaginable. Even Smith's most ardent Republican supporters in the Wiregrass began to turn against her. This would be a decision Smith would be forced to deal with in 2010.

After a great deal of discussion, the decision was made for Ross to go public with the conversation he had held with Harris. Our communications director, Philip Bryan, prepared a press release outlining the conversation and Ross penned an e-mail to the entire Republican State Executive Committee relaying the unfortunate news. The *Dothan Eagle* reported the story, which caused uproar across the district. Naturally, Smith denied the accusations, but Ross keeps proof of the Harris conversation under lock and key to this day.

Our phone system at the ALGOP headquarters was Voice Over IP, meaning all incoming and outgoing calls were transmitted via the Internet. Whenever someone would leave a member of the staff a voicemail, an electronic audio file was created and sent to the staffer's e-mail account. The night after the newspaper story ran, Harris called the office after hours and left Ross a long, rambling message. He was angry that Ross had let the cat out of the bag and proceeded to outline every detail of the deal Smith had accepted. Little did he know that the message was recorded and sent to Ross that evening on his smart phone.

After a hard-fought general election where Bright even admitted he supported Democratic presidential nominee Barack Obama, Love came up short on Election Day. Because of the extremely high turnout among African American voters, Love lost Montgomery County by 16,000 votes. Based on previous election history, both contenders should have split the vote in the county almost equally. The Bright lead was too much for Love to overcome—though he lost by only 1,766 votes—and the seat was now in Democratic hands for the first time since Lyndon Johnson was president.

This was a tough pill for Republicans across the state to swallow and, naturally, much of the blame was directed at me. As a whole, the 2008 general election was a GOP success, but the two congressional losses were inexcusable in the minds of many.

I remember sitting on the set in the studios of WSFA-TV in Montgomery the night of the election with my friend and counterpart, Joe Turnham, chairman of the Alabama Democratic Party. Joe and I had provided political analysis for the station's live election coverage throughout the night. After trying my best to put on a good face and spin the story on the air, I said to Joe during a break, "I'm not so sure this won't be my last appearance as Republican Party Chairman. Losing these two congressional races will definitely be blamed on me." Joe, a fellow Auburn resident whose son is the same age as and friends with my oldest son, Clayte, tried his best to console me. But he knew full well that party leaders get the blame when elections don't go well.

My political enemies, inside and outside the party, began openly questioning my ability to lead and suggested the goal set for Campaign 2010 was a pipe dream. This was the most difficult time for me in my four years as chairman of the party, but Governor Riley, our donors, our staff, and my allies within the party stood by me and my resolve was ultimately strengthened.

A SECOND OPPORTUNITY TO pick up a seat in the legislature presented itself in early 2009 when the longtime senator from District 22, Pat Lindsey, unexpectedly died. Senate District 22 is a large district covering all or parts of seven counties—Choctaw, Washington, Clarke, Mobile, Baldwin, Escambia, and Conecuh. The district presented a number of campaign challenges, most notably the delivery of advertisements via television due to the large number of cable systems in the district. There was also a natural rivalry between the eastern and western portions of the district as Choctaw, Washington, and Clarke counties were all part of the Black Belt region of the state.

Republicans again endured a spirited primary race between former State Representative Greg Albritton and perennial candidate Danny Joyner. Again, in typical fashion, Democrats had cleared their primary for their anointed nominee, 28-year-old State Representative Marc Keahey from Grove Hill.

Albritton emerged from the primary as the Republican nominee. I was pleased since we had served in the House together and I knew he was a man of character with a strong work ethic. Albritton had also brought Benjamin Lewis to us when we were recruiting a candidate to run against Joe Carothers in 2006. Since this was an opportunity for a pick-up in the Senate, my finance chairman and political partner Senator Del Marsh became engaged in the race.

Unfortunately, we almost immediately began to run into many of the same issues experienced in the House race between Willingham and Fields in Cullman County. Albritton, just as Willingham had, selected Chris Brown as his political consultant. Because it was a Senate race, Brown's prized client, Senator Scott Beason, insisted on playing a strategic role in the campaign. This presented an issue right out of the gate.

As was the case in the House District 12 race, ALGOP was the largest contributor to the Albritton campaign, eventually providing more than $100,000 in funding and in-kind services. After a post-primary benchmark survey, it was evident to us that Albritton needed to go on the attack. Keahey, who would ultimately spend in excess of $500,000 on the race, already had an advertisement airing on broadcast television out of Mobile. The ad was top-notch. In what would become another theme throughout 2010, there was no mention of Keahey's political affiliation, leading viewers to believe he was actually a conservative Republican.

While Keahey was doing a terrific job of building positive name identification in the district, we were having an internal fight over the direction of the Albritton campaign. Brown and Beason believed we needed to focus solely on improving Albritton's positive name identification while our team was convinced it was time to begin developing a contrast between the two candidates. We knew Keahey was going to outspend us by a large margin, so the sooner we could paint him as a Democrat being funded by the Montgomery liberal special interests, the better our chances of winning would be.

Unfortunately, just as in the House District 12 race, we found ourselves in another "darned if you do, darned if you don't" dilemma. Should we threaten to pull our funding if the consultants refused to follow the strategic direction we wanted for the campaign, or should we simply relent and let them have total ownership of it? In the end, Marsh and I relented. By doing so, we learned a hard lesson and would never again give in to consultants' advice when all evidence and polling data indicated we should go in another direction.

As is the case in virtually all special elections, a well organized Get Out the Vote (GOTV) effort can make a huge difference in the outcome. To his credit, Brown is talented in this area, so we hoped this might allow us to squeak out a win. In the days leading up to the election, I dispatched our staff to Atmore to assist in the turnout effort. They spent the Monday before the election knocking on doors in Atmore while Brown and his team of Albritton volunteers focused on Brewton. To win the race, we knew we would have to run up the score in Escambia County and hold steady in Conecuh, Mobile, and Baldwin counties. Keahey was going to be strong in the western part of the district, so we all but conceded it.

On Election Day, Marsh and I had volunteers and staffers monitoring turnout across the district. Over the course of the morning and early afternoon, our numbers were trending positive. We were seeing high turnout in our strong precincts and lower than projected turnout in the boxes where we knew Keahey would be strong.

Beginning around 3 o'clock that afternoon, however, we started to see a trend reversal. Turnout levels in our strong boxes were hitting a plateau while Keahey was experiencing an unusually strong wave of turnout increases in the western part of the district. Our cautious optimism gave way to frustration as it was becoming apparent our path to victory in the race was closing rapidly.

By eight o'clock that evening, Albritton had conceded and Keahey had won by a comfortable margin. Even though it was definitely a Democratic-leaning district and we were outspent by a three to one margin, we had publicly been a part of the race. As expected, the blame was being laid at our feet. This was our second special election loss in as many tries. Instead of shrinking the Democrats' margins in the House and Senate, they were beating us. The naysayers, again, were gloating over our failures. Republicans, our team, and my chairmanship desperately needed a victory.

AN OPPORTUNITY PRESENTED ITSELF only seven days later. A special election in Senate District 7 to fill the seat vacated by Democrat Parker Griffith, who had been elected to Congress, was in full swing. A political newcomer and local barbeque restaurant owner, Paul Sanford, emerged as the Republican nominee after yet another tough GOP primary battle.

As usual, the Democrats had cleared their primary for State Representative Laura Hall, who had been stockpiling funds and was lying in wait for Sanford. If Senate District 22 was a Democratic-leaning district, Senate District 7 was, at the time, a solid Democratic district.

We faced another decision. Should we invest a large amount of funds and resources in the race as we had done in Senate District 22 or, because of the tough demographics of the district, hold back to avoid another potentially embarrassing loss? The decision was easy for Marsh and me. If we were going to make history, we had to take some risks. So, the decision was quickly made to go all-in but not to repeat the mistakes of the past.

The Republican primary in this race had dealt another blow to Brown as his candidate was soundly beaten by Sanford, who had selected Public Strategy Associates, a little-known Montgomery-based boutique consulting firm, to run his race. Our team was excited about partnering with a new group looking to make their mark. It would also allow us to play the dominant role in the strategic decision-making process.

Sanford and his team traveled to the ALGOP Headquarters shortly after the primary to meet with Marsh and Ross. The purpose was to outline the party's financial commitment, which came in the form of in-kind contributions via a direct mail program, television and radio advertising, and providing a staffer to run the GOTV effort. After two disastrous campaigns that involved infighting between the campaign and the party, we wanted a meeting at the outset to allow the candidate and his team to understand fully our commitment as well to clearly define responsibilities and expectations. The manner in which this meeting was conducted with the candidate and his consultants ended up being a model for us during the 2010 election cycle. Our bad experiences in previous races had taught us a few things.

The GOTV operation was initiated shortly after the meeting in Birmingham. Sanford had done a nice job of putting together a strong organization, so our goal was simply to assist him in building upon it. We called up our trusty field representative from the Wayne Parker race, Ryan Adams, and he embedded himself in the campaign. Adams, a Mississippi native, had gotten to know the Huntsville area well and was able to tap into many of his contacts to get the voter identification effort off the ground.

Sanford was highly opinionated and quick to criticize. We understood that he had worked extremely hard to get to this point and we appreciated his desire to win, but his abrasive personality tested the patience of our team, including the even-tempered John Ross.

Working with the Public Strategy Associates team, however, was a breath of fresh air. We were in lockstep on the strategic direction of the campaign, messaging, and the demographics we needed to focus on to win. When the group inevitably had to inform Sanford the party was going to be sending a handful of direct mail pieces to a targeted group of voters that would probably be perceived as negative in nature, they did a good job of convincing him it was in best interest of the campaign. Sanford, in most cases, would come around.

In the days leading up to Election Day, however, tensions began to rise. ALFA, which had endorsed Sanford, had been performing tracking polls and informed us the Friday before the election that Sanford was down 18 points. This was troubling, to say the least, as our previous polling had suggested otherwise. This news, coupled with Sanford's sometimes contrarian attitude, added even more stress as we faced potentially losing yet another race.

From a strategic standpoint, our team believed Sanford needed to run a negative ad the remaining days leading up to the election. The purpose of the ad was to emphasize the contrast between him and Hall as well as to motivate conservative voters to head to the polls. Marsh had worked with a Montgomery association and received their commitment to pay for the ad, so everything had been carefully orchestrated to make it happen. But Sanford refused to put the ad on the air. He not only refused, but he did so dismissively. In our minds, the Alabama Republican Party had financed his race, yet Sanford didn't seem to care.

After receiving the news from Sanford on Friday morning prior to the Tuesday election, Ross called Marsh and me. He was exacerbated, which was totally out of character for him. Frustrated with Sanford throughout the race, the overwhelming pressure to win and the rejection of the ad that morning, he told us that he had had enough. After outlining his frustrations to us, we made the knee-jerk decision to pull Ryan Adams out of the campaign for the final three days.

Adams, whose girlfriend lived in Washington, D.C., bought a ticket to fly later that day from Huntsville to Washington and started packing his bags.

After a few hours of contemplation, I began having second thoughts. Despite the odds and even though Sanford's behavior was tiresome, I realized that seeing the race through, win or lose, was the right thing to do. I also received a call from my longtime friend and head of the Alabama Association of Realtors, Danny Cooper, who pleaded with me to rethink the decision, which I did.

I called Ross at the party headquarters in Birmingham. He had also had time to cool down and he agreed fully with me. After passing the news to the staff that we were now officially back in the race, Ross had the unenviable task of informing Adams. Only hours after packing up his things and happily leaving the Sanford campaign office, we would have to ask him to resume the GOTV efforts he had been developing for weeks. Ross reached Adams on his cell phone at the Huntsville Mall where he was in the process of buying some new clothes for his trip to Washington. Adams, always the team player, canceled his trip, returned the clothes, and reported back to the campaign that afternoon. I wrote Adams a personal check to cover the cost of his non-refundable plane ticket.

When Election Day arrived, there was actually a sense of optimism in the air, despite the fact that the most recent ALFA poll didn't support it. Our staff made the trip to Huntsville to assist with ballot security efforts and final phone calls to potential voters. Aside from the race itself, the news of the day was a flyer posted on the website of Dale Jackson, host of a popular conservative radio talk show in the area. It had jokingly stated that the election was to be held on the following day and insinuated that the flyer had been distributed in minority precincts.

What amounted to little more than a bad joke created a firestorm. The Democrats accused us of distributing the literature and were calling on Secretary of State Beth Chapman to investigate their claim of election fraud. Ross called Alabama Democratic Party executive director Jim Spearman to explain that we knew nothing about the flyer and would do all we could to put a stop to it. Philip Bryan drove from Huntsville to Birmingham and drafted a release from me condemning the act. We had a good working relationship with Jackson and, after we explained our position, he understood why we needed to publicly distance ourselves from his untimely joke. He issued an apology of his own.

As our team monitored turnout with Sanford's staff throughout the day, we were pleasantly surprised at what we were seeing in the district's strong Republican precincts. We remained extremely cautious, though, as the memory of the late afternoon turnout blitz in Senate District 22 was still fresh on our minds.

As the polls closed, our team headed to the Madison County Courthouse to monitor the returns while Sanford headed to his victory party at the Heritage Club only a few blocks away. Election officials in Madison County traditionally have a great setup for monitoring returns. In the main lobby of the courthouse, a projector is set up and seats are lined up theater-style so onlookers can watch as precincts report their results.

A small crowd of Republican and Democratic activists, along with staffers from the Hall campaign, had gathered in this area and were anxiously awaiting the news. As more and more precincts began reporting, our staff could not believe what they were seeing. Turnout levels in our bellwether precincts were through the roof. It appeared the hard work Sanford had put in going door-to-door, along with the Victory program we were slowly but surely perfecting, had worked like a charm. Once it was apparent Sanford was going to be victorious, Ross called Marsh and me, congratulated us on the win, and thanked us for working so hard to provide the resources we needed to be successful.

Our team then ran the few blocks to the Heritage Club to inform Sanford and congratulate him on becoming the newest Republican member of the Senate. Naturally, he was elated and all of the previous tensions disappeared. In his victory speech, Sanford singled out Ryan Adams for his efforts. While we had certainly had our differences, I believe a mutual respect grew out of the experience and Senator Sanford and I enjoy a healthy working relationship to this day.

To say this victory felt good would be an understatement. Not only were we one seat closer to a majority in the Senate, but we also finally had some confirmation that our efforts were not in vain. Strangely, the naysayers were nowhere to be found.

As THE SPECIAL ELECTION in Senate District 7 came to a close, yet another opportunity arose. The Republican primary in a special election for House District 6 had just come to an end and defense contractor Phil Williams had emerged as our nominee. A businessman who had never sought elected office before, Williams was a prototype candidate for us. We would be able to build a campaign around the message points that were striking a chord with voters—creating jobs, improving the economy, and doing away with career politicians responsible for the mess our country was experiencing. This simple message would carry us through the 2010 election cycle and, in this race, Williams was the perfect person to deliver it.

The need for this special election came as a result of unfortunate circumstances. State Representative Sue Schmitz, a Democrat, had been convicted on federal fraud charges related to the ongoing community college scandal that was rocking Alabama. Governor Riley called a special election to fill the vacancy resulting from Schmitz's conviction. While the circumstances surrounding the need for this election were unfortunate, it was a tremendous opportunity for us and the timing could not have been better. The demographics of the district were favorable to Republicans and we knew that with a strong candidate and adequate resources, we could win.

Fresh off the Sanford victory, Ross, Adams, and Kate McCormick traveled to Huntsville at my request to meet with Williams, his wife, Lisa, and consultant Joey Ceci. Ross was going to outline the ALGOP's financial and manpower commitments to the campaign, just as we had done with Sanford. Adams was going to assist with the GOTV efforts, and McCormick's job was to work with Williams's team on fundraising, specifically on a fundraiser that Governor Riley would headline and I would attend a few weeks later.

Ross had gotten to know Ceci during his time working in the Huntsville area for Congressman Aderholt. Ceci, who got his start working for Democratic Congressman Bud Cramer, was a federal lobbyist who dabbled in political consulting. Williams knew Ceci through his lobbying efforts on behalf of Huntsville defense contractors and asked him to run his campaign. The interesting part was that Ceci had traditionally been identified as a consultant for Democratic candidates, most notably Cramer, but also for other local Democrats in the Huntsville area. He also shared an office with another well-known Democratic lobbyist and consultant, Steve Raby.

In this race, however, as eventually in many others in the 2010 cycle, we teamed up with Ceci based on a common goal—seeing to it that Phil Williams became the 44th member of the House Republican Caucus. As the campaign progressed, I was struck by the talent Ceci displayed as he made important strategic decisions regarding the race as well as the fact that he understood and appreciated what we were doing with the party. I quickly realized that he was one of the sharpest and most capable consultants in the state. Our friendship grew and he continues to be one of my strongest allies in north Alabama. He also was instrumental in assisting me as I recruited his father-in-law, Lynn Greer, to come out of retirement and seek another term as the state representative in House District 2 in 2010.

Williams's Democratic challenger was a longtime activist, Jenny Askins, who took a leave of absence from her job as a member of the Madison

County Board of Registrars. She had deep political connections in the district as well as strong ties to the AEA, which meant that we would once again go head to head with the powerful union and its seemingly endless resources.

Following earlier struggles with consultants and candidates, working with Ceci and Williams was a pleasant experience and helped us define how the roles should work in future races. Our team melded perfectly with their team on message, direct mail, radio and TV ad production, and the GOTV effort. Williams's wife, Lisa, had a distinguished military background and had put together an impressive voter identification and turnout program in the primary election, using the skills she'd learned while serving in the Army. She and Adams worked well together and successfully combined her program with our Victory program, creating a formidable turnout mechanism.

Casting Williams as the outsider who wanted to reform Montgomery and use his experience as a small businessman to create jobs and improve the economy was well received by the voters of House District 6. We also subtly highlighted the fact that Askins's campaign was being driven by the liberal special interests in Montgomery who wanted the status quo to remain intact. This further developed the contrast we were striving to create in the race. Our polling confirmed this to be the case and our optimism began to grow as Election Day neared. We believed that if our GOTV organization delivered, we would be successful.

The day before the election, in July 2009, I again dispatched our team to the district to assist Adams with voter turnout. Ross, McCormick, Sidney Rue, and political director Michael Joffrion spent the day knocking on doors in targeted precincts. Bryan remained in Birmingham to coordinate the media effort. Their commitment to the plan, desire to win, and willingness to do whatever it took, even knocking on doors in the July heat, was on full display.

That night, the staff met Phil and Lisa Williams for dinner at the Mellow Mushroom at the Village of Providence in east Huntsville where the staff was staying and where the victory party would be held the following evening. As they recalled the activities of the day and made predictions on the outcome of the race, a couple sat down in the booth next to them. Ross recognized the man from his days as a staffer for Congressman Aderholt. It was Dan Williams, the mayor of Athens, and his wife, Kay. The mayor said hello to Ross and introduced himself to Phil Williams. They had a brief discussion about the race the following day and Mayor Williams mentioned in passing that he might have an interest in the House seat currently occupied by Henry White in Limestone County. Ross called me that evening and told me that we had, by accident, identified a potential candidate for a targeted House race for 2010.

In what would prove to be a classic case of foreshadowing, Mayor Williams, with the guidance of consultant Ceci, would defeat White and play an important role in the historic Republican legislative sweep.

The day of the election, the staff along with a handful of volunteers set up shop in the Board of Realtors building in downtown Huntsville. My friend Danny Cooper had arranged for a phone bank and war room to be set up in one of the meeting rooms. Throughout the day, the staff, volunteers, and members of the Realtors Association made calls to identified Williams supporters in the district reminding them to go vote. We were going to do all we could up until the polls closed at seven o'clock to get Republican voters to the polls.

By early evening, all indicators pointed to a solid victory for Williams. I received the news and called Williams to congratulate him and officially welcome him to the House GOP Caucus. Elated, he thanked me and my team for our efforts. This experience and victory had provided me, as well as our entire team, with a much-needed boost and strengthened confidence in our plan with back-to-back wins.

The *Huntsville Times* article that appeared the next morning highlighted the historic nature of the victory as well as the statewide implications of the race. For the first time, the media seemed to recognize that our goal of flipping the legislature just might not be so farfetched. Ross was quoted in the article stating, "With a resounding victory, I believe every Democrat in the state should know we're coming."

Indeed, we were.

IN LATE 2009, OUR confidence was growing. The special election for the House seat vacated by Keahey's election to the Senate earlier in the year had arrived. Jerry Reed, a popular former football coach and insurance agent, was the Republican nominee. The Democrats had selected Elaine Beech, a pharmacist from Chatom and member of the Washington County school board, as their nominee. The two were set to face off in early November.

With the national sentiment against President Obama increasing and with our recent successes in the two special elections, I decided to take a risk and get the ALGOP involved in the race despite the traditional Democratic leanings of the district. Adding to the intrigue was the fact that Beech's opponent in the Democratic primary, Ozell Hubert, had sent letters to everyone from the Clarke County probate judge to President Barack Obama claiming election fraud in the primary. His claims hadn't been substantiated, but it told us there might be some division in the ranks among Democratic voters in the district.

Winning a race we weren't supposed to win would not only send another strong message to the Democrats, but it would also greatly assist me with ongoing fundraising efforts. We developed a strategic plan that called for a stealth-like campaign on a budget of $50,000.

The first order of business was to find a consultant who would be willing to run the day-to-day campaign operations for a small fee. I decided to reach out to the guys at Public Strategy Associates who had consulted on the Sanford race in Senate District 7. Anxious to build their business and up for a challenge, they accepted. We would provide Reed with the funds to pay PSA a small consulting fee and their job was to be the conduit between our team and Reed.

Ryan Adams and Ryan Cantrell, who were now on staff full-time as deputy political directors under Joffrion in preparation of the 2010 election cycle, were sent to the rural district, which included parts of Clarke, Choctaw and Washington counties, to begin organizing a Victory program. Reed, his wife, Cheryl, and their 16-year-old son welcomed the two with open arms. They let them move into the basement of their home, which the two Ryans called home for five weeks. Not only was the Reed basement their residence, but it also served as the headquarters for our

Victory operation in the district. To this day, I appreciate the Reed family for embracing our team the way they did.

As we moved closer to Election Day, our polling suggested we were making progress. Our stealth campaign—based solely on a targeted direct mail program—was moving the numbers in Reed's favor. It was apparent, though, that we needed one strong hit in the final weeks to pull out the victory.

The good news was that we had a silver bullet-issue that tested off the charts when we polled it. The bad news was that we would not be able to fire it.

In 2008, a teacher at Leroy High School in Washington County, Charlene Schmitz, had been convicted of enticing a 14-year-old student to have sex with her. The scandal, not surprisingly, had rocked the small, rural county. To make matters worse, the Washington County school board, of which Democratic nominee Elaine Beech was a member, had let Schmitz continue to draw her teaching salary while she was serving her sentence. Alabama's teacher tenure laws, created and pushed by the AEA, were also to blame. (It was circumstances like this that would lead Republicans to reform the tenure laws in the 2011 legislative session.)

As one would imagine, and as our polling suggested, voters in the district would be much less likely to vote for Beech once they learned of the situation. Our path to victory in this race was crystal clear. But there was a problem.

Reed's son just happened to be close friends with the convicted teacher's son. They were the same age and had gone to school together for years. Reed also knew the boy and his family well, so the scandal hit particularly close to home. After presenting our plan to Reed, he struggled with how to proceed. He knew this issue could win him the race. But Reed also knew that making it a part of his campaign would be devastating to the young boy and his family, who were desperately attempting to put it behind them.

Reed decided not to use the issue against his opponent. Because of the circumstances and despite the resources we had allocated to the race, I did not question his decision. I wanted to win what would have been a monumental victory for the ALGOP and our Campaign 2010 efforts, but not at all costs.

As we moved forward, Cantrell and Adams focused on their GOTV efforts while we continued targeting voters with direct mail. In the end, Reed made a very commendable showing in the traditionally Democratic district, losing by 53 to 47 percent. In the *Mobile Press Register* article following the race, Beech remarked that she was surprised the election was so close given that the district was such a traditional Democratic stronghold.

Although no one will ever know what the outcome would have been if we had run the ad on the teacher sex scandal, I believe the results would have turned out differently. But I walked away with tremendous respect for Reed because he put the best interests of a young man over his own desire to represent the people of House District 65 in the Alabama House of Representatives.

ALSO IN LATE 2009, State Representative Lea Fite unexpectedly passed away. Fite, a Democrat from Jacksonville, was a well-liked member of the Alabama House, and I was saddened by the loss. I called his mother, a member of the Calhoun County Republican Party, shortly after his death to offer my condolences. The ALGOP also gave a donation in his honor to his favorite charity as a show of respect for his service and commitment to the state of Alabama.

As required by Alabama law, Governor Riley called for a special election to fill the vacancy. The election would be held in the middle of February 2010, making it a direct precursor to the main event in November. Interest in this race would come from across the state and would prove to be the most important race our team would be involved in to this point. All eyes were on us.

A win would not only put us one seat closer to a majority in the House but would add momentum as we prepared for the 2010 general election. There was no question this race would be a barometer race for the Campaign 2010 effort

A loss, on the other hand, would cause skepticism among the media, party members, and the individuals who had invested in Campaign 2010.

We were about to find out if our team could perform at a high level under the spotlight and a tremendous amount of pressure.

The Republican primary went smoothly. Senator Marsh represented this district in the Alabama Senate and was particularly helpful in working with the candidates to refrain from negative campaigning. The last thing we needed was a primary similar to the one in the Second Congressional District back in 2008 where the Republican nominee emerged so battered and bruised. To their credit, our candidates pledged to assist whoever the eventual nominee was in the interest of the district and the GOP.

When the results of the primary election were tallied, K. L. Brown, a funeral home owner from Jacksonville, had received 46 percent of the vote but was in a runoff with the second-place finisher, Anniston businessman Jay Dill, who received 19 percent. Because Brown had come so close to winning the election outright, I wanted to gauge Dill's willingness to drop out of the race. After all, chances were he would not be successful in the runoff and the additional six weeks of Republican intramural campaigning would only give the Democrats more time to prepare.

Fortunately, Marsh had a close relationship with Dill and agreed to broach the subject with him. Dill was a great candidate with a bright future in politics. He understood the magnitude of the race and its importance in the grand scheme of things for the Republican Party.

I visited with Dill on the phone and in person and went over the options. After a great deal of thought, Dill selflessly withdrew. He understood the stakes and the additional cost the state would incur in another election.

We held a press conference in Jacksonville. Dill, along with his wife, Phyllis, stood with Brown, Marsh, Calhoun County Republican Party officials, and me, and graciously dropped out of the race. He also pledged his full support to Brown in the upcoming general election. Marsh and I praised him for his act of service not only to the party, but also to the state. I was so moved by Dill's actions that I invited him to be the guest of honor at the Alabama Republican party's winter dinner the following week in Montgomery. After I introduced him to the crowd and outlined what he had done, the 700 guests gave him standing ovation. Jay Dill's contribution to the GOP effort to capture the legislature had not gone unnoticed.

The Democrats had, again, cleared the field for their nominee—Ricky Whaley, who in so many ways symbolized the stranglehold the Alabama Education Association held over the state for decades. He was Paul Hubbert's golden boy who served on the Hubbert-controlled state teacher's health insurance board (PEEHIP). Whaley was a teacher in Jacksonville who had been a longtime consumer of the AEA Kool-Aid. He had an air of confidence about him because, I assume, he was close with Hubbert and had been assured the union would do whatever it took to get him elected.

The race matched up a conservative, pro-business candidate who was seeking office for the first time against an active member of the AEA who epitomized the prototypical Democratic candidate in every way. I couldn't have imagined a more perfect storyline. It perfectly symbolized the epic battle Republicans and Democrats had been fighting for years over control of the legislature. It also would serve as a microcosm of the battle that would be waged later that year.

During the GOP primary, Brown had not hired a consultant but had instead asked his friend and former Goodyear public relations executive Gene Howard to advise him and put together a campaign plan. Whatever they did had worked in the primary, but Brown and Howard both knew they were in for a fight in the general election. They welcomed our experience and expertise.

In an unconventional move, I decided that the race would be run in-house by our team, with the counsel of Dax Swatek, my longtime advisor and Governor Riley's 2006 campaign consultant. Swatek was assisting our Campaign 2010 effort on a pro bono basis, so this race would be a warmup for the big show in November. I had all the faith in the world that our team was capable of handling the race. I also believed it would be strategically important for us to work directly with Brown once the other side began firing bullets.

As had been the case with previous special elections, we only had a six-week timetable prior to the general election in February. We polled the race in early January and it confirmed our suspicions that the race was going to be tight. It was vitally important that we follow our campaign plan that was based on message points tested in the survey.

After reviewing the data and following several lengthy discussions with pollster Jimmy McLaughlin, a campaign plan was created. It closely resembled the plan we had successfully followed in the House District 6 race that Phil Williams had won. Just as we had done with Williams, Brown was to be cast as the outsider, a fresh face who wanted to reform Montgomery and use his business experience to create jobs and improve the economy.

Conversely, our goal was to portray Whaley as the ultimate Montgomery insider, whose campaign was being funded by liberal special interest groups that wanted to raise taxes, which would result in killing jobs and hurting the economy.

The major difference between the two races was that House District 40 was not as attractive a district for a Republican as House District 6 had been. The old Yellow Dog Democrat roots were still very strong in the district. The demographics of the district, combined with a strong teacher's union presence, meant there was no room for mistakes.

A strong GOTV program was critical. Political director Michael Joffrion put together a calculated turnout plan and Cantrell and Adams went immediately to the district to implement it. Because of the heightened interest in the race around the state, they were able to tap into Young Republican groups, Republican women's groups, and GOP county executive committee members for door-to-door campaigners and phone volunteers. In fact, just after switching parties, Congressman Parker Griffith came to the district to go door-to-door as a show of loyalty. The Jacksonville State University College Republican group also played a big role in the campaign.

Quickly, our plan was being carried out by our team like a well-oiled machine. Ross was quarterbacking the effort with guidance from Swatek and McLaughlin while coordinating and relaying information to Brown. Bryan was managing communications and assisting with message development. Joffrion was overseeing the Victory program and coordinating with our mail vendor to ensure we were mailing to the universe of voters we needed to hit and the mail pieces were hitting mailboxes at right time.

Minda Riley Campbell, Kate McCormick, and Sidney Rue were coordinating video crews, as well as television and radio spot production. This system of McCormick planning, Campbell directing, and Rue shooting worked so well that it would eventually be repeated many times over on dozens of future campaigns.

With only a couple of weeks to go, "the Ryans" had moved into a Hampton Inn in Jacksonville and were coordinating the turnout program and ballot security effort from there.

I was busy raising money for the race and overseeing all of the campaign's elements. Governor Riley and I attended and spoke at a campaign rally in Jacksonville which generated an impressive and enthusiastic crowd. I was confident we were doing all we could to put Brown in the best position possible to win.

As expected, the attacks on Brown came with a couple of weeks to go. Instead of the Whaley campaign or the State Democratic Party delivering the attack, the AEA had created a third-party political action committee to do the dirty work. The group, called the Alabama Ethics Committee PAC, was created to mislead and confuse voters by insinuating the ads were being run by the Alabama Ethics Commission, the state's watchdog agency.

The content of the ads was equally misleading. They were claiming Brown somehow broke the law by not filing a campaign finance disclosure report 45 days before the election. This was particularly damaging because the ALGOP had been forced to remove a Calhoun County judicial nominee from the ballot the previous year for not filing a similar disclosure report, due between five and 10 days before an election, in time. The unfortunate situation was still fresh on the minds of the voters in Calhoun County and the Democrats were attempting to capitalize on it.

The good news was there was no basis to the claim that Brown had broken the law. His campaign had not yet hit the $5,000 threshold required to file a financial disclosure report, but this didn't stop the other side from running the ads anyway. Bryan, with the assistance from my friend and attorney Rob Riley, contacted the cable news outlets and radio stations airing the ads and convinced them to take them down or run the risk of a lawsuit for airing misinformation. After working diligently for a couple of days on this project, Bryan got most of the stations to take the advertisement off the air. It was an early and substantial victory.

Many of Whaley's other attacks were humorous and futile attempts claiming Brown was being controlled by party bosses and couldn't think for himself. Every chance he got, Whaley would talk about the "big wigs from Birmingham" who were controlling Brown's campaign. His goal was to convince voters that a group of people from outside Calhoun County was attempting to decide the race for them. It didn't work, of course, as Brown had been an upstanding and respected member of the community for years. I often thought it would have been amusing to see the looks on people's faces if they were shown a picture of these "big wigs." They would have been startled to see a group of fresh-faced young people, most of whom had not yet reached their 30th birthday.

As usual, our team was in the district on Election Day making phone calls to voters and Ross was providing updates from the field. Turnout was strong in our targeted precincts and we had a strong ballot security effort in place. Brown and his family were making calls to friends reminding them to go vote to make certain no stone was left unturned.

With a couple of hours remaining before the polls closed, Cantrell discovered that two of the poll watchers we had designated to observe activities in two of our weak boxes in Piedmont had unexpectedly not returned after lunch. Ross had Brown sign paperwork designating Ross and Bryan as poll watchers for those precincts, which all candidates are entitled to do. The two staffers rushed to Piedmont and spent the final hour and a half in the two polling places. The election officials were obviously surprised, and not amused, to have Ross's and Bryan's eyes fixed on them as the ballot boxes were sealed.

Ross later told me how quickly AEA members began showing up at the polling places as soon as the polls closed. He said the election officials alerted the union members to his presence in the polling place and all discussion regarding the election immediately ceased. While he never accused anyone of wrongdoing, I was, needless to say, glad he and Bryan decided to drive over and assume the role of polling place policemen that evening.

The other bonus of having the two of them at those particular boxes was their ability to report the final numbers back to Cantrell. He was keeping an elaborate spreadsheet to allow him to project the outcome of the race based on a handful of key precincts. The precincts where Ross and Bryan had served as poll watchers just so happened to be two he needed for an accurate projection. After relaying the numbers to Cantrell, Ross and Bryan drove back to Jacksonville with the belief Brown was going to win the race.

An hour later, Cantrell's projections proved correct. Brown had won. I received the news in Montgomery and excitedly placed a call to Brown to congratulate him on becoming the 45th member of the House Republican Caucus. He was thrilled, but also relieved. As I've grown to know Brown personally, I've found him to be a soft-spoken, gentle person. The hard-fought campaign had taken a toll on him and his family, but the reward of victory was sweet.

Our team was elated and I was elated for them. The win meant that our confidence, our supporters' confidence and the confidence of the candidates we had recruited was stronger than ever. This race was symbolic in so many ways as it was the first victory of the 2010 election cycle. It set the tone for the coming months.

As I reflect on the peaks and valleys we experienced leading up to the 2010 races, I honestly would not change a thing. We did not realize it at the time, but the defeats and challenges were valuable learning experiences. In addition to exposing areas of our plan that needed improving, they provided a clear picture of who our true supporters were as well as the ones who turned, ran, and started throwing stones at the first sign of trouble.

The peaks, including the special election victories, served as motivation and confidence builders for our team and for me. They also affirmed that what we were attempting to do was, indeed, possible.

We now had to take Campaign 2010 to a peak, not a valley.

∼ *In Their Own Words* ∼

JOE TURNHAM
ALABAMA DEMOCRATIC PARTY THREE-TERM CHAIRMAN

I remember Mike was very down on the night of the 2008 election. He turned to me during a break of the newscast where we were appearing and was worried because the Republicans had lost two congressional seats they were supposed to win along with the presidency of the Public Service Commission. But if anyone knows that two years is a lifetime in politics, it's me. I was hailed as a hero in 2006 and 2008 because the Democrats had performed well, but I was Robert E. Lee after Gettysburg in 2010. Mike probably thought he would have to resign after the 2008 elections, but in 2010 he was hailed nationally and elected Speaker of the House.

15

RECRUITING TROOPS FOR BATTLE

It is impossible to overestimate the importance candidate recruitment played in the success we enjoyed in 2010. Every man and woman we recruited made the decision to run for all of the right reasons and I believe they are some of the finest public servants Alabama has ever seen. Each has a fascinating story about how they came to run for the legislature. Many made sacrifices I am not sure most people would be willing to make to get involved in the plan to change Alabama. Space does not allow me to provide an in-depth look at each Republican House and Senate member, so I will highlight just a few as a representative sample of the group.

The district-by-district study by consultant Scott Stone told us which Democrats were the most ripe for defeat. Finding quality Republican candidates in those districts was our highest priority, but we also believed we could save considerable funding and resources if the Democratic incumbents filling those seats could be persuaded to retire. Achieving this required a bit of imagination.

My staff put together an impressive 88-page document entitled the *GOP Alabama State Victory Plan 2010* which included chapters on voter registration, voter identification, data information sharing, staffing, and other subjects. One important section listed 17 Democratic-held legislative districts aggressively targeted by the ALGOP—seven in the Senate and ten in the House—along with charts listing the impressive financial resources Campaign 2010 would devote to win each seat. Any incumbent, especially one who might be already contemplating retirement, would be disheartened to read the battle plan that awaited them should they seek reelection.

A copy of the *Victory Plan* document was mysteriously leaked to members of the press, and all 88 pages appeared in PDF format on the *Doc's*

Political Parlor gossip blog, which every lawmaker and lobbyist working in Montgomery seemed to check several times a day. The fact that our internal memo became public generated a great deal of snickering about our lax security measures.

Truth be known, the *Victory Plan* document had been written with every intention of it becoming public. The bold and sexy subjects heading each chapter overshadowed several pages of insignificant fluff that followed. Anyone who read it in totality would see the document was "all sizzle and no steak," and mostly focused on the 17 targets it contained, which was the plan all along.

To allow me plausible deniability with my Democratic colleagues in the House, John Ross and Philip Bryan had the document prepared and leaked its contents without my knowledge. Their hope that some on the "hit list" would decide not to run again bore fruit as three of the Democratic targets—Senator Hinton Mitchem of Albertville and Representatives Frank McDaniel of Albertville and Ron Grantland of Hartselle—announced their retirements shortly after the report became public. Bryan later explained to me how he placed the document with the media without leaving fingerprints.

ANOTHER LEGISLATIVE SEAT WAS also becoming vacant, but neither Del Marsh nor I were happy about this one. Ever since Jay Love defeated Senator Harri Anne Smith in the Second Congressional District run-off and Smith then endorsed Democrat Bobby Bright for that seat, members of the State Republican Steering Committee had her in their sights. The steering committee, a small group of influential Republicans who help determine party policy, has the authority to remove candidates from the GOP primary ballot when their qualifications are challenged. Reasons for removal may include any number of issues, but the cardinal sin is for a sitting Republican officeholder to publicly endorse a Democratic candidate over a Republican. Smith had done just that.

Smith had drawn Republican primary opposition in 2010 in the form of George Flowers, a prominent Dothan businessman whose father had founded the city's local hospital. Flowers had been a strong supporter of

Smith's congressional campaign and she had told him that she planned to retire from the legislature whether she won or lost the race to succeed Terry Everett. Smith encouraged Flowers to run for the State Senate in her stead, and he qualified for the seat. The only problem was that Smith changed her mind.

Smith had joined forces with Ronnie Gilley, the flamboyant developer of a legally questionable gambling hall smack in the middle of Smith's district. Gilley was working with other gambling interests to persuade the legislature to approve a constitutional amendment that would authorize the forms of electronic gambling he and others in the state were already openly offering. Smith was helping him gather the necessary votes. I can only surmise that with promises of campaign contributions and the full commitment of pro-gambling forces behind her, the temptation to seek another State Senate term was too much for Smith to resist.

Most of the steering committee members were determined to oust Smith for endorsing Bright. She told the committee that although her preference was to run as a Republican, she would seek reelection as an Independent if the anti-Smith forces prevailed. Ironically, Smith told anyone who would listen that Marsh and I were driving the effort to have her removed from the ballot, but Marsh and I actually argued as strongly as we could to let her remain a Republican.

While we were concerned that rumors of a pending federal indictment of Smith related to her pro-gambling activity might hurt the Republican brand if true, she had been a loyal vote for the GOP Senate caucus in most matters unrelated to Gilley's development. We told the steering committee members that plucking an incumbent Republican legislator from the primary ballot would set a bad precedent. When that argument failed, we appealed to their bloodlust. Smith, we explained, would stand a better chance of defeat if she met Flowers in a primary with purely Republican voters participating rather than in a general election where pro-gambling Democrats and Independents could support her.

Our request fell upon deaf ears and the committee voted by a wide margin to excommunicate Smith from the Alabama Republican Party. By doing so, they guaranteed a long and expensive general election fight against

an angry and aggrieved Independent candidate who was well-funded by
gaming interests. It was an unpleasant scenario any way you looked at it.

YET ANOTHER DISTRICT CAME open when Representative Bill Dukes, a
former mayor of Decatur who had been elected to the House as a Democrat in 1994, announced his retirement. Dukes was 82, and though he
was a fine man and popular among his House colleagues, members of
both parties were somewhat relieved as we all worried about his health.
With a political career that spanned four decades, I know that stepping
down was difficult for him.

In the years since Dukes was first elected, both the city of Decatur and
Morgan County had become increasingly conservative and Republican.
One of the few seats picked up by the ALGOP in 2006 was the Senate
seat vacated by the retiring Tommy Ed Roberts. Arthur Orr, a corporate
attorney in Decatur who had served overseas in the Peace Corps and had
founded the Habitat for Humanity effort in Bangladesh, was elected to
fill the void. Hearing of Orr's background in poverty-stricken third-world
countries, many people assumed he was a liberal "do-gooder," but he
actually is a conservative Republican to the core.

Given that in recent years Republicans had captured all of the public
offices in Morgan County, I knew Dukes's retirement opened a great opportunity to pick up the seat. I asked Tim Howe, the former Republican
Party executive director leading our recruitment efforts, to find a suitable
candidate to run in the district. Howe met with a group of Morgan County
party stalwarts, including Orr, attorney Barney Lovelace, and CPA David Scott, to seek their input. They suggested Wally Terry, a well-known
Decatur bank executive.

Howe made his pitch and Terry was intrigued enough to have a news
release announcing his entrance into the race drafted. But the day before
the release was to be sent to area media, he changed his mind. Terry suggested that Howe to speak with another bank employee, Terri Collins,
and seek her suggestions for possible candidates.

Collins, an attractive and intelligent woman with a personality as
robust and vivacious as her red hair suggests, met with Howe and the

two hit it off. She asked for some time to come up with names of those she might recommend to run. Reporting back to the group in Decatur, Howe said he had found an ideal candidate . . . Terri Collins. Howe said Orr, Lovelace, and Scott looked at each other and wondered why they had not thought of her first.

Later, Collins began to tell Howe her suggested candidates. He stopped her in mid-sentence and asked her to run. She was surprised but Howe explained that she would be a perfect candidate because her decades-long service as vice president at First America Bank, later bought by RBC, had provided her with countless contacts throughout the Decatur area. Civic involvements, including her personal mentorship of a young African American girl for several years, had made her even more visible. The fact that she had never thought about running for office or even considered politics, he added, made her more attractive because that's exactly what the Alabama Republican Party was seeking—fresh, new faces eager to bring change to Montgomery. Collins did not immediately accept, but she did not turn him down, either.

I was doing everything I could to support Howe's recruitment effort, so when he told me that Collins would be an excellent addition to our ticket, I put on the full court press. In addition to meeting with her and calling often to get updates on her thinking, I got Governor Riley and his salesman skills involved. While he and I were in New York City on political business, I had the governor call Collins on my cell phone as we were entering the United Nations building for a meeting. I figured she would be impressed that he had taken time out from an important event to touch base and encourage her to run.

Governor Riley, incidentally, played a major role in our candidate recruitment. In addition to making phone calls when we asked, he accompanied me to private dinners with potential candidates and their spouses and always was willing to allow me to pop into his office with a recruit to meet them. He used his skills of persuasion masterfully in convincing some great people to become engaged in our effort.

Collins's decision was not made easier when Dukes announced that he had changed his mind and would seek reelection rather than retire.

Knowing the Democrats were working to avoid primaries as often as possible, I told Collins he would likely bow out again once the qualifying period had closed. Few, if any, Democrats would consider a primary challenge against a local legend like Dukes, and if he quit the race once it was too late for other candidates to jump in, the Democratic State Committee could place their handpicked successor on the ballot. We call it a "placeholder" move.

That, in fact, turned out to be the case. An African American city councilman named Billy Jackson had indicated he would run for the House seat in Dukes's absence, but the Democratic leadership, working as hard as we were to elect a majority, wanted Drama Breland, the wife of a popular retired Morgan County district judge, to be their standard-bearer. The Dukes head fake worked, which allowed Breland—by coincidence, a sorority sister of Collins's—to grab the nomination uncontested. Jackson, however, was left somewhat embittered. The influential African American leader would sit on the sidelines throughout much of the race, a move that probably lost Breland some much-needed minority support.

While considering whether to run, Collins mentioned to me that she would like to talk with some female incumbents in the House to discuss how serving had affected their family life along with their experiences as women in a male-dominated political atmosphere. I put her in touch with Representatives Mary Sue McClurkin from Shelby County and Jamie Ison from Mobile, two of the most-respected members of the House Republican Caucus. They told Collins that their service had been very positive and encouraged her to run. I believe their words did more than anything to convince her because shortly after their talk, Collins told me she was in the race.

One Republican candidate had already qualified for the seat, Jason Puttman, a local businessman who was not as attractive a candidate for us as Collins. But, keeping to our pledge of not getting involved in primary elections, we told Collins she would have to raise her own money, run her own campaign and do what it took to win the primary without assistance from the ALGOP. If she was successful, we would do everything needed to help her win the general election. We did, however, team her with David

Azbell, the Montgomery political consultant who had helped guide the Barry Mask, Benjamin Lewis, and Arthur Orr campaigns.

Collins soon learned a hard lesson that often takes first-time candidates by surprise—running for office is a time-consuming, all-encompassing pursuit that requires you to put all other priorities on the back burner. Collins would work her normal 9-to-5 job schedule, close the bank and then hit the streets, often walking neighborhoods well past dark to knock on doors and ask for votes. Lunch breaks and weekends, too, were devoted to campaign events.

She found that the duties of her corporate job did not leave her adequate time to run the campaign she needed to run to win, so she made a tough decision. After 25 years of serving the financial needs of Decatur citizens, mostly at the same bank and the same location, she decided to quit her job and devote full-time to her legislative campaign. In her news release announcing the decision, Collins said, "If anything, the primary campaign demonstrated to me that running for office takes more hours than I ever imagined, and it would not be fair to the bank, my campaign, or the voters I seek to serve if I continue to split my time."

Though the public is often cynical about the elected officials who represent them, the truth is that each makes multiple sacrifices to serve. Time away from family and business are the most common, but many make financial sacrifices as well, often losing money, retirement and other security in exchange for their decision to hold office. I am amazed when candidates like Collins take such bold, life-changing steps just to have a chance at getting elected. Giving up a 25-year career to knock on doors, beg for votes, and sweat in Alabama's notorious summertime heat and humidity proved how committed Collins, and others like her, were to electing a Republican majority. Collins defeated Puttman in the primary and would be our nominee against Breland in the fall.

ANOTHER RECRUITED CANDIDATE, MARK Tuggle, would make a similar gut-wrenching decision and sacrifice in order to put his name on the ballot.

In addition to targeting open House seats in 2010, we also put a bulls-eye on several incumbent Democrats we believed we could defeat. One was Representative Betty Carol Graham, who represented a legislative district that happened to adjoin mine. First elected to the House in 1994, Graham was one of Paul Hubbert's main lapdogs in the body. If there was a bill he wanted sponsored, a vote he wanted cast or a motion he wanted made on behalf of the teachers' union, Graham was the first one to do it with no questions asked. A long-time employee of the state's two-year college system, she was also a poster child for double-dippers—elected officials who drew two taxpayer-funded paychecks and often faced ethical dilemmas for accepting both.

How could a community college administrator, most Republicans argued, discipline an employee who also served in the legislature and controlled their boss's budget? And how ethical was it for a lawmaker to vote on legislation directly affecting the public agency that employed them? The conflicts of interest and questions of propriety were, in my opinion, countless.

Although my colleagues across the aisle often label me as a partisan political animal, I believe I pale in comparison to the partisanship Graham demonstrated at every opportunity. On one occasion, when Democrats broke a Republican filibuster over a budget bill, Graham yelled like a cheerleader and celebrated by dancing a jig in the aisle of the chamber. Her blind allegiance to Hubbert and hatred of all things Republican placed her high atop our target list.

Howe and I began our search for a candidate to run against Graham by touching base with someone who had come within a hair of running four years earlier.

Mark Tuggle grew up in Alexander City, the heart of Graham's district, and attended Auburn University where he earned a degree in Forestry Management. After briefly working two jobs following his 1988 graduation, he was hired by the forestry division of Alabama Power Company in 1991.

Tuggle had served four years as the Tallapoosa County Republican Party chairman and in 2006 considered running for Graham's House seat when rumors indicated she might seek election to the Senate. In fact, he completed his qualifying papers and sent them to Howe, then employed by the party, and asked that they be held until instructed to file them.

Alabama Power, like many companies, has always had strict rules about its employees seeking elected office and provides a process for those who are interested to seek permission. Tuggle penned a letter to his manager stating the office he planned to seek and the time away from the job his campaign might require, just as the company asked. When his request was denied, he thought nothing of it since Graham had, by then, decided to stay in the House. Tuggle, following both his employer's directive and his own gut feeling, called Howe and told him to discard the paperwork.

More than a year before the 2010 elections, Howe and I met Tuggle for dinner at the Spring House Restaurant on Lake Martin. Tim Wellborn, a dues-paying member of the Governor's Circle who was helping our recruitment effort, joined us. Each of us hoped that almost four years of thinking "what if" had helped stoke Tuggle's political fire.

Tuggle told our group that he had recently considered running for the Senate seat held by Democrat Ted Little but believed voters in Lee and Russell counties, the largest in the district, would be reluctant to support a candidate from Tallapoosa County, one of the smallest. His thoughts, he admitted, had recently drifted back toward running against Graham. Those words were as beautiful as angels singing in our collective ears. While it would take him several months to commit to the race, we could tell that evening that Tuggle had the political itch and was dying to scratch it.

Almost two months before Republican qualifying closed in 2010, Tuggle wrote another letter to his bosses at Alabama Power signaling his intention to run against Graham. Unlike his note four years earlier, this one was more a notification that his decision was made than a request for permission. He heard nothing in reply, so Tuggle completed the paperwork necessary to appear on the ballot and left it with John Ross, just as he had done with Howe in 2006, telling him to hold it until further instructions.

On the morning of the last day to qualify, a Friday, Tuggle's boss called to tell him the request to run had been denied. Tuggle's reply, in return, was, "I'll have to give that some thought." By the end of the day, Tuggle had called party headquarters and told them to file his papers. He was running.

When his superiors learned his decision on Monday, Tuggle was summoned to Birmingham and asked to resign his $82,000-a-year job. He left after 19 years with two week's severance, his accrued vacation pay, and no guarantee he would ever serve a day in office.

Tuggle later told me that his wife, a schoolteacher and his high school sweetheart, was understandably nervous about his decision, but fully supported his candidacy even when they had to dip into his 401k account to make ends meet. He also told me he was proud of his years with Alabama Power and has great affection for the company to this day. They had rules, he admits, and when he did not agree with the rules, it was his decision to quit. I never had to question Tuggle's commitment to our mission of electing a Republican majority because he demonstrated it clearly from the day he qualified.

ANOTHER KEY RACE WAS in a House district held by Terry Spicer (D-Elba) in the Wiregrass area of Coffee County. Spicer was elected the same year as I, 1998. When elected, he was an air conditioning repair instructor at McArthur State Technical College in Opp. Following his election to the legislature, he was promoted to assistant to the president of Enterprise State Junior College and, for a while, simultaneously drew two paychecks from two different junior colleges.

Spicer was a hard-core Democrat and extremely loyal to Hubbert and the teachers' union. In 2006, we had targeted him in our first coordinated campaign effort but came about 300 votes short. The race had left a bad taste in my mouth because I knew in my heart that if I had diverted some resources from other campaigns that were less competitive and applied them against Spicer, we would have won the race. I would not make that mistake again.

We had to have a top-tier candidate to defeat Spicer because he would be heavily funded by the Democratic leadership and especially by the AEA. The perfect candidate would come to us by way of interweaving college friendships.

Mississippi State Senator Merle Flowers is an Alabama native and Auburn University graduate. I had sent my colleague, Representative Paul DeMarco of Homewood, to a National Legislative Leaders Foundation meeting in Naples, Florida. There, DeMarco, also an Auburn graduate, and Flowers hooked up. They talked about mutual friends from their college days and, as normally happens when two legislators get together, talk turned to politics. DeMarco explained to Flowers about Campaign 2010 and how we were actively seeking candidates to run for both open and challenge races.

"Well, if you're looking for a candidate in the Wiregrass, I know just the guy," Flowers said to DeMarco. "His name is Barry Moore and he lives in Enterprise. I was in school with him at Auburn and he's a smart guy, a great businessman and a true conservative."

DeMarco made a note of what Flowers told him and passed it along to me upon his return from the legislative conference. Enterprise is the population center of Spicer's district, so I got on the phone with Howe and told him to track this Barry Moore guy down. I wanted to win this seat badly and Merle may have just given us a huge tip.

Howe jumped on it right away, located Barry Moore, who operated a waste hauling and trucking business, and set up a time to meet in person. After meeting with Moore and his wife, Heather, Howe called me from his cell phone on the drive back to Montgomery.

"Mike, we have a winner," Howe said excitedly. "Barry Moore is the real deal. He's smart, he's never run for office, he's pro-business, and a good-looking family man. But best of all, his wife is a real fireball. If we can get him to run, she will make sure he wins!"

I made some calls to people I knew in Enterprise and asked if they knew Barry and if they thought he would make a good candidate for the House. Without exception, they all said he would be ideal.

Not long after Howe's initial meeting with the Moores, he arranged for a dinner meeting at a steak house in Troy. Barry, Heather, Tim, and I met at the Santa Fe Steak House on Highway 231 and visited for almost two and a half hours. I delivered my best sales pitch, outlining how the Alabama Republican Party was taking an unprecedented lead in fundraising, running campaigns, and providing services to our candidates.

I explained to Barry and Heather that this district was one of our top two targets in the House for the 2010 election and that I was absolutely convinced that we could take the majority. At the end of the conversation, I told the Moores that this would be a once-in-a-lifetime opportunity for the two of them to do the state a tremendous service—first of all by defeating a double-dipping Democrat like Spicer, and secondly by being a part of a historic Republican majority that would fundamentally change the way Montgomery operates.

In the parking lot afterwards, I asked Howe how I had done.

"You did a great job and have really perfected your sales pitch," Howe replied. "I think anyone I put in front of you will want to run."

I laughed and said it probably had to do with the fact that this was such a big deal for our whole effort. This was truly a critical district for us and I was committed to providing whatever resources were necessary. But, we had to have a worthy candidate to succeed and I knew Barry Moore was the right one.

I also agreed with Howe's initial assessment that Heather Moore was a fireball and would be key to her husband's political success if he were to run. I could tell from our conversation that she knew a lot about politics and was interested in it.

The next day, Moore called my office. He told me he and Heather had reviewed everything we had discussed over dinner the night before during their drive back home, late into the night once they were home, and again that morning. He said they were both lukewarm to the idea prior to our dinner meeting, but now they were both in the race with both feet.

I suspect Moore could hear the excitement in my voice, because the smile on my face was so big. I assured him that everything I promised the night before would be provided, including consulting assistance, polling data, opposition research, grassroots support, campaign media, and, of course, financial resources.

Defeating Terry Spicer, the prototype of what we were trying to change through Campaign 2010, was a top priority.

WE DIDN'T CONFINE OUR recruiting efforts to the House. Del Marsh, Howe, and I worked just as hard to recruit the same ideal, quality candidates to run for the State Senate. Unfortunately, to elect a Republican majority, we sometimes had to target friendly Democrats who had helped our efforts over the years.

Tom Butler, first elected to the Alabama House in 1982 and to the Senate in 1994, was one of the dissident Democrats who, unhappy with the legislative leadership at the time, had chosen to caucus with the Republican minority in the upper chamber. This bipartisan, conservative working group had almost gathered enough votes to capture the leadership in the Senate. The fact that a handful of Democrats would forgo the power and committee assignments that being part of the majority provided simply demonstrated just how liberal and unacceptable the Senate had become under leadership from the likes of Lowell Barron, Rodger Smitherman, and Hinton Mitchem.

Butler was perhaps most famous for passing the Anti-Obscenity Enforcement Act of 1998, a bill designed to combat the proliferation of nude strip clubs and adult shops that had popped up in the unincorporated areas of his legislative district, located around Huntsville. An adjunct effect of the law had resulted in a statewide ban on the sale of marital aids—sex toys— in Alabama, a move that pleased many social conservatives like me and generated much attention among members of the national news media, along with months of monologue jokes from late-night talk show hosts Jay Leno, David Letterman, and others. The ban, incidentally, was upheld in both state and federal courts.

With roughly two weeks remaining in the 2009 legislative session, Marsh privately sat down with Butler and asked that he seek reelection, but this time as a Republican. Marsh presented our poll that showed Butler's suburban district had become largely Republican during his time in office. The numbers showed that Butler could easily win even after switching parties. Marsh also told him that if he didn't switch parties, we would have no choice but to go after his seat with our own Republican candidate. Butler refused to commit one way or the other, so after several weeks of waiting, our search for a suitable Republican candidate began. Butler ultimately decided to run on the Democratic ticket.

Because Butler was a long-serving, well-known, and much-liked legislator, Howe initially had difficulty locating a willing candidate who met our established profile. Bumping up against a deadline and coming up empty-handed, Howe turned to the Internet in desperation. He began looking up local elected officials in Butler's district and found a biography for Bill Holtzclaw, a city councilman in Madison. As he read, Howe realized that if he had to build a background for a textbook candidate, Holtzclaw's would have fit perfectly.

Orphaned at birth and raised at the United Methodist Children's Home in Arkansas until his adoption at the age of five, Holtzclaw joined the U.S. Marine Corps following graduation from high school. A 13-year career as an enlisted Marine included two tours of combat duty, one in Iraq during Operation Desert Storm and another in Somolia. His stellar service led him to be chosen for the Marine Corps warrant officer program. Beginning his career as a private stationed at the Marine Ammunition School at Huntsville's Redstone Arsenal, he would return to the same posting 16 years later as the officer in charge. He retired after 20 years of service with numerous commendations and military awards.

When Howe stumbled upon him, Holtzclaw was working as a contracts specialist in the office of procurement at Marshall Space Flight Center, also located in Huntsville. He and his wife of 26 years, Pam, had moved to Madison a decade earlier and were raising their two daughters there. After being elected to the city council in Madison, Holtzclaw was now serving as its president.

Howe cold-called Holtzclaw to gauge his interest in taking on Butler.

Howe and Holtzclaw met for the first time at a Starbucks in Madison and the recruitment process began in earnest. We were all surprised when Holtzclaw was even willing to consider leaving a secure $75,000-a-year federal job with excellent benefits in order to run. Of course, he is a Marine, and those guys are famous for showing courage and taking chances.

Marsh and Howe later took Holtzclaw to dinner and began to outline the plan, but they warned that Campaign 2010 funding or assistance would have to wait until he won what looked to be a crowded primary. He discussed the possibility with his family, and his wife was reluctant. She remembered his time away during Marine Corps tours of duty and knew he would have to leave home for extended periods once again to campaign and, if elected, serve in Montgomery. She eventually acquiesced and his daughters offered their support as well.

Holtzclaw actually served as Butler's city councilman and told the incumbent senator he was thinking about entering the race. He also said that if Butler would switch parties he would give up any notion of running. As he had with Marsh, Butler kept his cards close to his chest.

Four other candidates had indicated they would run in the Republican primary and Holtzclaw spoke with each. He convinced two to pass on the race, while the other two waited until the last minute to back out. That left Butler as the only question mark.

Waiting until the last day of qualifying, Butler filed his paperwork to run as a Democrat. Despite the entreaties from Marsh, his other colleagues, and even the candidate who was prepared to run against him, Butler ran on the ticket with the same Democrats he voted against regularly in the State Senate. His decision baffles me until this day.

IN AT LEAST ONE case, I actively tried to discourage a candidate from running. It was, in part, for admittedly selfish reasons. Representative Gerald Allen of Cottondale had represented a rural portion of Tuscaloosa County for several terms and sat in the seat adjacent to mine in the House chamber. He had become a close friend and strong supporter, and I often leaned upon Gerald for his counsel and for reassurances when I had difficult decisions to make as minority leader. He had never let me down, and I valued his influence and positive presence in our caucus.

He approached me one day during the 2009 session and said he had decided to seek the State Senate seat then held by Phil Poole, a Democrat known to have a bad temper and sometimes erratic behavior. When Don Siegelman and Steve Windom were jousting over control of the Senate during my first term in Montgomery, Poole, who had indicated he would vote with a bipartisan group supporting the lieutenant governor, flipped his vote at the last minute in return for road projects and other rewards Siegelman promised for his legislative district. His move cost him a lot of trust in Montgomery and made him a prime Republican target in future races.

As much as I wanted to support Gerald's decision to run for the Senate, I had reservations. He was a good House member who had worked his district well and having him run for reelection would ensure we kept a seat in our column. If he ran for the Senate and lost, I knew Montgomery would lose a good man and an honest lawmaker in exchange for four more years of Poole's antics. Despite my efforts to nudge him back toward running for the House, Gerald threw caution to the wind and signed up for the Senate contest. I must sheepishly admit that I am glad my friend, sitting State Senator Gerald Allen, ignored my advice.

Recognizing that we had several first-time candidates running on the Republican ticket, each with clean backgrounds and no record to attack, we also knew that few were familiar with the labyrinth of issues that candidates for the legislature are expected to discuss in detail. Limiting the number of "gotcha" moments that Democratic incumbents might pull in public to highlight our candidates' limited knowledge of arcane issues was a top goal that Marsh and I shared.

We put together another *Republican Handshake with Alabama* agenda of issues that our caucus had supported in the past. Recent polling indicated that the public agreed with its contents. By having all of our candidates run on the same agenda, they could always turn the debate back toward this handful of important issues with which they were familiar. And, working in tandem with the ongoing "136 Years" campaign, it would differentiate our Republican brand from that of the Democrats.

After the primary election cemented our slate of candidates, we held a joint Republican House and Senate caucus news conference in Montgomery to announce the agenda. Our nonincumbent candidates from across the state participated in the event, which was broadcast via satellite to television stations across the state for inclusion in the evening newscasts.

Reminding the gathered reporters that Democrats had offered a similar agenda four years earlier, yet failed to pass 13 of the 16 items it contained, we outlined the five broad topics of our *Handshake* along with the specific bills that were included under each. They were:

Creating Jobs and Economic Opportunities—Alabama Republicans understand that creating jobs and putting our state on the right economic track is our top priority, and we are prepared to implement proven, conservative incentives and pro-business reforms to accomplish that goal.

We will work with the administration to build upon and expand the job-creation tax incentives that our gubernatorial nominee, Dr. Robert Bentley, successfully passed during the last legislative session. Those incentives will be targeted to both new and existing businesses alike.

In order to provide more capital needed to add new jobs Republicans will also push to expand the small business health insurance tax credit from 150 percent to 200 percent of the amount that both employers and employees pay for coverage premiums.

Similarly, the Bentley plan to create a cabinet-level *Office of Small Business Creation and Development* has been embraced by Republican legislative candidates who will work to dedicate the resources needed for its success. The office will be tasked with reducing regulations and red tape, unifying small-business orientated state programs under one roof and advocating on behalf of both new and existing small businesses.

We will fight to ensure that Alabama remains a right-to-work state in order to keep employment costs low and demand legislation that protects the right to a secret ballot in union elections so that no worker may be harassed or intimidated for voting his or her heart and conscience.

A Republican Legislature will work to put roadblocks in the way of the job-killing *"Cap and Tax"* legislation being pushed by liberal Congressional Democrats. If passed, such legislation will cause energy costs in Alabama to skyrocket and crash our economy. Businesses from our largest industrial employers to our smallest mom-and-pop operations rely upon affordable energy costs to keep doors open and workers employed in Alabama.

Controlling Wasteful Spending—Many of our national economic problems have been caused by a Democratic Congress and liberal president who are spending like drunken sailors. Alabama Republicans want to prevent that from happening on the state level. Our

Legislature has traditionally budgeted based on political convenience and unsustainable revenue estimates. When those estimates prove too conservative for the Democrats' tastes, they simply increase them to accommodate additional spending. The result is devastating proration.

Alabama Republicans believe that the legislature, like families and individuals across the state, should live within its means, and we propose passage of the Responsible Budgeting and Spending Act. Under this bill, state revenue estimates would be based upon a 15-year rolling average rather than unsupported projections, which will rein in spending and allow the budgets to more easily absorb changes in a cyclical economy.

Ending Corruption in Montgomery—Democrats have held the majority in Montgomery for 136 years, and during that time, they created an atmosphere that breeds corruption and encourages graft. The recent criminal convictions of numerous Democratic legislators and other Democratic officials provide ample evidence of that fact.

Republicans understand that we must limit the influence of special interests and other lobbyists who control much of what happens in Montgomery. Under existing law, lobbyists are allowed to spend up to $250 a day on each public official without having to file an ethics report. A Republican majority will introduce legislation to require all spending by lobbyists is reported—even down to a cup of coffee.

Alabama is one of only three states that do not provide subpoena power to its ethics watchdog agency, which makes it easy for public officials and others to hamstring investigations. Republicans not only support subpoena power for the Alabama Ethics Commission, they want to provide the agency with a statutorily defined level of appropriation that can be cut only by a two-thirds vote of both houses. That way, no legislator can retaliate against the agency and its work by cutting its annual budget.

Too many legislators and other public officials have been caught double-dipping or holding questionable contracts with government agencies and those wishing to do business with the state. Republicans will work to ban double-dipping and require public officials and their spouses to disclose any contracts they hold with government entities.

Combating Illegal Immigration—Because illegal immigration threatens our homeland security, reduces the quality of life for tax-paying citizens and places our schools, hospitals and other resources under tremendous burden, Alabama Republicans believe we must take immediate action. Politicians in Washington refuse to act, so we must bring the fight to the home front.

A Republican legislative majority will push an illegal immigration bill similar to the recently approved Arizona law. The Alabama bill will create a new state criminal trespass statute that allows local law enforcement to arrest illegal immigrants for simply setting foot in Alabama. Another provision will make it a crime to provide an illegal immigrant transportation anywhere in Alabama, whether it is a trip across the state or simply to the corner store.

Proof of citizenship or legal residency in order to access government services will also be required, and, because illegal immigrants and their allies are working to gather political power and influence, any illegal immigrant who registers to vote, or attempts to, or casts a ballot will be convicted of a Class C felony as will anyone aiding in those efforts."

Blocking the Washington, D.C. Power Grab—Many rights and freedoms previously reserved to the states and to individuals are under an unprecedented attack from D.C. liberals, and Alabama Republicans are prepared to take strong actions to repel their assault. It is important that the voices of the frustrated majority of Alabamians be heard, especially in the area of socialized health care programs recently implemented against our wishes by Obama and his allies.

An Alabama House and Senate controlled by Republicans will immediately introduce and work to pass a constitutional amendment that would "prohibit any person, employer or health care provider from being compelled to participate in any health care system." This amendment would be similar to measures introduced or passed in at least 30 other state legislatures across the country, and it is believed that such state amendments will assist in court cases questioning federal authority to force citizens to purchase something they do not wish to purchase, a mandate never previously forced on the populace.

PUT ON THE DEFENSIVE by not having followed through on their promise of passing their previous agenda, the Democrats never even offered a laundry list of their own initiatives or priorities during the 2010 cycle. They simply remained silent on the issues facing our state. In contrast, our *Handshake* unified our candidates, gave the rookies much-needed confidence, and provided our incumbents the ability to run under the reform label despite having been in office.

The ingredients for a successful 2010 election cycle were coming together for us. The Governor's Circle and our other fundraising efforts had provided the resources to pay for effective and competitive campaigns. The recruitment effort had provided the quality candidates needed to take on our top targets as well as lower-tier races that poll numbers indicated were vulnerable. The *Handshake* and the "136 Years" campaigns had provided the message and the rallying cries needed to pump up our base and give swing voters pause for thought before casting ballots for incumbent Democrats.

We had done everything we could to set the battlefield in our favor. Now it was up to God and the voters to decide the outcome. I prayed that both were on our side.

⁓ In Their Own Words ⁓

TERRI COLLINS
STATE REPRESENTATIVE HOUSE DISTRICT 8, 2010–

I had about five names on my list to recommend to him. I was not thinking me by any stretch of the imagination. When Tim came in and actually asked me, I was surprised . . . and speechless. I called my husband, Tom, about it on the way home, and we talked about it all night. We decided we needed to pray about it. We went to a football game that Saturday and I mentioned it to my children, all of whom were at the University of Alabama at the time, and they were all surprised but very supportive. The next weekend, I went to the lake with a group of about 20 or 30 friends and when I told them what I was considering, they circled and prayed for me and my decision.

MARK TUGGLE
STATE REPRESENTATIVE HOUSE DISTRICT 81, 2010–

Mike Hubbard explained that if I had primary opposition, I couldn't get any Campaign 2010 or ALGOP help unless I won the nomination. Shane Grimes, the brother of State Representative David Grimes at the time, qualified to run against me. I didn't have a consultant run my campaign. I ran my own race by going to events, speaking at volunteer fire departments and handing out signs and t-shirts. Our fundraising went well and I received lots of individual contributions and small donations from throughout the district. My parents put in a little money and I added about $2,000 of my own. I spent between $5,000 and $8,000 in the primary and won with 67 percent of the vote. In fact, I was the number two vote-getter in our primary behind U.S. Senator Richard Shelby.

BILL HOLTZCLAW
STATE SENATOR, DISTRICT 2, 2010–

Tim said, "I don't know you and you don't know me, but the Republican Party wants me to meet with you to see if you were interested in being a candidate for one of the races we are targeting." The first thing I did was get his name and number because I thought one of my friends was playing a prank on me. I called him back and we talked very briefly. I told him about the Hatch Act, which prevented federal employees like me from seeking offices like State Senate. I had a tough decision to make. He caught me off guard when he wanted me to run in a Senate race because I thought it would be a lot easier to start in a House seat.

16

THE CAMPAIGN TO CHANGE ALABAMA

The victory in House District 40 gave us 45 Republicans in the chamber and our intense candidate recruitment had produced a bumper crop. It was now time to turn our attention to the November general election. We were only about eight months away, and the amount of work awaiting us seemed quite daunting. The stakes were high, but we believed if we could remain focused and optimistic, we had a decent chance of creating a new political landscape in Alabama. The Campaign 2010 plan was solid, well-conceived, and in place. Our team was confident and motivated. Now, all we had to do was step on the field and follow the game plan.

In past election cycles, Alabama Republicans and Democrats traditionally allowed a three-month period for candidates to qualify to run for office. I had witnessed this policy work against Republican candidates, specifically in legislative races, because it gave the Alabama Education Association plenty of time to monitor where candidates were qualifying and in which districts. Their goal would be to identify races where they could sneak one of their candidates into a Republican primary at the last minute in hopes of forcing the "real" Republican candidate to expend funds unnecessarily. It was a great scheme that often worked because it would ultimately help the Democratic candidate they were really supporting win the general election. And, if the AEA-backed candidate happened to somehow win the Republican nomination, the union would be covered no matter which party came out on top in the fall.

To deter bogus candidates, I proposed shortening the 2010 Republican qualifying period to 30 days beginning March 2nd and ending on April 2nd and raising the qualifying fee for legislative candidates from $500 to $1,000. Marsh and I made that pitch to the State Republican Executive

Committee, of which we were both members, and they unanimously agreed with our logic. We had worked too hard to recruit solid, pro-business candidates to have to worry about them drawing illegitimate primary opposition from an AEA plant. While these steps would not prevent such moves, they would at least be a little more difficult.

Shortly after the qualifying period closed, John Ross e-mailed a complete list of qualifiers, and it was evident our candidate recruitment effort had paid off. We had a fantastic slate of candidates in every one of our targeted races. In many cases, as in Senate District 9 in Marshall County, we had more than one outstanding candidate. The goal of our candidate recruitment program had not been to handpick nominees, but rather to ensure we had quality candidates where we needed them. In races where we had more than one quality candidate, we would wait to see who emerged as the nominee and then put our full support behind them through the general election.

With our group challenging so many longtime Democratic incumbents, we knew beating them all was not realistic, but they were all certainly going to be in a fight. Our first, and possibly most important, goal of the Campaign 2010 plan had been achieved.

In anticipation of potential issues the steering committee would have to address, I called for a meeting the Saturday following the close of qualifying. Since the party had to certify its candidates with the Secretary of State the following week, all ballot-related decisions had to be resolved. The two major issues were denial of ballot access and, as crazy as it may sound, how candidates' names would appear on the ballot.

The ballot name issue involved two high-profile candidates. Unlike the Democrats, the ALGOP had a longstanding policy of not allowing nicknames or titles to appear on the ballot. This prevented situations where, for example, an incumbent judge could be listed as "Judge John Doe" giving him an unfair advantage over a challenger. Another example would be someone qualifying as "John 'No New Taxes' Doe." This policy had been followed closely over the years unless the candidate could demonstrate that a nickname was how people referred to them on a daily basis. An example would be the longtime sheriff in Baldwin County, Huey "Hoss"

Mack. Since Mack had been known as Hoss for years, the party allowed it on the ballot. A great deal of consideration was given to a candidate as long as the reason was legitimate and did not set a bad precedent.

The first candidate to come before the committee was Tea Party darling Dale Peterson, who would become known for a YouTube video in which he carried a rifle and proclaimed he was the man to clean up Montgomery. Peterson had qualified to run for Commissioner of Agriculture and Industries and wanted to be listed on the ballot as "Dale 'Cowboy' Peterson." Decked out in a pair of boots, a big belt buckle, and a large cowboy hat, Peterson made the case that he was known around the state as "Cowboy" and was using this nickname on all of his campaign literature.

At this point, one of the members of the steering committee asked him a question: "When you go to church on Sundays, do the people there greet you as 'Dale' or as 'Cowboy'?"

After some hesitation, Peterson truthfully answered, "Dale."

The committee voted to disallow him from using the nickname on the ballot, Peterson accepted the committee's decision without any protest and went on to run a very interesting race. He finished third behind our nominee and the eventual commissioner, John McMillan, and the runner-up, Dorman Grace.

Another candidate, a state representative from Tuscaloosa named Robert Bentley, was also asking the committee for a unique listing on the ballot. Bentley, who had served with me in the Alabama House for eight years, was seeking the nomination for governor and he was, indeed, a medical doctor, a successful dermatologist. In fact, he once wrote me a prescription to treat poison ivy while we were on the House floor.

Dr. Bentley, as everyone called him, wanted to be able to list his title on the ballot—"Dr. Robert Bentley." Like Peterson, he had already printed his campaign literature and was even running a very effective television ad proclaiming that Alabama was sick and needed a doctor.

Bentley made a compelling argument as to why his title should be allowed on the ballot. As the committee deliberated, it was apparent the group was genuinely torn. It was pointed out that a few years prior, Dr. J. Lee Alley, a veterinarian, ran for agriculture commissioner as a Republican and was not allowed to use his title on the ballot. In the end, the committee disallowed Bentley's title strictly on the basis that it would break precedent and cause problems for future committees.

When informed of the decision, Bentley was visibly disappointed, which troubled me. After all, he was a colleague and friend. Of course now that Bentley's title is now "Governor," it is obvious that our decision did not have an adverse affect on his campaign.

Later that afternoon, after what was an extremely stressful day, my cell phone rang on the drive home and Bentley's name popped up on my screen. As I answered, I prepared myself to receive an earful regarding the decision of the steering committee earlier in the day. I was pleasantly surprised to hear a calm, comforting voice on the other end. Bentley simply wanted to let me know that he had contemplated the decision on his drive home to Tuscaloosa and fully respected it. He went on to say that with all I had on my plate, he didn't want me to worry about it and that he appreciated the job I was doing as chairman. I hung up the phone with an even greater respect for him.

Following the Peterson and Bentley issues, the final items on the steering committee's agenda that day were much more stressful and uncomfortable, to say the least. They dealt with the potential denial of ballot access for two candidates. One, State Senator Harri Anne Smith, was very high-profile and the committee's decision was awaited by the media in the Wiregrass who had sent reporters up to cover the proceedings. The second was a candidate named Chip McCallum who had qualified to run in a House seat in Vestavia held by Representative Jack Williams (R-Vestavia).

As discussed earlier, the case against Smith was based solely on her endorsement of Democrat Bobby Bright in the 2008 Second Congressional District race. State Representative Jay Love (R-Montgomery), the GOP nominee for the congressional seat and the very person who was hurt the most by her endorsement of Bright, appeared in person before the committee urging us to allow Smith to remain on the ballot as a Republican. In the end, however, her actions—for which she never apologized—were an act of treason in the minds of a majority of the committee. Smith would not be allowed to run as a Republican.

McCallum's candidacy was being challenged on the premise that he was really a Democrat simply running as a Republican because it was the only way he could win in the very conservative district. Documentation was produced showing campaign contributions he had made to a variety of Democrats in the state. The kicker was a contribution to Barack Obama's campaign. Not surprisingly, the members of the committee had a hard time understanding how someone proclaiming to be a Republican could have sent a campaign contribution to Obama less than two years prior.

McCallum appeared before the committee and professed to be a "lifelong Republican." Yet, under questioning by the committee members, he could not recall ever having financially supported a GOP candidate, had never attended a Republican meeting of any kind, and did not know the name of the chairman of the Jefferson County Republican Party. Even though he was a lawyer, he was not convincing in presenting his case. McCallum, like Smith, was denied ballot access.

Both Smith and McCallum eventually qualified as Independent candidates for the general election. Smith was reelected to her Senate seat while McCallum was soundly defeated by the Republican incumbent.

Because the ALGOP could not involve itself in Republican primary races, our team spent the next three months preparing for the general election. The most pressing task now was assembling the field team needed to implement the Victory program that Michael Joffrion, our political director, had been devising for months.

We had already decided to bring two of our top field representatives from the 2008 election cycle, Ryan Adams and Ryan Cantrell, back on board to assume the roles of deputy political directors. Since Adams's experience and contacts were in the northern half of the state, he was assigned to oversee the field team for the races from Birmingham north. The majority of Cantrell's experience was in the southern half of the state, particularly Montgomery and the Wiregrass, so he would be responsible for the group working on races south of Birmingham.

Joffrion and Ross divided the state into seven regions. This would require hiring seven field directors to manage the voter identification, turnout, and ballot security efforts in their respective districts. The regions were designed to include no more than three targeted House races and two targeted Senate races. Travel time had also been taken into account when carving up the regions to minimize drive times between districts. These staffers needed to be spending as much time on the ground as possible, and since we were reimbursing travel expenses, this was viewed as a cost-savings measure as well as a time-efficiency one.

By late April, the political team was conducting interviews for the seven positions. Ross and Joffrion had veto power, but Adams and Cantrell would be the direct superiors so they had to be comfortable with the hires. Plus, the job performances of the field directors would be a direct reflection on Adams and Cantrell, so it was in their best interest to choose wisely. Ross provided reports on their progress and I was impressed by how seriously they were taking this responsibility. They interviewed more than 30 applicants for the seven positions.

Throughout the election cycle, Joffrion and Ross instigated competition between the two Ryans, reporting on which group was knocking on more doors, making more phone calls, and registering more voters. A friendly rivalry developed between the northern team and the southern teams, which led to each group constantly working to outperform the other. This was good for morale but also translated into a massive amount of phone calls and doors hit by our field directors and their army of volunteers.

Between June and Election Day 2010, this group of hard-working young people made close to 900,000 volunteer-based phone calls and knocked on more than 175,000 doors in our targeted legislative districts. Even more amazing was the result: compared to voter turnout levels in these districts in previous election cycles, the turnout in 2010 was an impressive 9 percent higher.

I believe this effort alone made the difference in several legislative races, especially the close ones. It also lifted Republican voter turnout on the statewide ballot. There was no question our investment in Joffrion and his Victory program beginning back in early 2008 paid incredible dividends.

The field team was in place by early May so they could spend a few weeks in their regions meeting the candidates and getting a feel for the lay of the land. It was during this period that I was forced to take my focus away from the Campaign 2010 effort to deal with a variety of issues surrounding the gubernatorial race.

THE ISSUE CAUSING REPUBLICAN Party leadership the biggest headache at the time was a political action committee (PAC) that had been created by Marengo County Republican Party chairman Andy Renner, with lobbyist Claire Austin assisting in the shadows. We discovered that True Republican PAC, as it was called, was being financed via backchannels by the Alabama Education Association with funds totaling $1.4 million. Its goal was simple—do whatever it took to keep Bradley Byrne from being elected governor.

Byrne had been at odds with the AEA and Paul Hubbert for years while he served on the State Board of Education, in the Alabama Senate, and as chancellor of the Alabama Community College System. He had declared war on AEA after announcing his candidacy for governor and pledged to do all he could to minimize its influence in Montgomery. With the winner of the Republican primary more than likely heading to the governor's mansion, Hubbert decided to take offensive action against Byrne. True Republican PAC would be the mechanism used to launch his attacks.

Approximately one month prior to the June primary, vicious TV ads appeared across the state. They claimed Byrne believed in only a portion of the Bible and highlighted the fact that, prior to becoming a Republican, he had been a delegate for Bill Clinton in 1996. The ads were nasty, hard-hitting, and caused a firestorm in the Republican primary.

They placed me in a precarious position. On one hand, I was the chairman of the Alabama Republican Party and charged with maintaining party neutrality in primaries. On the other hand, a well-known Democratic union was financing television ads under the guise of a PAC with Republican in its name, causing a great deal of confusion among voters. After consulting other leaders in the ALGOP, the decision was made to publically condemn the actions of True Republican PAC and expose the organization to voters as a farce.

Naturally, the moment the ALGOP took this position, various factions within the party began crying foul and claiming I had only done it because I was secretly assisting Byrne's campaign. He had been painted as the establishment candidate and was backed by many of Governor Riley's supporters. Some incorrectly assumed, or claimed, that I was using my power within the ALGOP as a tool to swing the race in his favor. This was far from the truth.

The other Republican candidates in the race for governor were made aware of the circumstances and each agreed the ALGOP could not stand idly by while Democrats tampered with our primary. If the other side was misleading voters and running ads attacking them, they would have expected me to react in the same manner. I continue to stand by our actions and the decision to expose the Democrats.

Suffice it to say, the June 6th primary couldn't arrive soon enough. Everyone was anxious to begin working with our nominees, and I was ready to focus totally on the goal we had worked toward for more than three years.

IN ANTICIPATION OF PUTTING the final phase of Campaign 2010 into action, we planned a series of events in Montgomery for the weekend immediately following the primary. We notified all of the legislative candidates a couple of weeks prior and told them to hold that weekend open because if they emerged as the nominee, we wanted to brief them on our plans to assist them.

The Friday evening event was held at the Governor's Mansion, a meet-and-greet of sorts for the legislative nominees and their spouses. The plan was for them to get to know our staff, Senator Marsh, me, and, of course, Governor and Mrs. Riley. We had obviously met and spoken with many of the nominees during the candidate recruitment process and the primary, but now they were officially the Republican candidates and our path to taking the legislative majority.

The night was a huge success highlighted by a brief speech, more like a pep talk, delivered by Governor Riley. He very poignantly described what was at stake in the upcoming election. Like me, he strongly believed Republicans were on the brink of making history and that we were prepared like never before. He warned that the other side would not go down without a fight, so it was important the nominees work together with our team. He was very gracious in praising our efforts to raise money, develop a plan, and put us in a great position. I believe it was at this point the candidates fully realized they were involved in a historic journey that could change Alabama forever.

The following morning, we met as a group at a local hotel. The purpose was to unveil the full Campaign 2010 plan to our nominees for the first time. I opened up by making it clear that the Alabama Republican Party was prepared to commit more resources, financial and otherwise, to legislative campaigns than ever before in party history. But I also told them that the assistance was not an entitlement and that much was expected from them.

I had invited pollster Jimmy McLaughlin down from New Jersey to paint the picture of the current political landscape in the state. He also led a discussion on the types of messages that were resonating with voters and the importance of remaining on message. While I always kid McLaughlin about his Yankee accent, he did a nice job of introducing and articulating the intricacies of polling and how it can be used as an effective tool in a campaign. This proved quite helpful as we worked with candidates later in the year and used polling data as the basis for strategic decisions as the campaigns evolved.

After hearing from our mail vendor about how his firm was partnering with the ALGOP and the type of material he needed to design quality mail pieces, each member of our staff gave a brief presentation of their roles and responsibilities as related to Campaign 2010. It was vitally important that the candidates become familiar with the staffers who would be working with them and their campaigns on a day-to-day basis.

Finally, after a long morning of strategy discussion and outlining the plan, it was time for Marsh and me to have a very candid conversation with the group. We spent some time outlining our efforts leading up to election cycle, specifically the record amount of money we had raised for Campaign 2010.

It was imperative that the nominees fully understood the lengths to which we had gone to ensure their campaigns would be well-funded and organized. We also wanted to underscore the fact that the ALGOP would not be simply sending them a check to cover expenses. Instead of cash, the party would be providing in-kind services including direct mail, contrast television and radio advertisements, polling, opposition research, strategy and message development, as well as field staff to assist with voter identification, voter turnout, and ballot security.

We made it clear that we foresaw only a couple of reasons for the party to send a check. One was when it was cheaper for the campaign to purchase their own television and radio ads since the campaign could get the lowest unit rate from the stations, and the other was to cover the cost of half of the consulting fees they would be paying on a monthly basis, a rate we had previously negotiated with our consultants.

Once this part of the Campaign 2010 process had been outlined, we discussed the most uncomfortable but most important topic of the weekend. Even though we had more than $4 million at our disposal, there was no way we could provide resources in every legislative race on the ballot. It would spread us too thin, and we had learned our lesson the hard way not to dump money into races we couldn't win.

Utilizing the ranking system we developed through demographic research, voting trends, and polling data, we prioritized the districts based on our ability to win the race. The candidates running in the top-tier races could expect a full commitment from the ALGOP. I pointed out, however, that the rankings were fluid and that top-tier races could move down and lower-tier races could move up, based on a variety of factors, including how hard a candidate worked, raised local financial support, and followed directions from us. If survey data indicated a positive movement, then we would move them up a tier. Conversely, if a candidate did not work or do what we asked and the polls moved the wrong direction, so would their level of support.

Setting up the process in this manner served a dual purpose. Not only did it incentivize the candidates in the lower tier to work hard in an effort to improve their numbers, but it also sent a message to the top-tier candidates that the resources we would be providing would stop if they weren't pulling their weight. It showed all of them that we had no intention of providing anyone with a free ride.

After hearing at length about the process, the candidates were bleary-eyed but no doubt fully understood our position. We were viewing it very pragmatically and were going to go about it with a business-like approach. Marsh and I had both been burned in the past when we allowed an emotional attachment to a candidate to blind us to the big picture and we ended up wasting resources that, in some cases, cost us close races elsewhere. We were determined not to let that happen again.

Even though some parts of the plan may have seemed harsh, I believe the candidates appreciated our candor and understood what we were doing. We were going to be great partners and provide unprecedented support to candidates, but we were doing so according to a well-thought-out plan.

IN THE WEEKS FOLLOWING the candidate meeting, we began an aggressive polling schedule. We had to get a feel for where our candidates stood and, since we would not be running cookie-cutter type campaigns as we had attempted in 2006, we had to develop a clear understanding of issues affecting voters in each district. The data was also used to confirm that our targeted districts were correctly accessed.

Armed with a stack of fresh survey data, Marsh and I scheduled one-on-one meetings with targeted district candidates in late June; candidates in runoffs had to wait until their races concluded in mid-July. Ross had designated an entire week for these meetings and had organized the scheduling process. I spent two full days meeting with House candidates and Marsh spent two full days meeting with Senate candidates. To show her support for the Campaign 2010 plan, State Treasurer Kay Ivey, our nominee to take on incumbent Lieutenant Governor Jim Folsom, took time out of her busy schedule to attend the meetings with the Senate candidates.

The purpose of these meetings was to share the polling data we had collected and analyzed as well as provide the candidates with a detailed outline of the ALGOP's commitment to their race. As we struggled to develop the most effective way to accomplish this goal, we had the idea to provide them with a baseline budget that included polling, a basic direct mail program, consulting fees, GOTV assistance, and funds allocated to a media program. In the House, every targeted campaign's baseline budget from the party was about $70,000, and $100,000 was allocated to each targeted Senate race.

Creating a uniform commitment to every candidate served two purposes. First, it gave a clear picture of what they could, at a minimum, expect from the party, which, in turn, allowed their consultants to fill in the gaps in their own campaign plan with funding the candidates were raising in their own districts. It also gave Marsh and me a large amount of discretionary funding, approximately $600,000 for each house, to allocate as we saw fit. This was particularly helpful because we knew that some races would be more expensive than others. For instance, a strong Democratic incumbent might have a large war chest or the cost of media in a larger district could require more money. It also let the candidates know that we had the ability to devote more resources if they did their jobs.

As THE COMMITMENTS WERE being made and the campaigns were now out of the gates, the Alabama Republican Party would face one of the most difficult issues in its history.

Bradley Byrne had emerged from the gubernatorial primary race as the leading vote-getter, with Dr. Robert Bentley, to the surprise of many, edging out Tim James by a mere 167 votes. For the race to determine the runner-up in a statewide primary to have come down to less than 200 votes meant it was essentially a tie.

As one can imagine, talk of a recount began immediately and James soon made a formal decision to pursue this route. While I didn't blame James, it created a nightmare for the party. Alabama law was relatively clear on how to conduct a recount in a general election, but it was vague when it came to a recount in a primary, which is run by the political parties, and not the state. The fact that the recount was to determine the second-place finisher to claim a position in a runoff simply added more confusion.

Discussions with Secretary of State Beth Chapman, the state's highest-ranking elections official, and the party's legal counsel, Ed Allen, began the same day James announced his intentions. The first order of business was to determine how the ALGOP should handle the certification process. The law required us to certify the candidates for the runoff by the following week and we all knew there was no way for a statewide recount to be concluded in that time frame.

After rounds of discussions by all involved parties, it was decided that the ALGOP should certify Byrne and Bentley, as the top two vote-getters, to meet in a runoff. The James campaign resisted this decision since it would create one more legal hurdle for them to overcome if the recount process showed James was, in fact, the candidate with the second-highest vote total. In the hours leading up to the certification deadline, the James campaign was secretly deliberating whether they really wanted to go through with the recount. The campaign, not the state, would be responsible for all of the costs and there was no question it would be expensive and difficult to coordinate the effort in all 67 counties.

With the noon deadline looming, Ross, Philip Bryan, and I waited patiently in my office at the State House for a final decision from James. Ross had received word from a campaign insider that he believed James was on the brink of conceding defeat. The clock was ticking, though, and if we missed the noon deadline, the Republican Party would have failed to certify its candidates, which would have created an entirely different set of even bigger issues. So, at 11:40, the three of us began walking toward the Capitol, paperwork in hand, with still no definite answer from the James campaign.

Bryan had been holding off the eager media. As we turned the corner into the hallway leading to the Secretary of State's office, we were notified that James had just announced he would remain in the race and assume the responsibility of funding a recount. With only a few minutes to spare and members of the press looking on, I officially signed the documents certifying Byrne and Bentley as the candidates for the gubernatorial runoff in mid-July. If a recount uncovered a different result, we would be in uncharted waters.

In retrospect, most would assume that implementing Campaign 2010 was the most difficult task our team faced that year. But it wasn't. Coordinating a statewide recount without precedent to follow, a vague law on the subject, and lawyers across the state offering differing legal opinions was the most difficult.

Working in conjunction with the Secretary of State's office, it was our job to educate election officials and party leaders in all 67 counties on how to conduct a legal recount. We held a seminar in the State House for probate judges and county chairmen, which brought about more questions than answers. Our field team was forced to set aside the Victory program to aid in this process as well.

For two weeks in the middle of July, controlled chaos was the only way to describe the activities at party headquarters. Not only was our team desperately attempting to keep the process out of the ditch, they were also being berated by supporters of both the James and Bentley campaigns, each accusing them of trying to steal the election for the other candidate.

The Bentley campaign had a group of people in the office at all times monitoring the staff's every move. While I understood the pressure everyone was under, I was also irritated that anyone would accuse our team of impropriety. They were, at my strict instruction, striving to do their jobs and conduct this process in the most efficient, effective, and honest manner possible. Ross later admitted to me that he barely slept during the two weeks surrounding the recount. We both knew that if the situation wasn't handled properly, the Alabama Republican Party could be faced with the sort of disastrous split that had resulted in the 1986 Baxley-Graddick debacle in the Democratic Party. At that time, the leadership of the Alabama Democrats took its party nomination for governor away from Attorney General Charlie Graddick, who had finished first in a run-off, and awarded it instead to the more liberal Lieutenant Governor Bill Baxley, claiming illegal Republican crossover votes as its reason. The move created a massive rift within the party that resulted in the surprising election of Guy Hunt as Alabama's first Republican governor since Reconstruction.

Miraculously, over a three-day period, all 67 counties recounted the gubernatorial primary election ballots. Even more miraculously, it went off without a hitch. This was a true testament to the party leaders, specifically the Republican county chairmen, across the state. While our team worked to coordinate the effort from the state level, the local leaders were the ones who carried it out and deserve to be commended.

The recount, to the chagrin of the James campaign, resulted in a net increase of votes for Bentley. James's team had put forth a valiant effort in organizing their part of the recount, as did the Bentley campaign. I believe everyone walked away from what could have been a disastrous situation satisfied with the result.

WHILE THIS EVENT WILL only be a small footnote in the history of Alabama, it had the potential to be one of the most significant political events in our state's history. Frankly, the fact it will be a footnote suits me just fine. We had dodged a major bullet but now had to focus on what was to be a heated gubernatorial runoff election.

Bentley went on to handily defeat Byrne in the runoff election. Despite arguments concerning crossover voting—people who voted in the Democratic primary but then voted in the Republican runoff—and claims by the AEA that they had tipped the election in Bentley's favor by turning out 50,000 Democratic voters, the fact is the people of Alabama were drawn to Bentley's kind, folksy demeanor. For my part, I was relieved that we finally had a gubernatorial nominee and I had not presided over the implosion of the Alabama Republican Party.

I was pleased when Bentley later told David Azbell that he thought the recount process had been well-handled. "The folks at the Party did not take sides in any way," he said. "We knew that Bradley wanted Tim James in the run-off because the polls showed Bradley beating Tim James. We also knew that the polls showed Bradley losing to me. So we knew who he wanted to run against. Do I blame Tim for wanting a recount? No. The good thing about the recount was that it proved we had an honest election in the Republican Party. There was no doubt on the part of Tim James's supporters that we had won it."

While he had his own general election to worry about, Bentley dedicated a great deal of time leading up to the November election helping our Campaign 2010 effort. As the old saying goes, a rising tide lifts all boats, and he realized a strong showing at the top of the ticket could help lift many of these legislative candidates. While it was the right thing to do for the state and our party, there was never any doubt in Bentley's mind that a Republican majority in the House and Senate would make his job as governor much easier.

IN EARLY JUNE, MARSH and I were generally focused on 14 House races and 8 Senate races. As we moved into late July and early August, however, these numbers jumped to 20 and 12 respectively. The fact that we had quality candidates across the board and sentiment against President Obama was growing at a rapid pace brought more races into play. Energized by this development, Marsh and I increased our efforts to raise additional funds to ensure the additional races would be adequately funded. We called on Governor Riley to assist us in this fundraising push and, as always, he did.

Once again, I asked Jimmy McLaughlin to fly down to Alabama to meet with our team. He and his staff had compiled all of the polling information, including a round of surveys conducted following the runoff, into a spreadsheet. Data was added to a formula that allowed McLaughlin to rank, as scientifically as possible, the races based on where they stood at that time.

Marsh and I scheduled separate House and Senate presentations because the information was so sensitive, and it was vital our priorities remain internal among a very tight group. The House presentation came first, and I asked Representatives Greg Canfield of Vestavia and Mike Ball of Huntsville, Dax Swatek, Minda Campbell, and Ross to sit in. McLaughlin carefully outlined where each race stood and how they stacked up against the other races on our radar screen. While the rankings were not all that surprising, I do recall realizing for the first time that we had a real opportunity of winning every single race.

The other benefit of this meeting was that it was helping me decide how to allocate the discretionary funds set aside for House races. It was safe to assume we were going to be victorious in races like House District 9 in Morgan County, where Ed Henry had a commanding lead. We were also pleased to see candidates like Mike Jones of Andalusia, who was running to fill the seat vacated by retiring House Speaker Seth Hammett, performing well. Kerry Rich in House District 26, Mayor Dan Williams in House District 5, and Bill Roberts in House District 13 were all performing at a level where, without a significant mistake, they should win.

I recall being pleasantly surprised to see Barry Moore in House District 91 and Richard Baughn in House District 14 leading in their races. I was particularly interested in these races because our nominees were running against two of the strongest Democrats in the legislature—Terry Spicer of Elba and House Majority Leader Ken Guin of Carbon Hill.

Moore and Tim Howe had hit it off so well during the candidate recruitment that I assigned Howe as Moore's consultant. I knew Spicer's campaign would be extremely well-funded, so a competent and savvy consultant was a necessity. Based on my previous experience with him, I had no doubt Howe was the man for the job. When our polling that summer showed Moore leading, I couldn't have been more pleased. Defeating Spicer was a key in our quest to take the majority and change Montgomery.

Guin, since he served as the ranking Democrat in the House behind Hammett, was near the top of our wish list as well. Just as I had gained the ire of Democrats due to my role as House Minority Leader, Guin, as Majority Leader, was not a favorite of House Republicans.

A couple of years prior to the 2010 Election Cycle, it had been reported that Guin had been turning in the same time sheet for work he had supposedly done while holding two separate jobs at community colleges in his legislative district. After further investigation by the media, it was discovered that Guin, a practicing attorney, was collecting three paychecks from the state totaling more than $130,000 per year. This, coupled with the fact his district had been trending more and more Republican, gave us the perfect opportunity to defeat him.

Our nominee, Richard Baughn, had taken an interesting path to securing the Republican nomination. Baughn had spent his career driving a delivery truck for United Parcel Service, and his route took him all over District 14 on a daily basis. A friendly, soft-spoken individual, Baughn, a native of Lynn in Winston County, wasn't well-known in the other parts of the district. For those who did know him, however, he was a well-respected member of the community with a solid reputation. For years, he had watched Guin. The community college scandal finally prompted him to step out and challenge the longtime incumbent.

Not long after Baughn qualified with the ALGOP, State Senator Charles Bishop announced his retirement from the Senate but indicated he was also considering a run against Guin out of his sheer disgust for him. A sitting senator announcing his retirement to run for a House seat was unusual, if not unprecedented.

Bishop, who may be best known for punching the powerful Senate Rules Committee chairman Lowell Barron of Fyffe on the Senate floor after being called an S.O.B., decided to qualify for the House District 14 race just prior to the deadline in early April. This would pit two individuals with a shared goal of defeating Guin against one another in the primary; Baughn, a political newcomer, and Bishop, a former state agriculture commissioner, gubernatorial candidate, and state senator.

Because of their shared mission, the primary race between Baughn and Bishop was very cordial. Both men spent the majority of their time discussing their vision and position on important issues, but both, especially Bishop, never missed an opportunity to cast a stone at Guin.

When the polls closed on June 2nd, the newcomer, Baughn, had upset the seasoned veteran, Bishop, by a margin of 53 to 47 percent. This came as a shock to onlookers outside the district, but the voters within, in what was a common theme throughout the entire 2010 election, preferred the outsider over the longtime politician.

The next morning, Bishop drove Baughn around the district showing him locations he could utilize for large campaign signs. In fact, he told Baughn that he could replace every Bishop sign with one of his. In the months that followed, Bishop proved to be one of Baughn's most ardent supporters, providing him with campaign funds and introducing him to people throughout the district.

All of the external factors were favoring Baughn, which, coupled with his intensely strong work ethic and likeable personality, meant there was no question he was going to give Guin all he could handle.

After McLaughlin concluded the House presentation at the party headquarters, I struggled to contain my optimism. With more than 90 days to go, I knew much could change. It was imperative that we keep our foot on the gas.

After a short lunch break, the Senate presentation began. I was forced to head back to Auburn, so this meeting included Marsh, Swatek, Ross, Campbell, and Senators Jabo Waggoner and Scott Beason. Beason had indicated to Marsh that he wanted to become more active in the takeover process and both agreed that there was no reason to duplicate efforts. Including him in this meeting was Marsh's way of offering a place on the team.

The polling data in the Senate wasn't as positive as in the House, but nonetheless it gave the people in the room plenty of reasons to be excited. The numbers that jumped off the projection screen were in Senate District 4, where Republican nominee Paul Bussman was leading Democrat Senate Majority Leader Zeb Little by 17 points.

Some 18 months earlier, Little was charged with a DUI after a hit-and-run along Interstate 65 just south of Birmingham. While he had gone through the motions of accepting responsibility for his actions, the incident didn't surprise many people in his home county of Cullman. The highly publicized DUI, along with the fact that Cullman County was becoming one of the most conservative areas in the state, had opened the door for a potential challenger.

Bussman, a local dentist and well-respected member of the Cullman community, was the perfect man for the seat. He had emerged from a hard-fought primary and runoff election against local Tea Party activist Patricia McGriff and a gentleman named Tom Beason—interestingly, the father of Senator Scott Beason.

The primary election had been particularly nasty as the elder Beason claimed that Bussman, the frontrunner, had operated his dental practice illegally without a license for a period of a few years. He also had researched a divorce Bussman had been involved in years before and discussed it with potential voters at every opportunity. Bussman, to his credit, patiently explained the details surrounding both issues anytime he was asked, but never attacked his opponents. He stayed true to this position even as Little launched vicious attacks in the general election.

McLaughlin's presentation also showed that former ALGOP Vice

Chairman and Jasper businessman Greg Reed had a comfortable lead over his Democratic opponent in Senate District 5. Reed, it was predicted, should cruise to victory in the general election as long as no devastating mistakes were made. This news had come as a relief to everyone as Reed had prevailed over University of Alabama football equipment manager, Thad Turnipseed, by a mere 93 votes in the GOP primary. After briefly considering a recount, Turnipseed conceded to Reed a week following the primary election. The seat, which had opened up as a result of Senator Charles Bishop's retirement, leaned Republican, and holding it was key to Republicans winning a majority in the Senate.

The other piece of exciting news was in Senate District 9 where a young chicken farmer from Arab, Clay Scofield, had a large lead over the sitting Democratic probate judge in Marshall County. A win in this district would be particularly symbolic as it had been held for many years by the former President Pro Tempore of the Senate, Hinton Mitchem. The district had also evolved into a solid Republican area and taking it was believed to be a necessary step toward a GOP majority.

Scofield, not yet 30 years old, had run a respectable race throughout a primary and a runoff. The primary pitted Scofield against three other exceptional candidates—Don Spurlin, an Albertville contractor, Tony Cochran, a CPA also from Albertville and John Wilson, a retired engineer living in Huntsville. After a hard-fought but clean primary, Scofield and Spurlin faced off in the runoff. Scofield beat Spurlin by a mere 613 votes.

At the conclusion of McLaughlin's presentation, it was apparent that there were 12 Senate races—10 targeted districts and two priority hold districts—where Republicans had a legitimate shot at winning. With the field of targeted districts growing in both the House and Senate, I instructed our team to began reworking budgets and expanding our Victory program to include the new targets.

As THE ELECTION SEASON moved from July into August, races began to heat up like an Alabama summer day. While the plan called for the majority of the campaigns to hold back until after Labor Day, we decided, after encouragement from Swatek and McLaughlin, for a handful of races to begin strategically running ads during August. In some races, we knew we were going to have to draw a deep contrast between our candidate and the Democratic incumbent. In other words, we knew we were going to have to go negative.

We spent a good amount of time and resources in August and early September building up positive name identification for our Republican candidates running in races that would be dominated by contrast ads in the last few weeks. This would help minimize the backlash that comes when a campaign goes negative. It would have been a fatal mistake for us to begin developing a contrast between candidates without first outlining all of the positive aspects of our Republican challenger, especially for first-time candidates who weren't well-known throughout their districts.

While we initiated this plan in a variety of races, two perfect examples come to mind. The first was in House District 27 in Marshall County where Wes Long was challenging Democratic incumbent Jeff McLaughlin.

McLaughlin was a respected member of the Alabama House of Representatives. A Harvard law graduate, his opinion on most matters was often taken into consideration. Back home in his district, McLaughlin fit the role of Jimmy Stewart in *Mr. Smith Goes to Washington* perfectly, and he had even landed the role of Atticus Finch in the Guntersville Community Theater production of *To Kill a Mockingbird*.

While portraying himself as a conservative Democrat back home in Marshall County, McLaughlin was, in fact, one of the most liberal members of the Alabama House. With Marshall County becoming a Republican stronghold, we knew Long could win if we could expose McLaughlin as the true liberal that he was.

Before we began developing the contrast between the conservative Long and the liberal McLaughlin, we had to tell Long's story. In late July, working with consultant Scott Stone, party staffers Sidney Rue, Kate McCormick, and Minda Campbell traveled to Guntersville to coordinate a film and photo shoot with Long and his family. This was done so positive television ads, radio ads, and direct mail pieces could run in the district throughout August.

This group was traveling the state performing the same services for the majority of our candidates in targeted races, just as they had in the House District 40 race for K. L. Brown. By coordinating production and handling the photo shoots in-house, we realized significant cost savings, allowing us to put more funds back into campaigns. These ladies spent a great deal of time away from home and worked in the summer heat to complete this massive endeavor. As someone who had spent his career in the advertising business, I was thoroughly impressed by the work ethic and the quality product.

The ads that began running for Long were evidence of the work by Campbell, McCormick, and Rue. After coordinating with Stone on scripts and content, Long's story of a high school star quarterback moving on to play under legendary Coach Gene Stallings at the University of Alabama was unveiled. Following his undergraduate years at Alabama, Long had gotten a law degree, started a law practice, and opened a variety of thriving businesses in the Guntersville area.

Long, 33, was a fresh face seeking elected office for the first time and a conservative, pro-business Republican who knew how to create jobs. He was cast as the outsider who wanted to reform Montgomery and do his part to improve the economy. The four-week "campaign within a campaign" worked like a charm as his positive name identification among voters grew significantly.

Interestingly, Ross had grown up and played sports with Long, but he also knew McLaughlin well and his family was close to McLaughlin's family. As the strategy was being developed for the final phase of the campaign, which included hammering McLaughlin on issues related to his votes on illegal immigration, the legislative pay raise, and tax increases, Ross knew his involvement could affect those relationships with McLaughlin. I noticed Ross taking added steps to ensure the attacks remained completely issue-based, which we did in all of our targeted races. He even coined a phrase we used throughout the campaign—"Jeff McLaughlin: A nice guy in Guntersville; a liberal Democrat in Montgomery."

McLaughlin, who had never faced a serious challenger, took it all very personally. His frustration at the fact that his record was being exposed was mounting, and it came to a head when there were reports of an automated call being placed in the district claiming McLaughlin beat his wife. While he and local Democrats immediately began pointing fingers in our direction, we were dumbfounded. We knew we had not been a part of the alleged call, but we could not imagine any other organization commissioning it either. To this day, the only reports of individuals receiving the call were from McLaughlin supporters.

To complicate matters, our polling firm was named McLaughlin & Associates; the firm had been conducting surveys in the district, as it had across the state. Shortly afterward, I received a stern letter from Jeff McLaughlin lambasting me for attempting to confuse voters. I wrote him back citing that I had no control over the fact that the owner of the polling firm we had been using for years happened to share the same last name as his. This was evidence that our efforts were working.

In an attempt to calm McLaughlin, Ross asked my permission to call him and explain that not only did we have nothing to do with the alleged robo-call, but that the surveys we had conducted were benchmark polls commissioned in all of our targeted races around the state. He believed he could reassure McLaughlin because of their relationship. I gave him the go- ahead and received a call back from Ross 10 minutes later. The conversation had not gone well.

After reaching McLaughlin, exchanging greetings and explaining the fact we had nothing to do with the call, Ross was taken aback when McLaughlin went into a tirade. He was upset about the mail pieces, television spots, and radio ads and refused to believe Ross. He had been looking for someone to tee off on and, unfortunately, Ross was the recipient.

It was obvious McLaughlin wanted to believe the alleged calls had actually occurred and the ALGOP was responsible for them because the controversy was allowing him to play the role of victim. Articles ran in the local newspapers, and, despite Long and the party denying any knowledge of the calls, and with no evidence to support it, the insinuation was made that we were responsible. This would be a common theme throughout the campaign as Long faced an uphill battle with the local media. It served as a reminder that changing the status quo is never easy.

ANOTHER HIGH-PROFILE RACE IN which we built early and strong identification for our candidate in preparation for later developing a contrast was in Senate District 27, which included parts of Lee, Russell, and Tallapoosa counties. This race pitted longtime Auburn resident Tom Whatley against five-term Democrat Ted Little, also of Auburn.

Whatley had an interesting journey to the Republican nomination even though he was unopposed in the primary.

Whatley had been known in and around Montgomery for years. After receiving a degree in public administration from Auburn University and graduating from the Thomas Goode Jones School of Law, he had served as a staffer at the Alabama Public Service Commission and later as chief of staff for State Supreme Court Chief Justice Sue Bell Cobb. Until 2010, Whatley, also a longstanding and decorated member of the Alabama National Guard, had been a Democrat. With a growing distaste for President Obama and the directions of the state and national Democratic Party, Whatley made the bold decision to run as a Republican against Senator Ted Little. This decision was questioned by many Montgomery insiders who knew him as a Democrat and, admittedly, by some Republicans in Lee County.

Senators Marsh and Waggoner spoke with Whatley on several occasions and felt confident of his motives, as well as his convictions regarding the Republican Party and its principles. I had known Whatley and his family for years and understood them to be conservatives at heart.

As a show of loyalty to his new party, Whatley drove to Jacksonville the weekend prior to the special election in House District 40 and spent the day knocking on doors throughout the district with our staff and a group of volunteers. He understood that actions would speak louder than words, and many leaders in the party were noticing. With the stamp of approval from Marsh and other Senate GOP leaders, Whatley qualified to run.

Since he had no primary opposition, Whatley used this time to raise campaign funds. A relentless worker on the campaign trail, he had impressive success at raising money, especially given the fact that he was running against an entrenched Democratic incumbent. He also put together a strong campaign team, which was to be led by my friend and former teammate on the Phil Williams campaign, Joey Ceci. Whatley had known Ceci for years and knew he was the kind of consultant who, with adequate resources, could put him in position to win.

In early August, we began working with Ceci and his team on a strategic plan. Marsh agreed to release a large portion of the funds he had allocated for the race with the understanding that if Whatley was unable to move the numbers over the next month, he might be forced to make a tough decision on whether to continue funding the race.

This motivated everyone. Rue, McCormick, and Campbell were dispatched to the district to handle the film and photo shoot. Ceci worked with our team to develop the concept and scripts for the ads that would air in the coming weeks. It was important we get the message exactly right immediately out of the gate.

As was the case with most candidates in our targeted races, Whatley was known in his hometown but our polling showed the large majority of respondents outside of Auburn had never heard of him.

Some political experts argue that poor name identification is bad, but in the current political climate our view was that it was a blessing. We believed it gave us the opportunity to cast the candidate in the best light because, as the old saying goes, you never get a second chance to make a first impression. If we played our cards right, we could substantially increase Whatley's positive name identification, a necessity if we had any hope of creating a believable contrast between him and the popular incumbent.

The television advertisement Ceci and our team produced was perfect, especially given the quick turnaround required to get on television through most of the month of August. Sticking with our theme, Whatley was cast as the outsider with the experience needed to fix the economy. We also had the added benefit of highlighting his military service and sense of country. The ad ran continuously for several weeks and was reinforced by direct mail pieces.

We polled the district again with just over six weeks remaining in the campaign. Our plan had worked. Whatley's positive name identification had been raised significantly and the data indicated that only 40 percent of poll respondents said they would support Little, so the path to victory was clear. If the second phase of our plan worked—to develop a deep contrast between the two candidates based on the issues the voters of District 27 cared most about—then Whatley could win. Our optimism continued to grow.

As LABOR DAY CAME and went, all the campaigns across the state were in full swing. Coordinating them was challenging, so the arrangement we had made with the consulting teams overseeing the day-to-day operations of each one was critical. Joffrion and our political team were having weekly calls with each campaign along with the field director over the candidate's region to discuss the progress of the Victory program in the district. We wanted to make certain the weekly goals were being hit and the candidate had ownership in the process. The last thing a field director wanted to do was get on one of these weekly calls and have to announce to the group that he hadn't met his weekly phone-call and door-knocking quotas, which at this point were in the thousands.

With the majority of the fundraising efforts and on-location film and photo shoots with the candidates complete, Rue and McCormick began to shift their talents more toward the political operations, including media production. Campbell was still writing scripts and producing television ads at a furious pace. During any given week, Campbell, with help from Rue and McCormick, was writing, producing, and editing as many as six different television ads for six different campaigns. The team produced more than 60 ads for 22 campaigns in a three-month period with an average cost of just under $1,000 each. In most campaigns, a single ad costs a minimum of $10,000, so we were putting out top quality products at literally a tenth the cost of most of our opponents' ads.

Our effort to produce quality television ads for our candidates was more successful than we could have imagined and resulted in the most public and effective display of our support. Campbell and her team went out of their way to make sure the needs of the candidates were met when shooting spots and gave them the "star treatment" whenever possible.

When Terri Collins filmed her television commercials in mid-summer, temperatures were over 100 degrees. But the ads would air in the fall, so

Collins needed to be dressed in sweaters and warm clothes. Campbell and the camera crew would set up each shot while Collins waited in the car with the air conditioner running full blast. At the last possible second, they would film her for a minute or two then put her back in the cool car. If they took too long to get a shot, Collins's make-up would begin to melt in the heat.

Campbell also showed great resourcefulness when needed, such as the time we got involved in Kurt Wallace's campaign in south Alabama late in the race and at the same time Lynn Greer was being attacked by his opponent near the Tennessee line. Joey Ceci, Greer's consultant, wanted to film an ad that showed his "opponent" from behind, so Campbell had Wallace serve as the stand-in when his commercial shoot was complete. Wallace, who had never met Greer, would appear in the ad for his future colleague in a race that was occurring hundreds of miles away.

We had also expanded our communications shop to coordinate the media relations efforts in multiple races. With Bryan coordinating, deputy communications director Meg Eldridge was responsible for all of the statewide GOP and individual campaigns online media. An elaborate e-mail system allowed us to send mass e-mails into specific districts, so Eldridge was constantly dropping press releases and messages into our candidates' districts. If their opponent came out with an ad attacking our Republican candidate, we would often have a response to the press and a large group of voters in the district within an hour. Our ability to quickly and effectively respond and stay one step ahead of the other side from a communications standpoint was critical. Bryan and Eldridge, with assistance from Blakely Logan, were mastering the craft and keeping the Democrats on the defensive.

With more than 20 campaigns running simultaneously, Joffrion and Campbell devised a system to coordinate the media spots and mail pieces. An extra-large dry erase board was mounted on the wall and color-coded calendars denoted when spots were to be filmed, edited, and aired as well as when each mail piece was to hit mailboxes in each district. Each member of the team consulted those calendars constantly to know what was happening when on each campaign. It wasn't sophisticated, but it worked.

While he was overseeing the party operations and coordinating with the campaigns to keep Marsh and me constantly updated, Ross was also responsible for tracking the budgets in each individual race. He developed a spreadsheet containing the budgets for all targeted races. Working with our bookkeeper, Kasie Nimm, Ross would attribute every campaign-related invoice our office received to the corresponding campaign. Nimm would pay the invoice and produce an in-kind letter to be provided to the campaign so they could show it on their campaign finance reports. Ross would then deduct the invoice amount from the working total for the specific campaign.

A few months before the election, Ross was sending updated budget information on all House races to me and of all Senate races to Marsh on a weekly basis. As we got closer to Election Day, budgets were updated and delivered daily. Ross also sent updates to the campaign consultants so they would know how much was left on their "tab." This was necessary for budgetary reasons, but it also served as a constant reminder to all candidates of the vast amount of money we were investing in them. In every targeted race, the Alabama Republican Party was by far the campaign's largest contributor.

As we reached mid-September, we discovered races that had not previously been in our top tier. These races were trending at levels that demanded a closer look, and one was House District 21 in Madison County where Jim Patterson was challenging Democratic incumbent Randy Hinshaw. Representative Mike Ball (R-Madison) had been telling me for days that we needed to poll the race. Based on information he was hearing on the ground, Patterson had been running a fantastic campaign, working extremely hard, and was in a position to win if he had the necessary resources. Because I trusted Ball's judgment, I made the call to survey the race. It would turn out to be a wise use of our resources.

Patterson had experience campaigning in Madison County. In 1988, he had been elected to the county school board, making him the first Republican elected countywide since Reconstruction. He was now working to be a part of flipping the legislature. I liked Patterson and wanted to help him win the seat, but I also knew I had to keep my emotions out of the process and make the decision strictly based on our ability to win the race.

When the polling data came back a few days later, it turns out that Ball, a former state trooper and investigator, was right on the mark. Patterson was slightly trailing but was in a position to win. Ross reached out to Patterson and campaign consultant Kal Barber on my behalf and told them we would make a large commitment to the race. It was music to their ears as they were confident in their ability to win and just needed the resources to make it happen. I was thrilled to help, and Patterson ended up being one of the candidates who was most appreciative of our efforts.

Because Patterson and Barber had done such a quality job with the campaign to this point, I told Ross to allocate the funds we had designated to them on an as-needed basis and provide any media resources required.

Soon, two more races we had originally viewed as long shots were looking to become real possibilities for Republican pick-ups in the House. One was in House District 7, which included Lawrence and a portion of Winston counties, where newcomer Ken Johnson was challenging Democratic incumbent Jody Letson. The other was in House District 29, in Etowah County, where another newcomer, Becky Nordgren, was facing longtime House incumbent Jack Page.

With a little over a month to go, signs were pointing toward a possible Republican sweep. I decided to take a chance on these two races. We informed both candidates that we would be sending funds for a direct mail program the final weeks of the campaign and also shifted our turnout efforts to include their districts. In the end, Patterson, Johnson, and Nordgren turned Democratic seats into Republican ones.

Marsh was also working on expanding into newly targeted districts. Most exciting to Marsh and the other members of the Republican leadership team was Senate District 8 in northeast Alabama where Shadrack McGill, a young man from the small town of Woodville, was giving the most powerful member of the Alabama Senate, Lowell Barron, all he could handle. After a poll, Marsh committed $125,000 to McGill's campaign. The possibility of taking out Barron had Marsh giddy.

There is no doubt that McGill was a political novice. A small-business owner, he was tired of added government regulation and disappointed in the current direction of the state and country. A principled person with a deep faith, he felt called to get involved to make a difference for his children and future generations. He was not motivated by power, prestige, or notoriety. All McGill wanted to do was his part to make Alabama a better place to live.

McGill qualifying to run against Barron back in April had gone largely unnoticed by many of the political insiders around the state. After all, Barron would have access to unlimited financial support and was likely the best-known politician in northeast Alabama. He was renowned for "bringing home the bacon" to his district, so the politicos were quick to dismiss McGill's candidacy. What transpired can only be described as a modern-day David vs. Goliath contest.

Like many first-time candidates, McGill spent the first several months of the campaign doing all he knew to do—meeting and talking to anyone he could find. He accepted speaking engagements at every nook and cranny across the district and spent afternoons and weekends campaigning door-to-door. McGill's work ethic, coupled with an honest and likeable demeanor, was quietly resonating with voters. He was the antithesis of Barron, which for many in the area was a breath of fresh air.

Unfortunately, Barron and his cronies soon caught onto the fact that McGill was gaining ground and resorted to their old tricks. For example, late one night, two intoxicated prostitutes knocked on McGill's door. Whether there was a photographer hiding in the bushes, no one will ever know, but after consulting with his wife, he felt the best thing for him to do was to take them home, which he did. More incidents followed. A frivolous lawsuit was filed against McGill's business, a car was driven through the front door of his office, and McGill felt that he was being followed. While nothing was directly traced back to Barron, it didn't take a rocket scientist to realize it was not simple happenstance.

Undeterred, McGill pushed forward, determined to rise above the backward political practices that had haunted that part of the state for decades.

As news of McGill's unrelenting campaign spread, Marsh, Waggoner, and Beason had taken notice. Beason traveled to the district to begin mentoring McGill, Waggoner set him up with a quality consulting team, and Marsh decided to fund the race. Two impressive television ads were quickly produced to increase his name identification in the district. A full-fledged campaign had been initiated. While we knew we would never be able to match the money Barron would spend, we did believe that McGill and his story, if properly delivered to the voters in the district, would put him in a position to win. If we were successful, it would be one of the greatest upsets in the history of Alabama politics.

ANOTHER SENATE RACE THAT had come into play was Senate District 10, which encompassed Etowah and a portion of Cherokee counties. Perhaps one of the most impressive candidates the Republican Party fielded in 2010 was running as our nominee in this race. His name was Phil Williams, not to be confused with the Phil Williams who had won the special election in House District 6 in 2009. Williams was the in-house counsel for a Fortune 500 company located in Gadsden where he also had been an area Young Life leader as well as a decorated member of the U.S. military. He was challenging Larry Means, a reasonably popular Democratic incumbent.

Williams, an extremely intelligent and well-spoken individual, had met with Ross and Waggoner earlier in the year to discuss his intentions to seek the Senate seat. The three were highly impressed. In fact, one Republican senator told me that Means had remarked that he would vote for Williams if he were not also running. This was a testament to the kind of person Williams is and, after meeting with him, Marsh wanted to do all he could to assist him.

Williams's consultant was Tim Howe, and our team worked with him to develop a plan to close the gap that existed between Williams and Means. We believed that if the voters got to know Williams, he would instantly become a hit.

Marsh released funding, and we pounded all the message points we needed to introduce Williams to the voters of Senate District 10. When we received the poll we had commissioned to gauge Williams's progress, it indicated his positive name identification had risen dramatically, but a large voter support gap remained between him and Means.

At this point, Marsh was faced with a very tough decision. He met with Williams shortly thereafter and informed him that he was having a hard time justifying continued funding of the race, especially with so many other hotly contested races around the state. He told Williams that if something changed or if he was able to close the gap on his own, we would get back in the race. Williams, always the gentleman, fully understood and graciously thanked Marsh for all he had done for him up until that point. They agreed to stay in close touch, with Ross and Howe also monitoring his progress.

One month later, Williams caught the break he needed. Senator Means, along with 10 other individuals, was indicted on federal charges alleging he was a part of a vote-buying scheme to legalize electronic gambling in Alabama. This news not only sent shock waves throughout the state, but particularly throughout Senate District 10. As one would imagine, having Means on the front page of the local papers allegedly connected with a corruption scandal had a tremendous negative impact on his reelection campaign. It also drew a stark contrast between Means and the squeaky-clean Williams. Marsh quickly reengaged Campaign 2010 into Williams's campaign. This was yet another opportunity we had to capitalize on if we were going to make history.

WITH NOVEMBER 2ND FAST approaching and our campaign plans being implemented, we also began bracing ourselves for the attacks on our candidates we knew would inevitably come. In preparation, Swatek had plotted out as many of the attacks that he could anticipate so we would be prepared for any scenario. While the onslaught of coordinated attacks we expected from the Democrats never materialized, they did begin to come in some of the higher-profile races.

One was in House District 14 where Richard Baughn continued to have a solid lead over Democratic House Majority Leader Ken Guin. Up to this point, our campaign plan against Guin was working like a charm.

Because Guin had been collecting more than $130,000 a year from the taxpayers, we believed it important to point out the lifestyle he was leading as a result. We hired a helicopter to fly with a photographer over his mansion in Carbon Hill and also took a photo of the Porsche SUV he had recently purchased for his wife. A mail piece sent into the district pointed out that the car cost more than double the average household income in the district.

In an attempt to get his campaign back on track, Guin had convinced Baughn's ex-wife to appear in a television commercial to talk about what a bad person she thought he was. According to Baughn, he had gone through a difficult divorce following his now ex-wife's battle with some personal issues. Baughn had been awarded full custody of their two children, whom he was raising as a single father.

When Guin's ad began airing on Birmingham television stations and on cable systems throughout the district, Baughn and his children were devastated. Not only did it stir up a sea of emotions for them, but their unfortunate family troubles were now on the air for all to see.

> [Video: Lisa Baughn sitting in office setting speaking to camera]
> Lisa Baughn: Richard Baughn is not the man he pretends to be.
> [Graphic: Lisa Baughn—Married to Richard Baughn for 25 years]
> Lisa Baughn: The night that I told my husband, Richard, that I had been diagnosed with lupus, he gave me a set of car keys, and he showed me the door.
> Richard told me you wouldn't believe the power and the perks he would have if elected to this job.
> [Graphic: Photo of Richard Baugh in UPS delivery uniform with words Richard Baughn—Power Perks Money Control]
> Lisa Baughn: He's in it for the power, the money and the control.

Because we were so interested in the race, but more importantly because our team and I had grown to truly care for Baughn and his children, we sprang into action. A media buyer had tipped us off to the general content of the ad the night before it began running, so we had a little more time than usual, but not much. Campbell immediately scheduled a film crew for the following morning. The plan was to meet Baughn and his two children, Katie and Cory, both college students, at the Birmingham Botanical Gardens as early as possible to film a response ad.

After the film shoot was planned, we needed a script. It was decided that the proper response would simply feature Baughn's children talking about their father. No mention at all of the ex-wife and mother. At around 11 P.M. the night before the shoot, Ross, who generally was involved in simply reviewing and approving scripts written by Swatek, Campbell, and me, e-mailed a draft that was right on target. It called for the children to talk about the character traits Baughn had instilled in them as they grew up, witnessing the manner in which he treated others. The ad closed with the two stating how proud they were of their father. I refined the script, editing it for time, assigned lines to the two children and sent it back via e-mail. Swatek and Campbell made some minor changes and within 20 minutes, we had a finished script ready to shoot the next day.

It may have been the fastest television script I've ever been involved in writing, but it turned out to be one of the most effective ads of the entire campaign.

> Richard Baughn For State Representative
> :30 Television "Family"
> Katie and Cory on camera
> Katie: *Growing up, our dad Richard Baughn taught us some important lessons in life.*
> Cory: *Christian values . . . and to lead by example*
> Katie: *To have strength and courage when you face adversity*
> Cover video of Katie, Cory and Richard on front porch
> Katie Voice Over: *Like all families, we've had our share good times and tough times.*
> Cover video of Richard and family with puppies; Richard and Cory loading wood
> Cory Voice Over: *But our dad taught us that honesty and integrity are true tests of a person's character.*
> Cover video Richard with farmer and tractor; video of Richard at firehouse

Katie Voice-Over: *As we've watched Dad campaign, we've seen him practice what he's preached to us for so many years.*
Cory and Katie on camera
Cory: *We're proud of you, Dad.*
Announcer: *Richard Baughn. A new direction for Alabama.*

Campbell met Baughn, his children and the film crew the following morning. Campbell drove the video to G2 Productions in Montgomery, where most of our television spots were produced, and directed the editing process. By 3 P.M., the spot was approved by our team and out the door to the television station. Amazingly, we had our response on the air only one day after Guin's attack ad had been launched. Our ad pulled the rug out from underneath Guin's campaign ploy.

AT THE SAME TIME, our party's gubernatorial nominee and my House colleague, Robert Bentley, was polling through the roof and outdistancing his Democrat opponent by a mile. His campaign ads, in which he looked at the camera and spoke directly to the voters in a very sincere and heartfelt manner, were proving effective as was his unique pledge to forgo his salary as governor until Alabama's unemployment rate had dropped. Bentley was proving so popular that we enlisted him to aid our Campaign 2010 efforts. In addition to appearing with and touting our legislative candidates during his travels, Bentley recorded a radio ad that we ran on stations across the state. In the ad, he stressed the need for voters to elect a Republican legislature to work with him in Montgomery. I am sure the coattail effect that resulted helped many of our candidates into office.

The final ten days of the campaign cycle were a complete blur. Our team, myself included, was exhausted, but the smell of victory was keeping us intensely motivated. It is at this stage of the campaign process where the GOTV program goes into full swing. We had been identifying our voters in districts across the state since early June and it was now time to begin the process of turning them out to vote.

This is accomplished through a variety of avenues, including television, radio, automated telephone calls, and direct mail. In my opinion, however, there is nothing more effective than direct person-to-person contact either over the phone or at their front door. You simply cannot put a price tag on it.

It was for this reason that I had set aside $500,000 for the Victory program developed by Michael Joffrion. We knew we could spend all the money in the world attempting to convince voters to vote for our candidates over the airways and through the mail, but it would all be worthless if we couldn't convince those voters to go and vote on Election Day.

Fortunately for us, President Obama had created a great deal of voter intensity among Republican voters. This meant we could count on voters who regularly turned out to vote, even in non-presidential election years, to show up at the polls. We could also motivate a good portion of the ones who don't normally vote in every election to turn out as well. The focus of our Victory program, therefore, was on the identified Republican voters we knew only rarely turned out to vote. If we could inspire them to show up on Election Day then, not only would our legislative candidates benefit greatly, but so would all Republican candidates.

The excitement surrounding Campaign 2010, along with the frustration with Obama, had also made it easier for us to recruit volunteers. Our field directors had amassed armies of them across the state, all of whom were ready to make as many phone calls and knock on as many doors as possible in the days leading up to the election. I had no doubt that this would be a very significant advantage for us over the Democrats.

The evidence of this could not have been clearer the morning of Election Day. I had been forced to remain in Auburn that morning and had planned to head up to ALGOP Headquarters after lunch. Birmingham's WBRC, one of the state's most powerful television stations, had invited both Alabama Democratic Party Chairman Joe Turnham and me to appear on the widely viewed "Good Day Alabama" morning show and make election predictions. Because I could not be there, I had asked Ross to attend in my absence.

Ross met Turnham in the green room where they nervously discussed the topic of the day. As they were brought onto the set, Rick Journey, longtime anchor and the station's main political reporter, outlined the direction of his questioning as he had just wrapped up an interview with Birmingham-Southern political science professor Natalie Davis. Ross couldn't suppress a grin because she had predicted the Democrats would remain in power. He had been following the polling data closely and was getting numbers from the field throughout the week that suggested otherwise.

As the live interview began, Journey directed a question to Turnham on what his party had been doing in preparation for Election Day. Turnham explained that he was excited about all of the volunteers they had knocking on doors and making phone calls across the state to increase turnout among Democratic voters.

The Alabama Democrats had issued a press release the week prior bragging that their team had knocked on more than 20,000 doors over the course of the campaign. Ross knew this, so when the same question was directed to him, he gave a similar response but added that the Alabama Republican Party had knocked on more than 32,000 doors . . . the weekend prior to the election. This was an incredible number and the look on Turnham's face said it all. They had knocked on 20,000 doors during the entire campaign and we had hit 32,000 in just one weekend.

As Campaign 2010 was winding down, I was confident it had been carried out perfectly. It was a great plan, but we had backed it up by assembling an outstanding team, setting fundraising records, recruiting an unparalleled class of candidates, and running multiple campaigns in targeted districts . . . all in a coordinated effort to make history by taking control of the Alabama Legislature for the first time in 136 years.

I was confident that Campaign 2010 had worked. Only when the polls closed in a few hours would we know just how well.

17

UNPRECEDENTED SUCCESS

After years of planning, thousands of miles traveled across the state, and countless man hours invested into hundreds of personal meetings, fundraising, and recruiting of candidates, the Campaign 2010 plan had been closely followed and fully implemented. The campaign mail had been delivered, the radio and television spots aired, the phone calls made, the doors knocked on, and the campaign messages delivered.

It now came to down to one day. November 2, 2010. Election Day.

I knew that nothing of this magnitude had been attempted in Alabama politics, so our team was operating in uncharted waters. But I also knew that the plan was solid and that we had put ourselves in the best possible position to make history. Now, all that remained was for the voters of Alabama to decide if we would be successful. In a larger sense, they would decide if the culture of politics in Montgomery would change or if champions of the status quo would prevail.

When the ballots were counted, voters left little doubt that they had overwhelmingly rejected the status quo. Campaign 2010 was not just a success—it was a success of historic proportions.

In a single election cycle, the most overwhelming victory in the history of the Alabama Republican Party had taken place. Our polling data the week leading up to Election Day indicated that we could experience a large number of significant wins up and down the ballot, but the magnitude of what did happen was beyond even our most optimistic projections.

In 2010, Republicans:

- won every state constitutional office, including Governor, Lieutenant Governor, Attorney General, Secretary of State, State Treasurer, State Auditor, and Commissioner of Agriculture and Industries;
- won every court race on the ballot, including the State Supreme

Court, Court of Criminal Appeals, and Court of Civil Appeals;
- won the U.S. Senate seat by a wide margin, keeping it in GOP hands;
- won six of the seven congressional seats, including regaining the seat lost two years earlier;
- won both open seats on the Public Service Commission;
- and, for the first time in 136 years, won control of both houses of the Alabama Legislature.

The magnitude of the Republican sweep was initially difficult to comprehend. Never before had Republicans held every single constitutional office. Not only did Robert Bentley's landslide win ensure that the governor's office would remain in Republican hands, but Kay Ivey had taken out an iconic name in Democratic circles by unseating Lieutenant Governor Jim Folsom Jr. For the first time in modern Alabama history, the top two executive positions in the state would be held by Republicans.

The deep wounds and disappointments from 2008, when Republicans lost the Second Congressional District for the first time since 1964, were healed. Martha Roby, a member of the Montgomery city council, soundly defeated incumbent Democrat Bobby Bright, ending his congressional career after a single two-year term. This win was especially satisfying to me personally since the loss of the seat in 2008 had caused some to question my ability to lead the party and the overall viability of Campaign 2010. The Roby victory also soothed the sting of Harri Anne Smith's 2008 endorsement of Bright over my friend and colleague Jay Love.

The Fifth Congressional District, the seat Republicans had failed to capture in 2008, was now finally in the GOP column. Mo Brooks, a former Madison County district attorney and county commissioner, defeated longtime Democratic lobbyist and campaign consultant Steve Raby to give Republicans six of Alabama's seven U.S. House seats. With both U.S. Senate seats held by Republicans, the result was the widest Republican federal delegation majority in the history of the state.

BUT OF ALL THE historic records set by Republicans on November 2,

2010, the one that sent shockwaves throughout the state was the change in control at the Alabama State House. After all, taking the majority of the legislature was the stated goal of Campaign 2010. Republicans had held each of the constitutional offices at one time or another in the modern era and already enjoyed a majority on the courts and in Congress, and it was definitely rewarding to take control of those offices to the next level. But not since 1874 had Republicans held the majority of the seats in the Alabama Legislature. The Democrats' streak of 136 years had slammed to a close.

Republicans entered the 2010 election holding 45 of the 105 seats in the House and emerged with 62. A few days later, four conservative Democrats officially changed parties, swelling the GOP ranks to 66. In the 35-member State Senate, the GOP numbers increased from 13 to 22.

Not only had Republicans taken the majority in both houses, a feat unimaginable just two years earlier, but we had moved from the minority to a supermajority in both houses, meaning that if Republicans stuck together, Democrats could not kill our legislation with filibusters. After 12 years of being forced to play defense against bad Democratic bills, I could not dream of anything better than finally being in a position to pass Republican bills.

And, as we would soon prove, we would indeed pass the measures we promised.

The comprehensive, aggressive, ambitious, well-funded and highly sophisticated campaign effort had become much larger and more far-reaching than I, or anyone involved in its creation, could have imagined when I first uttered the "Campaign 2010" phrase in my 2007 acceptance speech as party chairman. The small-scale yet effective experiment to gain seats in the 2006 legislative elections was the genesis of Campaign 2010, but that basic concept had evolved into an effort unmatched in Alabama politics.

Mistakes we had made in the 2006 campaigns and in the special elections that followed turned out to be blessings in the form of valuable lessons. We continually refined our campaign plans to avoid repeating the mistakes of the past and to build upon what worked well.

For the 2010 legislative campaigns, I was determined to make sure we had the resources to give Republicans a shot at taking the majority. Despite naysayers inside and outside the party, more than $5 million, a record by many multiples, was raised and devoted to the effort. We had also spent time and resources recruiting quality candidates—another lesson learned from past losses—and we took a more business-like approach to avoid making costly emotional decisions.

A key element of Campaign 2010 was building a centrally based approach to achieving a lofty and historic goal. Having dozens of campaigns coordinated in message, strategy, tactics, polling, and even media production was invaluable. The ability to package the elements from multiple campaigns also led to tremendous financial savings by taking advantage of economies of scale.

But the most important component was having an outstanding team. From top to bottom, Campaign 2010 combined the talents of an incredible group of people devoted to winning races and making history.

Now that our campaign goals were realized and history made, we had another challenge before us. Leading.

In Alabama, House and Senate members take office at 12:01 A.M. the morning following the election, which means that a brand new legislature is immediately seated. The newly elected constitutional officers, on the other hand, don't take office until the second Tuesday in January, as required by the Alabama Constitution.

Since Republicans had been in the minority in the legislature, we had no committee chairmanships, much less a Republican Speaker of the House or Senate President Pro Tempore. Now that we were in the majority, we had to determine who would lead our branch of government.

My job, as chairman of the Alabama Republican Party, was to elect Republicans to every office at every level. Of course, since the legislature was the last bastion of Democratic control in the state and a longtime powerbase for Democrats and the liberal special interests that controlled them, taking it over was a top priority. That was my goal, which I plainly stated when I was elected chairman.

My goal was not to become the first Republican Speaker of the House in 136 years. But I did believe my experience serving as House minority leader for six years and GOP party chairman for four years had prepared me for the position and that I was qualified, so I decided to seek the job.

The Speaker of the House in Alabama is a powerful position. The Speaker is the presiding officer of the House, third in line of succession to the governor, and assigns committee chairs, designates the members of all committees, and makes selected appointments to boards and commissions. Just as in Congress, the Speaker is a member of the House of Representatives and is elected by the entire body.

Since we now had 66 Republican members of the House, my task was to get at least 53 of them to support me for Speaker. I hoped that my days of taking bullets as minority leader and as party chairman would be recognized by my colleagues and would help my cause. But I did have competition.

Representative Paul DeMarco (R-Homewood) had also thrown his hat into the ring for Speaker. DeMarco, an attorney in Birmingham, is an intelligent and effective lawmaker. He was elected in a special election in 2005 and quickly became a leader within our caucus, serving on the steering committee. I liked DeMarco and, as minority leader, had recognized his leadership qualities, nominating him to attend an Emerging Legislative Leaders conference in Virginia and also sending him to another leadership event in Florida. The Florida conference is where he visited with Mississippi Senator Merle Flowers and was told about future candidate Barry Moore.

DeMarco had every right to run for Speaker; the position is open to any member of the Alabama House. I just believed that I was the right person for the job and that my experience in leadership had prepared me to lead this new GOP legislature.

The race for Speaker is not a traditional political campaign. You know exactly who the voters are, the 105 members of the House. DeMarco and I both made phone calls and personal visits to members and stated our cases. There was no animosity or bad-mouthing on either side, just vote counting.

A couple of weeks prior to the election, I had called a meeting of our

caucus to be held on November 4 in Montgomery. I knew that no matter the outcome of the election, we would have to make some decisions
as a group on how to move forward. As it turned out, time was of the
essence because now that we were in the majority, there was a great deal
of organizing to be done.

The meeting was held at the RSA Plaza across the street from the State
House and every GOP House member was in attendance. Everyone clearly
wanted to be a part of the first meeting of this new majority. One of the
most humbling and unexpected experiences of my time in the legislature
occurred when I entered the room. I was greeted with a long and enthusiastic standing ovation from my colleagues, veterans and freshmen alike.
Tears came to my eyes, as this reception by my fellow House members let
me know that my efforts to elect a Republican majority were appreciated.
I was momentarily overwhelmed by emotion as smiling members came
forward to shake my hand and pat me on the shoulder.

Once we convened the meeting, Congressman Mike Rogers, who had
once served as minority leader, spoke to the group. Rogers had supported
our effort in 2006 and had contributed $100,000 toward Campaign 2010,
so he played a big role in helping us attain a dream. He had driven from
his home in Anniston that day just to be with us.

"I just couldn't pass up the opportunity to see what a Republican
majority in the Alabama House of Representatives looks like," said Rogers, fresh from his own victory for a fourth term in Congress. "This is
something I've dreamed about for years and let me tell you, it looks better
than I could have ever imagined!"

Governor-elect Bentley, who had been a member of the House just
two days before, addressed the group as well. To say it was a celebratory
meeting would have not done it justice. Bentley, too, knew full well what
being in the minority is like as he had experienced it for eight years.
Now, he would soon enjoy something no other Republican governor
in Alabama had benefited from in more than a century—a Republican
House and Senate.

Following Bentley's remarks, each member stood up and introduced
themselves so freshmen and veterans could get to know each other. Then,

it was time to for the group to determine who, as a caucus, we would nominate for Speaker. Since we now held a majority of the seats, more than the 53 required, whoever our caucus decided to support would be the Speaker-designate.

My name was placed into nomination and the motion seconded. Then a motion that nominations be closed was quickly made and seconded. The voice vote was unanimous and in a matter of a few minutes, I was our caucuses' choice for Speaker of the House. It was a surreal moment.

As I stated earlier, I am a friend and admirer of Paul DeMarco, and no hard feelings resulted from the Speaker's race. In fact, I named DeMarco to serve as chairman of the House Judiciary Committee, a powerful position and one especially coveted by those in the legal community. He is a valued member of my leadership team and a trusted advisor.

At the same time we were making our choice for leadership in the House, the Senate Republican Caucus was doing the same thing. Del Marsh, my Finance Chairman and Campaign 2010 partner at the Republican Party, was challenged by Senator Scott Beason for President Pro Tempore, the top ranking position in the Senate.

Just like the House, the Senate membership selects the President Pro Tem. The position is the Senate equivalent to the House Speaker, but there are a few differences. The presiding officer of the Senate is, by State Constitution, the Lt. Governor, even though the Lt. Governor is actually a member of the executive branch, not the legislative.

The Pro Tem position is a critical one and, as the top ranking member of the Senate, has a great deal of influence over the operations of the body. It was important for me that it be held by someone I knew I could work with closely. Under the Democrats, the House and Senate never worked well together and, in fact, I'm not sure the leadership of the two houses even liked one another. Under Republican leadership, we wanted that to change.

I knew Marsh held the same philosophy as me and the two of us had worked closely together for four years to get a GOP majority in place. The two of us spoke on the phone multiple times a day and our relationship had gotten so close that we actually knew what the other would think on issues and situations. Nothing against, Beason, but Marsh was clearly the man I hoped would get the nod from the Senate Republicans to lead that chamber.

At the Senate GOP Caucus meeting, held at the Alabama Forestry Association building not far from where we were holding our House Caucus meeting, the votes were taken and Marsh was the choice by a 15-7 vote to be the President Pro Tem-designate.

Although members of the legislature take office immediately following the election, we would not officially become the two leaders of the legislature until a full vote of our respective bodies, and the constitutionally-mandated Organizational Session would not be held until January. Marsh and I would become a footnote in history by becoming the first Republican legislative leaders since Reconstruction. But we had no idea at the time that we would also assume our roles earlier than anticipated.

∼ *In Their Own Words* ∼

ROBERT BENTLEY
STATE REPRESENTATIVE 2002–10; GOVERNOR, 2011–

Mike Hubbard had worked so hard to get us this point, I just felt like he should be the leader. It was his turn and he had the leadership abilities to be a good Speaker. Mike was very fair when he divided up the chairmanships and even put people on some committees who probably didn't initially support him. He was very fair to the Democrats as well.

18

Promises Made, Promises Kept

D el Marsh and I first discussed the possibility of a special session with Governor Riley within an hour of our becoming the next leaders of the legislature. At the time, though, it wasn't really a serious consideration.

Marsh and I walked together from the State House to the Capitol following the caucus meetings where the votes had just been conducted. The governor was a major reason we were now in the majority, and we wanted to celebrate our most recent news with him. Of course, by the time we arrived in his office, he already knew.

I don't believe I've ever seen Riley so happy and excited. He told us that having me as Speaker and Del as President Pro Tem was a dream come true for him. There was no doubt he meant it.

We recalled the details of our respective caucus meetings for him and threw out some ideas we each had for the organizational session to be held in January. Marsh commented that it was really a shame the governor would not be able to sign a bill passed by the new legislature after all he had done to help the cause.

Almost as a joke, I responded that since he would still be the governor until the Inauguration in January, he could always call us into special session. No one followed up with a comment, and we moved onto another topic before Marsh and I asked to have our photo made with the governor and left the Capitol. It had been quite a day.

For a week or so afterwards, I was thinking that calling the new Republican-led legislature into special session was really not a bad idea. I spoke with Marsh and he had been thinking the same thing. We both broached the topic with some of our members and, to a person, they liked the idea.

Everyone also agreed on the subject matter that should be covered. For the eight years Riley had been governor, he had pushed for ethics reform legislation only to have the Democrats kill it. Some years, a bill would simply get killed in committee while another would make it through one chamber only to die in the other. Other years, the routine would be reversed. The orchestrated game was played to appear as if the legislature was actually considering Riley's ethics legislation when, in reality, there was never any intent to give the bills a fair hearing.

Ethics was a subject that set Republicans apart from the Democrats. The Siegelman indictment and subsequent conviction, the two-year school scandal, and legislators being sent to prison was evidence that ethics reform in Alabama was way past due.

Unfortunately, Alabama had gained a reputation of being a corrupt state, or at least having a corrupt government. That hurt economic development, created cynicism in the minds of the public and, quite simply, was not fair to the citizens and taxpayers of the state. Alabamians are, after all, not a corrupt people. They are honest, hard-working, God-fearing folks who deserved to have a government that reflected their values. Politically, strengthening the ethics law and providing the Alabama Ethics Commission with some real teeth was a perfect way for this new legislature to set the tone for the quadrennium. It would send a loud and clear message to the people of Alabama, and to the special interest groups that had run Montgomery for decades, that things would be different from here on out.

Eventually, I discussed the idea with Dave Stewart, Riley's chief of staff. He said the governor had already been thinking along the same lines and was open to the idea. Only the governor can call a special session of the Alabama Legislature, so Marsh and I had subsequent conversations with Riley and urged him to make the call. We promised him that we would work with the membership of the House and Senate to make sure it was a success.

A special session prior to the constitutionally mandated organizational session had only happened once before in Alabama, and that was during World War II. This brought up some interesting issues. Since it was a brand new legislature, there were no rules in effect, no leaders, and no committees. If a special session was indeed called, we would have to adopt rules and elect leaders before we could conduct any business. But, according to Greg Pappas, the longtime clerk of the House, it would require some dusting off of that section of the Alabama Code to figure it all out, but could be done.

Governor Riley, at our urging, called for the legislature to go into special session beginning December 7, 2010. In the session's "call," he clearly outlined the purpose: to strengthen the state's ethics law.

Ahead of time, Marsh and I, along with other members of the House and Senate, worked with the governor's staff to craft the bills to be introduced. It was an aggressive but sorely needed agenda. We also discussed the proposed bills with Governor-elect Bentley, who was solidly supportive of the session and pledged to help pass the bills. From his eight years in the Alabama House, he knew the weak ethics laws needed to be strengthened. He publicly stated that he fully supported Governor Riley's decision to call the session.

EVERY FOUR YEARS, THE newly seated legislature meets at the University of Alabama Law School, the home of the Alabama Law Institute, for orientation. It's a time for new members to get to know the veterans and to learn about the legislative process. This year, the new members had to do some quick learning, because they were about to be thrown into the fire. The orientation ended at noon on December 7 in Tuscaloosa, and we would be in session just a few hours later in Montgomery.

At 4 P.M., the seats of the House Chamber located on the fifth floor of the Alabama State House were occupied by the 105 members, 66 of whom were members of my party. Seth Hammett, who had served as Speaker for 12 years, slammed the gavel and called the House to order. In a quirk of the Alabama Constitution, this is the only time a non-elected person is allowed to preside over the body. Since we had not yet set rules or selected leaders, the Constitution calls for the previous Speaker to preside until a new Speaker is elected.

After some procedural matters were dispensed with, Hammett called for nominations for Speaker. My friend Mike Hill of Columbiana, who

had met me for dinner in Auburn 1998 to urge me to run for the legislature, placed my name into nomination. The motion was seconded by
Jim Barton of Mobile. Phil Willliams of Huntsville, who won the 2009
special election in Madison County, moved that nominations be closed.

Hammett then called for each member to cast their vote for Speaker
viva voce (by voice). As the clerk called their names, each member of the
Alabama House of Representatives stood and responded "Mike Hubbard."
At the end of the roll call, it was a unanimous vote.

With Susan at my side holding my Dad's Bible, Clayte and Riley
standing next to us, and my father sitting a only few feet away, Alabama
Supreme Court Justice Mike Bolin administered the oath of office to me.
In what was one of the most humbling moments of my life, I had been
elected Alabama's first Republican Speaker in 136 years.

In my comments to the membership afterward, I set as our goal maintaining the tradition of two words that are so important they appear in
the seal of the Alabama House of Representatives. *Vox Populi*—Voice of
the People.

"The phrase does not say voice of the special interests, voice of the
powerful, or voice of the campaign contributors," I said. "It means voice
of all of the people. Whether you are Republican or Democrat, black or
white, rich or poor, I will work to ensure that your voice is heard in the
Alabama House chamber."

My first official act as Speaker was to preside over the election of Speaker
Pro Tempore. My good friend Victor Gaston of Mobile, the longest-serving
Republican in the legislature, was unanimously elected. First elected to
the House in 1982, Gaston has been a mentor to me and countless other
Republicans through the years. A retired school administrator, Gaston is
a former Marine who earned his doctorate from Auburn University. He
is well liked and respected by members of both parties, so I affectionately
refer to him as "the Godfather." It was a great honor for me to administer
the oath of office to Dr. Gaston.

After we adopted new rules and handled a few other housekeeping
requirements, it was time to work. I'm proud to say that legislators in
both chambers and on both sides of the aisle stepped up to the plate and

passed more reform in just seven days than was approved in many previous decades.

Because of the laws passed in the special session and proudly signed into law by Governor Riley, Alabama ethics laws are now among the strongest in the nation. In fact, Alabama Ethics Commission Director Jim Sumner stated that we now have a "platinum" package of guidelines. I firmly believe the dramatic reforms will be an important part of Governor Riley's legacy.

The ethics package included:

- A prohibition on public officials holding two or more taxpayer-funded jobs, also known as "double-dipping," that led to conflicts of interest and scandals in the two-year college system;
- A measure providing subpoena power to the Ethics Commission, ensuring that public officials are forced to answer when accused of questionable behavior;
- Legislation that lowered the amount lobbyists and their clients may spend on entertaining public officials from $250 a day to $250 a year, a dramatic decrease designed to lessen special interest influence on the political process;
- Campaign finance and budget transparency reforms to prevent the camouflaging of the sources of political contributions and to eliminate pork barrel spending;
- Mandatory ethics training for public employees that ensures they understand the rules under which they may operate;
- A ban on allowing government employees to collect union dues and political donations through payroll check-offs while working on taxpayer time.

It is my hope that future historians will say that this was the legislature that brought the reforms Alabama had needed for so long and that fundamentally changed how state government operates.

THE SPECIAL SESSION PROVED to be a fitting warm-up for the new legislature. When the 2011 regular session convened in March, our first order of business was clear.

Most voters in Alabama had become used to hearing politicians say one thing on the campaign trail and do something else once elected. That kind of empty rhetoric and broken promises has given Alabamians a serious distrust of state government for decades.

We vowed to change that. We had made specific promises during the 2010 campaign and we had every intention of delivering.

We first dealt with the "*Republican Handshake with Alabama*," the series of reforms addressing everything from combating illegal immigration to taking control of long-abused state finances that all GOP candidates vowed to pass during the campaign. All of the bills addressed in the *Handshake* were pre-filed and assigned to the proper committee so they could be considered at the very first committee meeting. Then, we placed the bills at the top of the calendar and pledged to consider no other issue until we passed every one of them.

Not only did we pass every bill, thanks to our supermajority, but, in the House, we passed them by the tenth legislative day, something the Democrats has promised to do with their *Covenant for the Future* back in 2006 but had failed to deliver. The Senate also passed each bill and Governor Bentley signed the package into law.

Newspaper editorial writers, even ones who disagreed with some of the issues, praised the new legislature for doing something that was un-usual—delivering on promises made. Clearly, they reported, there was a new mindset in Alabama.

If we had done nothing more than pass our Handshake bills, it would have been a huge increase in productivity over previous legislative ses-sions. We didn't stop there. We took up issues and passed bills dealing with budgeting reform, tort reform and, for the first time in my legislative career, passed the state budgets well before the final day of the session. We addressed congressional and state board of education redistricting in the regular session instead of having to address it in a special session as had been done in the past, saving the taxpayers at least half a million dollars.

One of the most contentious but most important issues we dealt with was teacher tenure reform. The tenure law in Alabama protected the worst teachers and educators by making it nearly impossible and cost-prohibitive for a local school board to dismiss poorly performing education employees, even those who broke the law. In fact, there had been widely publicized cases of teachers sitting in prison yet still receiving taxpayer-funded paychecks and benefits. Over the years, the Alabama Education Association had vigorously opposed and successfully defeated attempts to change the tenure law. But in another sign that things were now different, we passed, and Governor Bentley signed into law, a streamlined process that now puts students and taxpayers ahead of employees who break the law and abuse our classrooms.

When the final gavel of the 2011 regular session sounded and the legislature adjourned, it ended the most productive legislative session in decades, if not ever. We had made bold promises during our Campaign 2010 effort. We promised the people of Alabama that a Republican majority in the legislature would be different, and in the very first year of the quadrennium, we delivered on those promises in a triumph of historic proportions.

And we're just getting started.

Contested Races = 44 Page 2 GOP win ✓ OTH win ✓

	HD GOP	Demo	Indep
1	1 Hanson	Burdine	
2	2 Greer	Curtis	
3	4 Hammon	Goodwin	
4	5 Williams	White	Hill
5	7 Johnson	Letson	
6	8 Collins	Breland	
7	9 Henry	Goodwin	
8	12 Buttram	Fields	
9	13 Roberts	Sherrer	
10	14 Baughn	Guin	
11	16 Bowman	Thigpen	
12	21 Patterson	Hinshaw	
13	22 Johnson	Taylor	
14	24 Greeson	Ledbetter	
15	26 Rich	White	
16	27 Long	McLaughlin	
17	29 Nordgren	Page	
18	30 Galliher	Burns	
19	32 Struzik	Boyd	
20	35 Mean	Hurst	
21	36 Wood	Bearden	
22	37 Fincher	Laird	
23	38 Bridges	Long	
24	39 Sprayberry	Lindsey	
25	40 Brown	Whaley	
26	42 Wallace	Martin	
27	43 McClurkin	Sweet	
28	45 Drake	Cannon	
29	47 Williams		McCallum
30	61 Chandler	Harper	
31	62 Merril	Kneussle?	
32	63 Poole	Hammil	
33	73 Grimes	Hubbard	
34	75 Wren	Allen	
35	80 Dudley	Vance	
36	81 Tuggle	Graham	
37	84 Perrin	Forte	
38	85 Singleton	Grimsley	
39	86 Lee	Carothers	
40	90 Hartin	Newton	
41	91 Moore	Spicer	
42	92 Jones	Darby	Cotton
43	93 Clouse	Helms	
44	98 Powe	Bracy	

November 2, 2010
Oh, What a Night!

This tally sheet was kept by State Rep. Jim McClendon of Springville as election returns came in on the historic night of November 2, 2010, when Republicans took control of the Alabama legislature. The sheet is now on display in Hubbard's State House office.

APPENDIX

A. CAMPAIGN 2010 TARGETED RACES

Alabama House of Representatives

Dist.	Republican	Opponent(s)	Type Race	Result	Vote %
1	Quinton Hanson	Greg Burdine (D)	Open	Lost	49%
2	Lynn Greer	Mike Curtis (D)	Challenge	Won	55%
5	Dan Williams	Henry White (D)	Challenge	Won	57%
		Jerry Hill (I)			
7	Ken Johnson	Jody Letson (D)	Challenge	Won	51%
8	Terri Collins	Drama Breland (D)	Open	Won	56%
9	Ed Henry	Kathy W. Goodwin (D)	Open	Won	73%
12	Mac Buttram	James Fields (D)	Challenge	Won	54%
13	Bill Roberts	Tommy Sherer (D)	Challenge	Won	61%
14	Richard Baughn	Ken Guin (D)	Challenge	Won	69%
16	Dan Boman	William Thigpen (D)	Challenge	Won	54%
21	Jim Patterson	Randy Hinshaw (D)	Challenge	Won	52%
22	Wayne Johnson	Butch Taylor (D)	Challenge	Won	65%
26	Kerry Rich	Randall White (D)	Open	Won	60%
27	Wes Long	Jeff McLaughlin (D)	Challenge	Won	53%
29	Becky Nordgren	Jack Page (D)	Challenge	Won	52%
35	Steve Dean	Steve Hurst (D)	Challenge	Lost	48%
38	DuWayne Bridges	Huey Long (D)	Hold	Won	51%
40	K. L. Brown	Ricky Whaley (D)	Hold	Won	63%
42	Kurt Wallace	Jimmy Martin (D)	Challenge	Won	63%
45	Owen Drake	Charlene Cannon (D)	Hold	Won	63%
47	Jack Williams	Chip McCallum (I)	Hold	Won	63%
63	Bill Poole	Susan Pace Hamill (D)	Open	Won	64%
73	David Grimes	Joe Hubbard (D)	Hold	Lost	49%
81	Mark Tuggle	Betty Carol Graham (D)	Challenge	Won	56%
85	Jody Singleton	Dexter Grimsley (D)	Open	Lost	48%
86	Paul Lee	Merritt Carothers (D)	Open	Won	58%
91	Barry Moore	Terry Spicer (D)	Challenge	Won	64%
92	Mike Jones	David Darby (D)	Open	Won	52%
		Don Cotton (I)			
			Won-Loss	**24-4**	

Alabama Senate

Dist.	Republican	Opponent(s)	Type Race	Result	Vote %
2	Bill Holtzclaw	Tom Butler (D)	Challenge	Won	59%
4	Paul Bussman	Zeb Little (D)	Challenge	Won	58%
5	Greg Reed	Brett Wadsworth (D)	Open	Won	73%
7	Paul Sanford	Jeff Enfinger (D)	Hold	Won	55%
8	Shadrack McGill	Lowell Barron (D)	Challenge	Won	51%
9	Clay Scofield	Tim Mitchell (D)	Open	Won	69%
10	Phil Williams	Larry Means (D)	Challenge	Won	54%
11	Ray Robbins	Jerry Fielding (D)	Open	Lost	47%
13	Gerald Dial	Greg Varner (D)	Open	Won	51%
21	Gerald Allen	Phil Poole (D)	Challenge	Won	51%
27	Tom Whatley	Ted Little (D)	Challenge	Won	55%
29	George Flowers	Harri Anne Smith (I)	Challenge	Lost	45%
30	Bryan Taylor	Wendell Mitchell (D)	Challenge	Won	57%
35	Ben Brooks	Scott Buzbee (D)	Hold	Won	59%
			Won-Loss	12-2	

B. Alabama Legislature, Post 2010 Election

House of Representatives

Dist.	Member	Hometown	Party	Dist.	Member	Hometown	Party
1	Greg Burdine	Florence	R	16	Daniel Boman+	Sulligent	R
2	Lynn Greer	Rogersville	R	17	Mike Millican*	Hamilton	D
3	Marcel Black	Tuscumbia	D	18	Johnny M. Morrow	Red Bay	D
4	Micky Hammon	Decatur	R	19	Laura Hall	Huntsville	D
5	Dan Williams	Athens	R	20	Howard Sanderford	Huntsville	R
6	Phil Williams	Huntsville	R	21	Jim Patterson	Meridianville	R
7	Ken Johnson	Moulton	R	22	Wayne Johnson	Huntsville	R
8	Terri Collins	Decatur	R	23	John Robinson	Scottsboro	D
9	Ed Henry	Hartselle	R	24	Todd Greeson	Ider	R
10	Mike Ball	Huntsville	R	25	Mac McCutcheon	Capshaw	R
11	Jeremy Oden	Vinemont	R	26	Kerry Rich	Albertville	R
12	Mac Buttram	Cullman	R	27	Wes Long	Guntersville	R
13	Bill Roberts	Jasper	R	28	Craig Ford	Gadsden	D
14	Richard Baughn	Lynn	R	29	Becky Nordgren	Gadsden	R
15	Allen Farley	McCalla	R	30	Blaine Galliher	Gadsden	R

31	Barry Mask	Wetumpka	R
32	Barbara Boyd	Anniston	D
33	Ron Johnson	Sylacauga	R
34	Elwyn Thomas	Oneonta	R
35	Steve Hurst*	Munford	D
36	Randy Wood	Anniston	R
37	Richard Laird	Roanoke	D
38	DuWayne Bridges	Valley	R
39	Richard Lindsey	Centre	D
40	K.L. Brown	Jacksonville	R
41	Mike Hill	Birmingham	R
42	Kurt Wallace	Maplesville	R
43	Mary Sue McClurkin	Indian Springs	R
44	Arthur Payne	Trussville	R
45	Owen Drake**	Leeds	R
46	Paul DeMarco	Homewood	R
47	Jack Williams	Birmingham	R
48	Greg Canfield#	Vestavia Hills	R
49	April Weaver	Brierfield	R
50	Jim McClendon	Springville	R
51	Allen Treadaway	Morris	R
52	John Rogers Jr.	Birmingham	D
53	Demetrius Newton	Birmingham	D
54	Patricia Todd	Birmingham	D
55	Rod Scott	Fairfield	D
56	Lawrence McAdory	Bessemer	D
57	Merika Coleman	Birmingham	D
58	Oliver Robinson	Birmingham	D
59	Mary Moore	Birmingham	D
60	Juandalynn Givan	Birmingham	D
61	Alan Harper%	Aliceville	D
62	John Merrill	Tuscaloosa	R
63	Bill Poole	Tuscaloosa	R
64	Harry Shiver	Bay Minette	R
65	Elaine Beech	Chatom	D
66	Alan Baker	Brewton	R
67	Darrio Melton	Selma	D
68	Thomas E. Jackson	Thomasville	D
69	David Colston	Hayneville	D
70	Christopher England	Tuscaloosa	D
71	A.J. McCampbell	Demopolis	D
72	Ralph Howard	Greensboro	D
73	Joe Hubbard	Montgomery	D
74	Jay Love	Montgomery	R
75	Greg Wren	Montgomery	R
76	Thad McClammy	Montgomery	D
77	John Knight	Montgomery	D
78	Alvin Holmes	Montgomery	D
79	Mike Hubbard	Auburn	R
80	Lesley Vance*	Phenix City	D
81	Mark Tuggle	Alexander City	R
82	Pebblin Warren	Tuskegee	D
83	George Bandy	Opelika	D
84	Barry Forte	Eufaula	D
85	Dexter Grimsley	Newville	D
86	Paul Lee	Dothan	R
87	Donnie Chesteen	Geneva	R
88	Paul Beckman	Prattville	R
89	Alan Boothe*	Troy	D
90	Charles Newton	Greenville	D
91	Barry Moore	Enterprise	R
92	Mike Jones, Jr.	Andalusia	R
93	Steve Clouse	Ozark	R
94	Joe Faust	Fairhope	R
95	Steve McMillan	Bay Minette	R
96	Randy Davis	Daphne	R
97	Yvonne Kennedy	Mobile	D
98	Napoleon Bracy	Mobile	D
99	James Buskey	Mobile	D
100	Victor Gaston	Mobile	R
101	Jamie Ison	Mobile	R
102	Chad Fincher	Semmes	R
103	Joseph C. Mitchell	Mobile	D
104	Jim Barton	Mobile	R
105	Spencer Collier &	Irvington	R

+ Daniel Boman was elected as a Republican in the 2010 election but switched to the Democratic Party on May 26, 2011.

*Reps. Boothe, Hurst, Millican and Vance were elected as Democrats in the Nov. 2, 2010 election but all four became Republicans on Nov. 22, 2010.

** Rep. Owen Drake died of cancer on June 27, 2011; He was succeeded by his brother, Rep. Dickie Drake, who was elected in a Special Election on November 29, 2011.

Rep. Greg Canfield was named Director of the Alabama Development Office by Governor Robert Bentley on July 6, 2011. His seat was filled by Rep. Jim Carns, who won a Special Election on August 30, 2011.

%Rep. Alan Harper was elected as a Democrat but switched to the Republican Party on February 7, 2012.

& Rep. Spencer Collier was named to the position of Director of Homeland Security by Governor Robert Bentley. His House seat is now held by Rep. David Sessions who won a Special Election on May 10, 2011.

Senate

Dist.	Member	Hometown	Party	Dist.	Member	Hometown	Party
1	Tammy Irons	Florence	D	19	Priscilla Dunn	Bessemer	D
2	Bill Holtzclaw	Madison	R	20	Linda Coleman	Birmingham	D
3	Arthur Orr	Decatur	R	21	Gerald Allen	Cottondale	R
4	Paul Bussman	Cullman	R	22	Marc Keahey	Grovehill	D
5	Greg Reed	Jasper	R	23	Hank Sanders	Selma	D
6	Roger Bedford	Russellville	D	24	Bobby Singleton	Greensboro	D
7	Paul Sanford	Huntsville	R	25	Dick Brewbaker	Montgomery	R
8	Shadrack McGill	Woodville	R	26	Quinton Ross	Montgomery	D
9	Clay Scofield	Guntersville	R	27	Tom Whatley	Auburn	R
10	Phil Williams	Rainbow City	R	28	Billy Beasley	Clayton	D
11	Jerry Fielding	Sylacauga	D	29	Harri Anne Smith	Slocomb	I
12	Del Marsh	Anniston	R	30	Bryan Taylor	Prattville	R
13	Gerald Dial	Lineville	R	31	Jimmy Holley	Elba	R
14	Cam Ward	Alabaster	R	32	Trip Pittman	Montrose	R
15	Slade Blackwell	Birmingham	R	33	Vivian Figures	Mobile	D
16	Jabo Waggoner	Birmingham	R	34	Rusty Glover	Semmes	R
17	Scott Beason	Gardendale	R	35	Ben Brooks	Mobile	R
18	Rodger Smitherman	Birmingham	D				

C. Legislative Districts as of 2010 Election

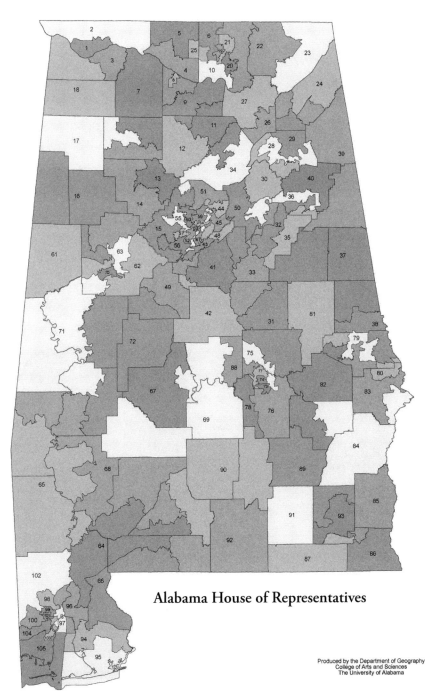

Alabama House of Representatives

Produced by the Department of Geography
College of Arts and Sciences
The University of Alabama

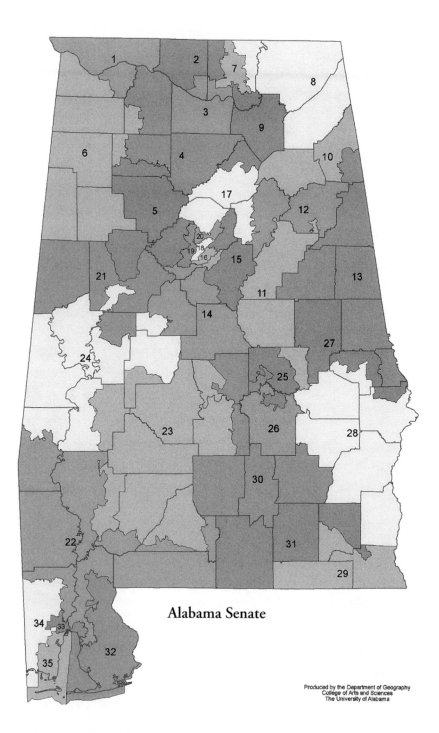

Alabama Senate

Produced by the Department of Geography
College of Arts and Sciences
The University of Alabama

Index